Test Bank

to accompany

International Business Competing in the Global Marketplace

Third Edition

Charles W. L. Hill
University of Washington

Prepared by
Bruce R. Barringer
University of Central Florida

Boston Burr Ridge, IL Dubuque, IA Madison, WI New York San Francisco St. Louis
Bangkok Bogotá Caracas Lisbon London Madrid
Mexico City Milan New Delhi Seoul Singapore Sydney Taipei Toronto

McGraw-Hill Higher Education

A Division of The McGraw-Hill Companies

Test Bank to accompany
INTERNATIONAL BUSINESS

1 2 3 4 5 6 7 8 9 0 BKM/BKM 9 0 9 8 7 6 5 4 3 2 1 0 9

ISBN 0-07-234850-X

http://www.mhhe.com

PREFACE

INTERNATIONAL BUSINESS: COMPETING IN THE GLOBAL MARKETPLACE, 3rd Edition

This Test Bank has been prepared to provide comprehensive testing material for Professor Hill's textbook. There are 60 multiple-choice, 30 true-false, and 10 essay questions per chapter.

Categories of Questions

The multiple choice, true-false, and essay questions are labeled either easy, medium, or hard. Each chapter contains a full range of questions.

Page Numbers

For the convenience of the adopters of the book, the page number where the correct answer appears in the text is provided for each question.

Bruce R. Barringer
University of Central Florida
Orlando, Florida
E-mail: Bruce.Barringer@bus.ucf.edu

TABLE OF CONTENTS

TEST BANK

INTERNATIONAL BUSINESS: COMPETING IN THE GLOBAL MARKETPLACE, Third Edition

CHAPTER 1

GLOBALIZATION

MULTIPLE-CHOICE QUESTIONS

INTRODUCTION

Answer: C
Easy
Page: 4

1. The rate at which globalization is spreading around the world has:

   A. remained stable in recent years
   B. slowed down in recent years
   C. accelerated in recent years
   D. virtually stopped in recent years

Answer: B
Medium
Page: 4

2. The emergence of a global telecommunications market should have which of the following effects on the prices paid for telecommunications services?

   A. prices should increase sharply
   B. prices should plummet
   C. prices should increase modestly
   D. prices should decrease modestly

Answer: A
Medium
Page: 5

3. The two main components of globalization are:

   A. the globalization of markets and the globalization of production
   B. the globalization of finance and the globalization of accounting
   C. the globalization of advertising and the globalization of services
   D. the standardization of technology and the globalization of markets

THE GLOBALIZATION OF MARKETS

Answer: B
Easy
Page: 5

4. The globalization of markets refers to the fact that in many industries historically distinct and separate markets are merging into:

   A. markets defined by a common language
   B. one huge market
   C. markets defined by a common culture
   D. several distinct regional markets

Answer: A
Medium
Page: 5

5. Which of the following markets has experienced the highest degree of globalization?

A. industrial goods and materials
B. services
C. consumer products
D. intellectual capital

Answer: D
Hard
Page: 5

6. The most global markets currently are not markets for __________, where national differences in tastes and preferences are still often important enough to act as a break on globalization, but markets for __________ that serve a universal need the world over.

A. services, consumer products
B. industrial goods and materials, intellectual capital
C. intellectual capital, services
D. consumer products, industrial goods and materials

Answer: C
Easy
Page: 6

7. Globalization results in a greater degree of __________ across markets than would be present otherwise.

A. variety
B. diversity
C. homogeneity
D. heterogeneity

THE GLOBALIZATION OF PRODUCTION

Answer: D
Medium
Page: 7

8. The globalization of production refers to:

A. the tendency among firms to recruit production workers from foreign countries
B. the tendency among firms to move production facilities to foreign countries where wage rates are lower
C. the tendency among firms to use similar production methods
D. the tendency among firms to source goods and services from locations around the globe to take advantage of national differences in the cost and quality of factors of production

Answer: C
Medium
Page: 7

9. In producing its latest jet airline, the 777, Boeing purchases goods and services from different suppliers around the globe in an attempt to take advantage of national differences in the cost and quality of factors of production. This practice is made possible by the globalization of:

A. markets
B. commerce
C. production
D. finance

Answer: B
Medium
Page: 7

10. An international firm like General Electric may design a product in one country, produce component parts for the product in another country, assemble the product in a third country, and export the product to several other countries. This scenario is made possible by:

A. the globalization of finance
B. the globalization of production
C. the globalization of marketing
D. the globalization of management

Answer: D
Easy
Page: 7

11. According to former Secretary of Labor Robert Reich, the propensity for firms to outsource many of their productive activities to different suppliers around the world has resulted in the creation of __________ products.

A. multi-domestic
B. cross-national
C. cross-cultural
D. global

Answer: B
Hard
Page: 7

12. Which of the following is not an impediment that makes it difficult for firms to achieve the optimal dispersion of their productive activities to locations around the globe?

A. formal and informal barriers to trade between countries
B. a slowdown in the trend towards globalization worldwide
C. issues associated with economic and political risk
D. transportation costs

DECLINING TRADE AND INVESTMENT BARRIERS

Answer: A
Hard
Page: 8

13. The two macro factors that seem to underlie the trend towards greater globalization are:

A. the decline in barriers to the free flow of goods, services, and capital that has occurred since the end of World War II, and technological change
B. the decline in political tensions around the world, formal and informal barriers to trade between countries
C. the increase in barriers to the free flow of goods, services, and capital that has occurred since the end of World War II, the decline in economic pressures around the world
D. a convergence in consumer tastes around the world, an increase in political tensions around the world

Answer: C
Easy
Page: 8

14. The exporting of goods or services to consumers in another country is referred to as:

A. foreign direct investment
B. countertrade
C. international trade
D. cross-boarder exchange

Answer: A
Medium
Page: 8

15. Aircraft manufacturers like Boeing, Airbus, and Lockheed-Martin export goods and services to consumers in other countries. This practice is referred to as:

A. international trade
B. country-to-country exchange
C. global salesmanship
D. cross-national barter

Answer: B
Easy
Page: 8

16. A firm's decision to invest resources in business activities outside its home country is referred to as:

A. international diversification
B. foreign direct investment
C. cross-national investment
D. transnational commerce

Answer: D
Medium
Page: 8

17. American firms like Procter & Gamble, General Motors, and IBM have substantial business activities outside the United States. This practice is referred to as:

A. transnational diversification
B. international investment expansion
C. cross-national commerce
D. foreign direct investment

Answer: A
Medium
Page: 8

18. The __________ is a treaty designed to remove barriers to the free flow of goods, services, and capital between nations.

A. General Agreement on Tariffs and Trade
B. United Nations Treaty on Trade
C. Tariff Buster Trade Agreement
D. North Atlantic Agreement on Trade and International Business

Answer: B
Medium
Page: 8

19. Under the umbrella of GATT, there have been eight rounds of negotiations among member states. The most recent round of negotiations was referred to as the:

A. North Atlantic Round
B. Uruguay Round
C. Pacific-Basin Round
D. Singapore Round

Answer: D
Hard
Page:

20. All of the following were accomplishments of the 1993 Uruguay Round, with the exception of:

A. extended GATT to cover services as well as manufactured goods
B. provided enhanced protection for patents, trademarks, and copyrights
C. established the World Trade Organization
D. established a common currency for international trade

Answer: C
Hard
Page: 8

21. As a result of GATT and other international trade initiatives, the average tariff rate on manufactured goods should fall to approximately __________ by the year 2000.

A. 9.5 %
B. 6.2 %
C. 3.9 %
D. 1.7 %

Answer: B
Easy
Page: 8

22. The acronym GATT stands for:

A. Global Association for Technology and Trade
B. General Agreement on Tariffs and Trade
C. General Agreement on Taxation and Trademarks
D. Global Agreement on Taxation and Tariffs

Answer: B
Medium
Page: 9

23. Which of the following statements in incorrect in regard to trends in international trade?

A. the lowering of barriers to international trade enables firms to view the world, rather than a single country, as their market
B. the volume of world trade has grown consistently at a similar rate as world output since 1950
C. the economies of the world's nation states are becoming more intertwined
D. foreign direct investment is playing an increasing role in the global economy

Answer: A
Hard
Page: 9

24. According to data from the World Trade Organization, the volume of world trade has grown faster than the volume of world output since the 1950s. This relationship suggests all of the following except:

A. nations are becoming increasingly self-sufficient for important goods and services
B. more firms are dispersing different parts of their overall production process to different locations around the globe to increase quality
C. more firms are dispersing different parts of their overall production process to different locations around the globe to drive down costs
D. FDI is playing an increasing role in the global economy

Answer: C
Medium
Page: 10

25. According to our textbook, the growing integration of the world economy is:

A. narrowing the scope of competition in a wide range of service, commodity, and manufacturing industries
B. increasing the intensity of competition in manufacturing industries, and decreasing the intensity of competition in services
C. increasing the intensity of competition in a wide range of manufacturing and service industries
D. decreasing the intensity of competition in manufacturing industries, and increasing the intensity of competition in services

THE ROLE OF TECHNOLOGICAL CHANGE

Answer: B
Easy
Page: 10

26. According to our textbook, the single most important technological innovation that has impacted international trade has been the:

A. fax machine
B. microprocessor
C. development of optic fiber
D. communications satellite

Answer: A
Medium
Page: 10

27. According to __________, the power of microprocessor technology doubles and the cost its production falls in half every 18 months.

A. Moore's Law
B. Brennan's Theorem
C. Stephen's Theorem
D. Berkeley's Law

Answer: D
Medium
Page: 10

28. According to our textbook, __________ promise to develop into the information backbone of tomorrow's global economy.

A. CNN and other cable television channels
B. fax technology and videoconferencing
C. fiber optics telephone and teletype service
D. the Internet and World Wide Web

Answer: C
Medium
Page: 11

29. Which of the following statements is not an accurate depiction of the impact of the World Wide Web on international trade?

A. the web allows businesses to expand their global presence, at a lower cost than ever before
B. the web frees firms from some of the constraints of location, scale, and time zones
C. the web has been used successfully by large firms, but is of little use to smaller firms
D. the web makes it easier for buyers and sellers to find each other

Answer: A
Medium
Page: 13

30. What does the term "global village" refer to?

A. the convergence of consumer tastes and preferences around the world
B. the increasing concern worldwide about the health of the environment
C. the Internet, which makes it possible for people all over the world to communicate with one another easily
D. the possibility of creating free trade across the world through the elimination of all trade barriers

THE CHANGING WORLD OUTPUT AND WORLD TRADE PICTURE

Answer: C
Hard
Page: 13

31. Although the characteristics of the global economy have changed dramatically over the past 30 years, as late as the 1960s all of the following demographic characteristics were true except:

A. the U.S. dominated the world economy and the world trade picture
B. roughly half the world was governed by centrally planned economies of the Communist world, and was off-limits to Western international business
C. small, U.S. entrepreneurial firms dominated the international business scene
D. the U.S. dominated the world foreign direct investment picture

Answer: A
Easy
Page: 13

32. The percentage of world output accounted for by the United States has __________ since the early 1960s.

A. fallen sharply
B. fallen slightly
C. increased sharply
D. increased slightly

Answer: B
Medium
Page: 14

33. If we look 20 years into the future, most forecasts now predict a __________ in the share of world output accounted for by developing nations such as China, India, Indonesia, and South Korea, and a __________ in the share enjoyed by rich industrialized countries such as Britain, Germany, Japan, and the United States.

A. rapid rise, slight decline
B. rapid rise, rapid decline
C. sharp rise, sharp decline
D. slight rise, slight decline

Answer: C
Medium
Page: 14

34. According to our textbook, the dramatic shift that is taking place in the economic geography of the world suggests that many of tomorrow's economic opportunities may be found in __________, and many of tomorrow's most capable competitors will probably also emerge from these regions.

A. traditional industrial powers such as Germany, Japan, and the U.S.
B. Western Europe, including Britain, France, Germany, and Belgium
C. the developing nations of the world
D. Eastern Europe and the republics of the former Soviet Union

Answer: A
Easy
Page: 14

35. The following is an example of a developing nation.

A. Indonesia
B. Japan
C. Britain
D. Germany

Answer: C
Easy
Page: 14

36. All of the following are examples of developing nations with the exception of:

A. Brazil
B. Thailand
C. Germany
D. China

THE CHANGING FOREIGN DIRECT INVESTMENT PICTURE

Answer: C
Medium
Page: 14

37. In the 1960s, the two most dominant countries in terms of foreign direct investment were:

A. Japan and the United States
B. Germany and Britain
C. Britain and the United States
D. China and Japan

Answer: A
Medium
Page: 15

38. During the 1970s and 1980s, the foreign direct investment by non-U.S. firms was motivated primarily by the following two factors:

A. the desire to disperse production activities to optimal locations; and the desire to build a direct presence in major foreign markets
B. the desire to disperse production activities to optimal locations; and the desire to influence foreign exchange rates
C. the desire to influence foreign exchange rates; and the desire to influence political developments in foreign countries
D. the desire to build a direct presence in major foreign markets; and the desire to influence political developments in foreign countries

Answer: D
Medium
Page: 15

39. The "stock of foreign direct investment" refers to:

A. the total number of foreign direct investments exceeding $10,000
B. the nations in the world that have the potential to participate in foreign direct investment
C. the nations in the world that participate in foreign direct investment
D. the total cumulative value of foreign direct investments

Answer: B
Hard
Page 16

40. Among developing nations, __________ has received the greatest volume of inward FDI in recent years.

A. Indonesia
B. China
C. India
D. South Korea

Answer: D
Medium
Page 16

41. During the 1990s, the percentage of foreign direct investment flowing into developing countries has:

A. fluctuated widely
B. remained constant
C. decreased
D. increased

THE CHANGING NATURE OF MULTINATIONAL ENTERPRISE

Answer: A
Easy
Page: 16

42. A __________ is any business that has productive activities in two or more countries.

A. multinational enterprise
B. international conglomerate
C. international consortium
D. global endeavor

Answer: C
Easy
Page: 16

43. Companies such as Sony, General Electric, and British Petroleum have operations in two or more countries. These types of firms are commonly referred to as __________ enterprises.

A. global
B. cross-boarder
C. multinational
D. diverse-national

Answer: D
Medium
Page: 16

44. Since the 1960s, there have been two notable trends in the demographics of the multinational enterprise. These two trends have been:

A. the rise of U.S. multinationals and the disappearance of mini-multinationals
B. the decline of non-U.S. multinationals and the decline of mini-multinationals
C. the rise of U.S. multinationals and the growth of mini-multinationals
D. the rise of non-U.S. multinationals and the growth of mini-multinationals

Answer: A
Easy
Page: 16

45. Since the 1960s, one of the most notable trends in the demographics of the multinational enterprise has been the rise in __________ multinationals.

A. Japanese
B. United States
C. Russian
D. British

Answer: D
Easy
Page: 17

46. Mini-multinationals are:

A. multinational firms that obtain less than 10 percent of their revenues from investments in foreign countries
B. multinational firms from relatively small countries
C. multinational firms that operate in three or less foreign countries
D. small and medium-sized multinationals

Answer: A
Medium
Page: 17

47. Lubricating Systems Inc. is a small firm that generates more than $2 million in annual revenues through exports to a number of different foreign countries. Lubricating Systems Inc. and similar firms are referred to as:

A. mini-multinationals
B. secondary-multinationals
C. emerging-multinationals
D. subordinate-multinationals

THE CHANGING WORLD ORDER

Answer: D
Hard
Page: 19

48. Which of the following statements is not accurate in regard to many of the former communist nations of Europe and Asia?

A. many of these countries seem to share a commitment to democratic politics and free market economies
B. in these countries, the opportunities for international business may be enormous
C. the economies of most of the former communist states are weak
D. the risk of doing business in these countries is minimal

Answer: A
Hard
Page: 19

49. Which of the following statements is not accurate in regard to China?

A. China seems to be moving progressively towards greater trade isolationism
B. if current trends continue, China may move from Third World to industrial superpower status even more rapidly than Japan did
C. China represents a huge and largely untapped market
D. China's new firms are proving to be very capable competitors

Answer: B
Medium
Page: 19

50. Which of the following statements is not true regarding the majority of Latin American countries?

A. governments are selling state-owned enterprises to private investors
B. neither democracy nor free market reforms have seemed to take hold
C. foreign investment is welcome
D. debt and inflation are down

GLOBALIZATION, JOBS, AND INCOMES

Answer: B
Hard
Page: 22

51. Many influential economists, politicians, and business leaders argue that the twin engines that are driving the global economy toward greater prosperity are:

A. political reforms, information technology
B. falling barriers to international trade, investment
C. strong currencies worldwide, political reforms
D. investment, information technology

Answer: C
Easy
Page: 22

52. Economists argue that increased international trade and cross-boarder investments will result in __________ prices for goods and services.

A. stable
B. higher
C. lower
D. unstable

Answer: B
Hard
Page: 22

53. One frequently voiced concern about globalization is that it destroys manufacturing jobs in wealthy advanced economies such as the U.S. The basic thrust of the critics' argument is:

A. the governments of developing countries will heavily subsidize their primary industries, making competing products produced in advanced economies less attractive
B. falling trade barriers allows firms to move their manufacturing activities offshore to countries where wage rates are much lower
C. globalization increases the pace of the shift from a world economy based on manufactured goods to a world economy based on services
D. developing nations will recruit employees from the more advanced economies, thereby depleting their labor pools

Answer: B
Medium
Page: 23

54. In general, supporters of globalization argue that free trade benefits __________ that adhere to a free trade regime.

A. all but the largest countries
B. all countries
C. all but the smallest countries
D. all but the countries with the highest wage rates

GLOBALIZATION, LABOR POLICIES, AND THE ENVIRONMENT

Answer: C
Medium
Page: 23

55. Critics use the following argument to suggest that globalization is a contributing factor to an increase in pollution.

A. globalization results in an increase in the amount of activity that takes place in companies that do not have adequate pollution controls
B. globalization results in increased commerce between countries, which results in an increase in the amount of transportation activity (e.g., trains, barges, air cargo, trucks, and so on)
C. firms that operate in countries that have adequate pollution regulations have a tendency to move their manufacturing operations to countries that have less stringent or no pollution controls to avoid the cost of regulation
D. globalization results in increased production, which has the undesirable side-effects of increased pollution

Answer: A
Easy
Page: 23

56. Supporters of free trade argue that tougher environmental regulations and stricter labor standards __________ economic progress.

A. go hand in hand with
B. have no impact on
C. diminish
D. are incompatible with

GLOBALIZATION AND NATIONAL SOVEREIGNTY

Answer: B
Medium
Page: 24

57. What is the primary purpose of the World Trade Organization?

A. monitor the implementation of trade agreements such as NAFTA
B. arbitrate trade disputes
C. act as a "watchdog" for countries that lower their pollution standards in an effort to attract more foreign manufacturing activity
D. set tariffs for countries that signed the GATT agreements

Answer: D
Easy
Page: 24

58. The __________ was founded in 1994 to police the world trading system established by the General Agreement on Tariffs and Trade.

A. United Nations Trade Administration
B. Global Trade Monitoring Commission
C. International Trade Enforcement Agency
D. World Trade Organization

Answer: D
Hard
Page: 24

59. In what way can the World Trade Organization (WTO) penalize member countries that are found to be engaged in unfair trade practices?

A. the WTO can impose sanctions on the transgressor
B. the WTO can bring the employees of offending companies to court
C. the WTO can restrict the membership of the offending country in other world organizations such as the United Nations
D. the WTO panel can issue a ruling instructing a member state to change trade policies that violate GATT regulations, and if the policies are not changed, allow other states to impose sanctions

MANAGING IN THE GLOBAL MARKETPLACE

Answer: D
Easy
Page: 25

60. The minimum that a firm has to do to engage in international business is to:

A. license products to companies in other countries
B. establish joint ventures or strategic alliances with companies in other countries
C. invest directly in operations in another country
D. export or import

TRUE-FALSE QUESTIONS

INTRODUCTION

Answer: F
Easy
Page: 4

61. The rate at which globalization is spreading around the world has slowed down in recent years.

Answer: T
Easy
Page: 4

62. The global economy is moving towards a world in which national economies are merging into an interdependent global economic system, commonly referred to as globalization.

Answer: F
Easy
Page: 4

63. The trend towards a more integrated global economic system is a very recent phenomenon.

THE GLOBALIZATION OF MARKETS

Answer: F
Medium
Page: 5

64. Globalization has two main components: the globalization of markets and the globalization of finance.

Answer: F
Hard
Page: 5

65. Because of the global presence of widely accepted products like Citicorp credit cards, Coca-Cola, and McDonalds, national markets are all but disappearing.

Answer: T
Medium
Page: 5

66. The most global markets are the markets for industrial goods and materials.

THE GLOBALIZATION OF PRODUCTION

Answer: T
Easy
Page: 7

67. The globalization of production refers to the tendency among firms to source goods and services from locations around the globe to take advantage of national differences in the cost and quality of factors of production.

Answer: F
Medium
Page: 7

68. Although many companies have lowered their overall cost structure and have improved the quality of their products by dispersing their production activities to locations around the world, this activity is confined primarily to large firms.

Answer: F
Hard
Page: 7

69. As a result of the great promise of the globalization of production, very few impediments make it difficult for firms to achieve the optimal dispersion of their productive activities to locations around the world.

DECLINING TRADE AND INVESTMENT BARRIERS

Answer: T
Easy
Page: 8

70. International trade occurs when a firm exports goods or services to consumers in another country.

Answer: T
Easy
Page: 8

71. Foreign direct investment occurs when a firm invests resources in business activities outside its home country.

Answer: F
Medium
Page: 8

72. Although many countries have reduced trade barriers in recent years, a similar easing in restrictions on foreign direct investment has not occurred.

Answer: F
Hard
Page: 9

73. There is fairly compelling evidence that the lowering of trade barriers has had little effect on the globalization of production.

THE ROLE OF TECHNOLOGICAL CHANGE

Answer: T
Medium
Page: 10

74. According to Moore's Law, the power of microprocessor technology doubles and its cost of production falls in half every 18 months.

Answer: T
Easy
Page: 11

75. Due to containerization, the transportation costs associated with the globalization of trade have declined.

Answer: F
Medium
Page: 13

76. Largely as the result of globalization, very few national differences remain in culture, consumer preferences, and business practices between countries around the world.

THE CHANGING WORLD OUTPUT AND WORLD TRADE PICTURE

Answer: F
Medium
Page: 14

77. Over the past thirty years, U.S. dominance in export markets has increased, while the influence of Japan, Germany, and a number of newly industrialized countries such as South Korea and China have diminished in importance.

Answer: T
Medium
Page: 14

78. Notwithstanding the financial crisis that is gripping some Asian economies, if we look 20 years into the future, most forecasts now predict a rapid rise in the share of world output accounted for by developing nations such as China, India, and South Korea.

Answer: T
Medium
Page: 14

79. The globalization of the world economy, together with Japan's rise to the top rank of economic power, has resulted in a relative decline in the dominance of the United States in world trade.

Answer: T
Easy
Page: 14

80. South Korea is an example of a developing nation.

THE CHANGING FOREIGN DIRECT INVESTMENT PICTURE

Answer: F
Hard
Page: 15

81. The stock of foreign direct investment refers to the nations in the world that participate in direct foreign investment.

Answer: T
Medium
Page: 16

82. Among developing nations, China has received the greatest volume of inward FDI in recent years.

THE CHANGING NATURE OF MULTINATIONAL ENTERPRISE

Answer: T
Easy
Page: 16

83. A multinational enterprise is any business that has productive activities in two or more countries

Answer: T
Easy
Page: 17

84. Although most international trade and investment is still conducted by large firms, small to medium sized firms are increasingly involved in international trade and investment.

THE CHANGING WORLD ORDER

Answer: F
Medium
Page: 19

85. Many of the former communist nations of Europe and Asia seem to share a commitment to democratic politics and free market economics. As a result, the risks involved in doing business in such countries are relatively minor.

Answer: T
Medium
Page: 19

86. Throughout most of Latin America, debt and inflation are down, governments are selling state-owned enterprises to private investors, foreign investment is welcomed, and the region's economies are growing rapidly.

Answer: F
Easy
Page: 21

87. Current trends suggest that the world is moving rapidly toward an economic system that is not favorable for international trade.

Answer: F
Hard
Page: 22

88. Although there are many benefits to globalization, economists argue that increased international trade and cross-boarder investments will result in higher prices for goods and services.

Answer: T
Medium
Page: 23

89. One concern associated with globalization is that free trade may encourage firms from advanced nations to move manufacturing facilities offshore to less developed countries that lack adequate regulations to protect labor and the environment by abuse by the unscrupulous.

Answer: T
Medium
Page: 24

90. The World Trade Organization was founded in 1994 to police the world trading system established by the General Agreement on Tariffs and Trade.

Answer: F
Easy
Page: 25

91. An international business is any firm that employs people from more than one country.

ESSAY QUESTIONS

Medium
Page: 4

92. Describe the concept of globalization. What are the major opportunities and challenges that globalization has created for business organization?

Answer: Globalization refers to a fundamental shift that is occurring in the world economy. The world is progressively moving away from a structure in which national economies are relatively isolated from each other, towards a structure in which national economies are merging into one huge interdependent global economic system. This trend is commonly referred to as globalization.

The trend towards globalization is creating many opportunities for businesses to expand their revenues, drive down their costs, and boost their profits. For example, many American firms are now exporting to previously closed foreign markets. By doing so, these firms are simultaneously expanding their sales and driving down their costs through additional economies of scale. Globalization has also created challenges for business organizations. For example, managers now have to grapple with a wide range of globalization related issues. Examples of these issues include should we export, should we build a plant in a foreign country, should we modify our products to suite the tastes of each of our foreign customers, and how do we respond to foreign competition? These questions often do not have easy answers, but are very important to the future competitiveness of business organizations.

Medium
Page: 5

93. Describe the two main components of globalization. Explain how each of these components of globalization has helped create the shift towards a more integrated world economy.

Answer: The two main components of globalization are the globalization of markets and the globalization of production. The globalization of markets refers to the fact that in many industries historically distinct and separate national markets are merging into one huge global marketplace. The globalization of production refers to the tendency among many firms to source goods and services from different locations around the world in an attempt to take advantage of national differences in the cost and quality of factors of production (such as labor, energy, and capital).

Both of these components of globalization have helped create the shift towards a more integrated world economy. The globalization of markets has created a "global" interest in many products, such as Coca-Cola, the Sony Walkman, and Levi jeans. This "sharing of interest" in products across national boarders has facilitated the trend towards a more integrated world economy. The globalization of production has resulted in a substantial increase in the number of business relationships between companies from different countries. This increase in the number and intensity of interrelationships between companies from different countries has also facilitated the trend towards a more integrated world economy.

Easy
Page: 8

94. Define the term "foreign direct investment." How does the term "foreign direct investment" differ from the term "international trade?"

Answer: Foreign direct investment occurs when a firm invests resources in business activities outside its home country. For example, an American firm may invest in a production facility in Great Britain. International trade occurs when a firm exports goods or services to consumers in another country. The difference between the terms is that the term "international trade" does not necessarily mean that a firm is investing resources in business activities outside its home country. The firm could be simply exporting domestically produced products to a foreign country.

Easy
Page: 8

95. What has been the impact of the General Agreement on Tariffs and Trade (GATT) on average tariff rates for manufactured goods worldwide? In your judgment, has GATT been successful?

Answer: Since GATT was put in place, average tariff rates have fallen significantly. As shown in Table 1.1, average tariff rates have fallen dramatically since 1950 and under the Uruguay agreement should hit 3.9 percent by the year 2000. Most students will argue that GATT has been successful. Under the auspicious of GATT, tariff rates have declined worldwide which has been one of the major drivers of globalization.

Hard
Page: 8

96. Describe the meaning of the term "trade barriers"? What measures have been taken by the world community to reduce the impact of trade barriers on international trade?

Answer: Trade barriers are the regulations, tariffs, and other activities that are put in place by governments for the purpose of protecting their domestic industries from "foreign competition." For example, a country may impose a stiff tariff on the import of foreign produced automobiles. That makes it very difficult (i.e. creates a substantial barrier) for foreign produced cars to be sold in their country.

The world community has taken a number of measures to not only lessen the impact of trade barriers on international trade, but to remove trade barriers altogether. The General Agreement on Tariffs and Trade (GATT) has been an ongoing effort to remove and reduce trade barriers worldwide. Under the umbrella of GATT, there have been eight rounds of negotiations among member states, which now number 120, designed to lower and/or reduce all forms of trade barriers. To provide the GATT treaty some teeth, the recently completed Uruguary Round of GATT established the World Trade Organization (WTO) which polices the international trading system. Although the WTO cannot compel a nation to comply with the GATT treaty, it can recommend that other member nations impose sanctions on the offending party.

Other business organizations, governments, trade groups, and not-for-profit organizations are working hard to reduce and remove trade barriers.

Medium
Page: 11

97. The author of our textbook describes the World Wide Web as the "great equalizer." In the context of international trade, in what ways does the World Wide Web act as an equalizer?

Answer: The World Wide Web is an equalizer because it is relatively inexpensive and it is allows small firms the same opportunity as large firms to expand their global presence through a web site. Prior to the development of the web, only large firms like Sony and General Electric could afford to achieve a "global reach." Now, the vast majority of firms can afford to create a website and provide information about their products and services to a global audience.

A related way in which the World Wide Web is an equalizer is that websites can be accessed by potential customers' 24 hours per day, 365 days per year. As a result, a firm can offer information to potential customers (through the website itself or through downloads) around the clock. This lets a firm's employees go home at night, while its website is still "spreading the word" about the firm's products and services. Prior to the advent of the web, only larger firms with more resources could afford to have operators on duty 24 hours per day to answer questions about a firm's products or services or to send out information.

Easy
Page: 14

98. In we look 20 years into the future, how will the share of world output that is produced by industrial countries compared to developing nations differ from what it is today? In your answer, identify some of the industrial countries and some of the developing countries of the world.

Answer: If we look 20 years into the future, most forecasts now predict a rapid rise in the share of world output accounted for by developing nations such as China, India, Indonesia, Thailand, South Korea, and Brazil, and a commensurate decline in the share enjoyed by rich industrialized countries such as Britain, Germany, Japan, and the United States.

Hard
Page: 16

99. What is a multinational enterprise? What have been the two most notable trends in multinational enterprises since the 1960s? What is a mini-multinational? Do you expect the role of mini-multinationals to gain momentum or wane in the future? Why?

Answer: A multinational enterprise is any business that has productive activities in two or more countries. There are many multinational enterprises, including General Motors, Sony, General Electric, Exxon, and Toyota. The two most notable trends in multinational enterprises since the 1960s have been (1) the rise of non-U.S. multinationals, particularly Japanese multinationals; and (2) the growth of mini-multinationals.

Mini-multinationals are small and medium-sized international firms. The role of these firms is likely to gain momentum in the future. Many small and medium-sized companies are becoming increasingly involved in international trade, in a variety of different contexts. As these companies expand their international activities, they will increasingly take their place as mini-multinationals on the world stage.

Medium
Page: 22

100. Discuss the primary advantages and disadvantages of globalization. Do you believe the advantages outweigh the disadvantages? How can the effects of the disadvantages of globalization be reduced?

There are many advantages of globalization. From a broad perspective, globalization creates economic activity (which stimulates economic growth), creates jobs, raises income levels, and provides consumers with more choices in regard to the products and services that are available to them. From the perspective of an individual firm, globalization has the potential to increase revenues (through expanded market potential), drive down costs (through additional economies of scale), and boost profits.

Conversely, critics argue that globalization destroys manufacturing jobs in wealthy countries and contributes to pollution. In regard to destroying manufacturing jobs, the basic thrust of the critics argument is that falling trade barriers allow firms in industrialized countries to move their manufacturing activities offshore to countries where wage rates are much lower. This activity, if it occurs, has the undesirable side-effect of eliminating manufacturing jobs in the industrialized country. In regard to pollution, the critics of globalization argue that globalization encourages firms from advanced nations to move manufacturing facilities offshore to less developed countries to avoid the more stringent pollution controls in place in their home countries. This activity increases worldwide pollution.

The final section of the question is designed to encourage classroom discussion and/or to encourage students to "think" about how these undesirable side-effects of globalization can be reduced.

Medium
Page: 25

101. What are the main differences between managing an international and a domestic business?

Answer: Managing an international business is different from managing a purely domestic business for at least four reasons.

- Countries are different.
- The range of problems confronted by the manager of an international business is wider and the problems are more complex than those confronted by the manager of a strictly domestic business.
- An international business must find ways to work within the limits imposed by government invention into the international trade and investment system.
- International transactions involve converting money into different currencies.

CHAPTER 2

NATIONAL DIFFERENCES IN POLITICAL ECONOMY

MULTIPLE-CHOICE QUESTIONS

INTRODUCTION

Answer: D
Easy
Page: 34

1. Every country has a political, economic, and legal system. Collectively we refer to these systems as constituting the _________ economy of a country.

   A. civic
   B. public
   C. administrative
   D. political

Answer: B
Easy
Page: 34

2. Japan, England, and the United States all have unique political, economic, and legal systems. A country's political, economic, and legal system is collectively referred to as its _________ economy.

   A. administrative
   B. political
   C. civic
   D. official

POLITICAL SYSTEMS

Answer: D
Hard
Page: 34

3. Political systems can be assessed according to two related dimensions. These are:

   A. the degree to which they emphasize individualism opposed to totalitarian and the degree to which they are individualistic versus democratic
   B. the degree to which they are market oriented opposed to production orientated and the degree to which they are democratic verses individualistic
   C. the degree to which they are social democrats opposed to communists and the degree to which they emphasize collectivism opposed to individualism
   D. the degree to which they emphasize collectivism opposed to individualism and the degree to which they are democratic or totalitarian

Answer: A
Easy
Page: 34

4. By political system we mean the system of:

A. government in a nation
B. economic standards in a nation
C. cultural values and norms in a country
D. military and economic might in a country

Answer: C
Easy
Page: 35

5. The term __________ refers to a system that stresses the primacy of collective goals over individual goals.

A. individualism
B. democracy
C. collectivism
D. capitalism

Answer: A
Medium
Page:35

6. When collectivism is emphasized:

A. the needs of society as a whole are generally viewed as being more important than individual freedoms
B. the interests of the individual take precedence over the interests of the state
C. one person or political party exercises absolute control over all spheres of human life
D. the needs of society and the needs of individuals are equally balanced

Answer: B
Medium
Page: 35

7. Which of the following political systems is consistent with the notion that an individual's right to do something may be restricted because it runs counter to "the good of society" or "the common good."

A. capitalism
B. collectivism
C. democracy
D. individualism

Answer: D
Hard
Page: 35

8. In the early 20th century, the socialist ideology spit into two broad camps. The __________ believed that socialism could be achieved only through violent revolution and totalitarian dictatorship, while the __________ committed themselves to achieving socialism by democratic means and turned their backs on violent revolution and dictatorships.

A. individualists, collectivists
B. social democrats, communists
C. collectivists, individualists
D. communists, social democrats

Answer: C
Easy
Page: 35

9. The last major communist power left in the world is:

A. Hungry
B. Brazil
C. China
D. India

Answer: A
Medium
Page: 35

10. The group that was committed to achieving socialism by democratic means were referred to as:

A. social democrats
B. communists
C. collectivists
D. individualists

Answer: C
Medium
Page: 36

11. Experience has demonstrated that state owned companies in basic industries such as oil refining, steel, airlines, and auto production have performed:

A. well
B. about the same as privately owned companies in the same industries
C. poorly
D. at break even levels

Answer: A
Easy
Page: 36

12. The philosophy that is based on the idea that an individual should have freedom in his or her economic pursuits is called:

A. individualism
B. socialism
C. totalitarianism
D. collectivism

Answer: A
Hard
Page: 35

13. Individualism is built on two central tenets. These are:

A. an emphasis on the importance of guaranteeing individual freedom and self-expression, and the belief that the welfare of society is best served by letting people pursue their own economic self interests
B. an emphasis on suppressing the rights of individuals if they interfere with the rights of society, and the welfare of society is best served by distributing wealth equally
C. an individual's right to do something may be restricted on the grounds that it runs counter to "the good of society," and the welfare of society is best served by distributing wealth equally
D. an emphasis on the importance of guaranteeing individual freedom and self-expression, and the welfare of society is best served by distributing wealth equally

Answer: C
Easy
Page: 37

14. The political system in which government is "by the people", exercised either directly of through elected representatives is referred to as:

A. totalitarianism
B. despotism
C. democracy
D. individualism

Answer: B
Easy
Page: 37

15. __________ is a form of government is which one person or political party exercises absolute control over all spheres of human life and opposing political parties are prohibited.

A. Capitalism
B. Totalitarianism
C. Collectivism
D. Democracy

Answer: C
Medium
Page: 38

16. Which of the following restrictions is not consistent with the spirit of a representative democracy?

A. relatively free access to state information
B. free speech
C. a court system that is supervised by the political system
D. free media

Answer: B
Medium
Page: 38

17. Which of the following is not one of the four major forms of totalitarianism that exist in the world today?

A. tribal totalitarianism
B. collective totalitarianism
C. right-wing totalitarianism
D. communist totalitarianism

Answer: C
Medium
Page: 38

18. The form of totalitarianism that is found in states where political power is monopolized by a party, group, or individual that governs according to religious principles is referred to as:

A. right-wind totalitarianism
B. tribal totalitarianism
C. theocratic totalitarianism
D. communist totalitarianism

Answer: A
Medium
Page: 38

19. In which region of the world is tribal totalitarianism found?

A. Africa
B. South America
C. Asia
D. Australia

Answer: B
Medium
Page: 38

20. __________ totalitarianism generally permits individual economic freedom but restricts individual political freedom on the grounds that it would lead to the rise of communism.

A. Tribal
B. Right-wing
C. Theocratic
D. Communist

ECONOMIC SYSTEMS

Answer: B
Medium
Page: 40

21. The four broad types of economic systems are:

A. market economy, collective economy, production economy, and political economy
B. market economy, command economy, mixed economy, and state-directed economy
C. collective economy, production economy, mixed economy, and politically-controlled economy
D. market economy, production economy, politically-controlled economy, and command economy

Answer: C
Medium
Page: 39

22. In a pure __________ economy all productive activities are privately owned, as opposed to being owed by the state.

A. mixed
B. command
C. market
D. production

Answer: D
Medium
Page: 39

23. In a pure command economy, the goods and services that a country produces, the quantity in which they are produced, and the prices at which they are sold are all planned by:

A. private industry
B. individual entrepreneurs
C. local trade associations
D. the government

Answer: A
Medium
Page: 40

24. In a __________ economy, certain sectors of the economy are left to private ownership and free market mechanisms, while other sectors have significant state ownership and government planning.

A. mixed
B. state-directed
C. market
D. command

Answer: B
Hard
Page: 40

25. Which of the following group of countries can be classified as mixed economies?

A. Japan, South Korea, and Thailand
B. France, Italy, and Sweden
C. Canada, United States, and Great Britain
D. Brazil, Columbia, and Chile

Answer: C
Medium
Page: 40

26. A __________ is one in which the state plays a significant role in directing the investment activities of private enterprise through "industrial policy" and in otherwise regulating business activity in accordance with national goals.

A. mixed economy
B. market economy
C. state-directed economy
D. command economy

Answer: B
Hard
Page: 41

27. The infant industry argument suggests that:

A. in select industries, new firms should be given tax abatements to provide them an evenhanded chance of succeeding given the market share currently controlled by larger firms
B. in some industries, economies of scale are so large and incumbent firms from developed nations have such an advantage that it is difficult for new firms from developing nations to establish themselves
C. in the majority of cases, infant industries in developing countries must be started by firms from developed countries that have experience in the industry
D. firms in infant industries are more prone to failure than firms in more mature industries

LEGAL SYSTEMS

Answer: D
Easy
Page: 41

28. The __________ of a country refers to the rules, or laws, that regulate behavior along with the processes by which the laws are enforced and through which redress for grievances is obtained.

    A. political system
    B. bureaucratic system
    C. economic structure
    D. legal system

Answer: D
Easy
Page: 41

29. __________ rights refer to the bundle of legal rights over the use to which a resource is put and over the use made of any income that may be derived from that resource.

    A. Equity
    B. Authoritative
    C. Statutory
    D. Property

Answer: A
Easy
Page: 43

30. __________ refers to property, such as computer software, a screenplay, a music score, or the chemical formula for a new drug, that is the product of intellectual activity.

    A. Intellectual property
    B. Proprietary goods
    C. Exclusive ownership
    D. Restrictive goods

Answer: C
Medium
Page: 43

31. The legal instrument that grants the inventor of a new product or process exclusive rights to the manufacture, use, or sale of that invention is referred to as a:

    A. trademark
    B. intellectual property certificate
    C. patent
    D. copyright

Answer: C
Medium
Page: 43

32. McDonalds is able to prevent other companies from opening fast-food restaurants with the McDonalds name and the McDonalds golden arches because McDonalds has obtained __________ protection on its name and distinctive designs.

A. copyright
B. patent
C. trademark
D. intellectual property certificate

Answer: B
Hard
Page: 43

33. The purpose behind intellectual property rights is that they:

A. discourage people from working on inventions or novel ideas that have no commercial potential
B. provide an incentive for people to search for novel ways of doing things and they reward creativity
C. place a dollar value on patents, copyrights, and trademarks
D. standardize patent regulations worldwide

Answer: D
Medium
Page: 45

34. Product liability involves holding a firm and its officers responsible when:

A. a product is sold for less than its cost of production
B. a product is sold for more in one part of the country than another
C. a product fails to meet the expectations of its users
D. a product causes injury, death, or damage

Answer: D
Medium
Page: 46

35. There are two main legal traditions found in the world today. These are:

A. administrative law system and civil law system
B. common law system and mutual law system
C. interdependent law system and independent law system
D. common law system and civil law system

Answer: C
Hard
Page: 46

36. The legal framework referred to as __________ law is based on tradition, precedent, and custom. In contrast, __________ law is based on a very detailed set of laws organized into codes.

A. bureaucratic, administrative
B. jurisdictional, civil
C. common, civil
D. administrative, jurisdictional

Answer: A
Medium
Page: 46

37. The legal system based on tradition, precedent, and custom that evolved in England over hundreds of years and is now found in Britain's former colonies, including the United States, is called:

A. common law
B. civil law
C. administrative law
D. jurisdictional law

THE DETERMINANTS OF ECONOMIC DEVELOPMENT

Answer: B
Easy
Page: 47

38. GNP is an acronym that stands for:

A. General National Profile
B. Gross National Product
C. Geographic National Preference
D. Geneva National Petition

Answer: A
Medium
Page:

39. The United Nations __________ index is based on life expectancy, literacy rates, and whether the average income is sufficient to meet the basic needs of life in a particular country.

A. Human Development
B. Quality of Life
C. Humane Living
D. Economic Vitality

Answer: D
Hard
Page: 50

40. The United Nations Human Development Index is based on the following three measures.

A. standard of living, quality of transportation, and life expectancy
B. access to medical care, access to education, and life expectancy
C. access to education, literacy rates, and whether average incomes, based on PPP estimates, are sufficient to meet the basic needs of life in a country
D. life expectancy, literacy rates, and whether average incomes, based on PPP estimates, are sufficient to meet the basic needs of life in a country

Answer: C
Hard
Page: 50

41. The Human Development Index is scaled from 0 to 100. Countries scoring less than __________ are classified as low human development (i.e. the quality of life is poor).

A. 10
B. 30
C. 50
D. 70

Answer: B
Medium
Page: 50

42. There is general agreement that __________ is the engine of long-run economic growth.

A. economic policy
B. innovation
C. basic manufacturing
D. agriculture

Answer: A
Medium
Page: 50

43. It has been argued that the economic freedom associated with a __________ economy creates greater incentives for innovation than alternative economic systems.

A. market
B. command
C. mixed
D. state directed

Answer: B
Easy
Page: 53

44. __________ is the process of selling state-owned enterprises to private investors.

A. Capitalization
B. Privatization
C. Downsizing
A. Simplification

STATES IN TRANSITION

Answer: A
Hard
Page: 55

45. Since the late 1980s there have been two major changes in the political economy of many of the world's nation-states. These two changes have been:

A. a wave of democratic revolutions have swept the world, and there has been a strong move away from centrally planned and mixed economies and toward a more free market economic model
B. a wave of socialistic revolutions have swept the world, and there has been a strong move away from mixed economies and towards a more centrally planned economic model
C. a wave of communist revolutions have swept the world, and there has been a strong move away from free market economies and towards more mixed and centrally planned economic models
D. a wave of democratic revolutions have swept the world, and there has been a strong move away from centrally planned economies and towards more mixed economic models

Answer: D
Hard
Page: 56

46. What percent of the world's population presently lives under democratic rule?

A. 5 percent
B. 20 percent
C. 40 percent
D. 55 percent

Answer: D
Hard
Page: 56

47. Which of the following is not one of the reasons that democracy has spread around the world?

A. many totalitarian regimes have failed to deliver economic progress to the vast bulk of their populations
B. many information and communications technologies have broken down the ability of the state to control access to uncensored information
C. in many countries the economic advances of the last quarter century have led to the emergence of increasingly prosperous middle and working classes who have pushed for democratic reforms
D. the global spread of democracy has not been challenged economically or politically

Answer: C
Easy
Page: 61

48. __________ involves removing legal restrictions to the free play of markets, the establishment of private enterprises, and the manner in which private enterprises operate.

A. Privatization
B. Simplification
C. Deregulation
D. Downsizing

Answer: B
Easy
Page: 63

49. The transfer of the ownership of state property into the hands of private individuals, frequently by the sale of state assets through an auction, is referred to as:

A. Deregulation
B. Privatization
C. Simplification
D. Downsizing

Answer: B
Medium
Page: 63

50. The privatization movement started in __________ in the early 1980s when then prime-Prime Minister Margaret Thatcher started to sell state-owned assets.

A. Canada
B. Britain
C. Germany
D. France

IMPLICATIONS FOR BUSINESS

Answer: D
Easy
Page: 66

51. Advantages that accrue to early entrants into a business market are referred to as:

A. prime-mover advantages
B. proactive advantages
C. standard-class advantages
D. first-mover advantages

Answer: C
Easy
Page: 66

52. __________ advantages accrue to early entrants into a business market.

A. Prime-mover
B. Proactive-mover
C. First-mover
D. Standard-class

Answer: A
Easy
Page: 66

53. Handicaps suffered by late entrants into a business market are referred to as:

A. late-mover disadvantages
B. last-in-class disadvantages
C. late-mover difficulties
D. late-mover miscues

Answer: B
Medium
Page: 66

54. Countries with __________ economies in which property rights are well protected tend to achieve greater economic growth rates than command economies and/or economies where property rights are poorly protected.

A. mixed
B. free market
C. state-directed
D. totalitarian

Answer: B
Medium
Page: 67

55. The likelihood that political forces will cause drastic changes in a country's business environment that adversely affect the profit and other goals of a particular business enterprise is referred to as:

A. governmental risk
B. political risk
C. administrative risk
D. democratic risk

Answer: A
Medium
Page: 67

56. The likelihood that economic mismanagement will cause drastic changes in a country's business environment that adversely affect the profit and other goals of a business enterprise is called:

A. economic risk
B. commercial risk
C. legal risk
D. industrial risk

Answer: C
Medium
Page: 68

57. The likelihood that a trading partner will opportunistically break a contract or expropriate property rights is referred to as:

A. political risk
B. moral risk
C. legal risk
D. economic risk

Answer: C
Medium
Page: 68

58. The overall attractiveness of a country as a potential market and/or investment site for an international business depends on:

A. tariff rates
B. the type of economic system in place
C. balancing the benefits, costs, and risks associated with doing business in the country
D. the receptivity of the host government

Answer: A
Medium
Page: 70

59. The __________ is a U.S. law enacted in 1977 that prohibits U.S. companies from making "corrupt" payments to foreign officials for the purpose of obtaining or retaining business.

A. Foreign Corrupt Practices Act
B. Federal Mercenary Practices Act
C. Federal Corrupt Behavior Act
D. Federal Ethical Standards Act

Answer: C
Hard
Page: 70

60. The Foreign Corrupt Practices Act is a U.S. law enacted in 1977 that prohibits U.S. companies from:

A. making products in overseas markets that do not comply with the same safety and environmental regulations as domestically produced products
B. exporting to countries that do not comply with United Nations human rights regulations
C. making corrupt payments to foreign officials for the purpose of obtaining or retaining business
D. selling products for corrupt, unethical, or illegal purposes

TRUE-FALSE QUESTIONS

INTRODUCTION

Answer: F
Easy
Page: 34

61. The political, economic, and legal systems of a country are independent of each other.

POLITICAL SYSTEMS

Answer: T
Hard
Page: 34

62. Political systems can be assessed according to two related dimensions. The first is the degree to which they emphasize collectivism as opposed to individualism. The second dimension is the degree to which they are democratic or totalitarian.

Answer: F
Medium
Page: 34

63. Political systems that emphasize collectivism tend to be democratic.

Answer: T
Easy
Page: 35

64. The term collectivism refers to a system that stresses the primacy of collective goals over individual goals.

Answer: F
Medium
Page: 35

65. When collectivism is emphasized, the interests of individuals take precedence over the interests of the state.

Answer: T
Easy
Page: 36

66. Individualism is the opposite of collectivism.

Answer: T
Easy
Page: 37

67. Totalitarianism is a form of government in which one person or political party exercises absolute control over all spheres of human life and opposing political parties are prohibited.

Answer: F
Hard
Page: 38

68. Four major forms of totalitarianism exist in the world today. These are communist totalitarianism, collective totalitarianism, theocratic totalitarianism, and right-wing totalitarianism.

Answer: F
Medium
Page: 38

69. Right-wind totalitarianism is found in states where political power is monopolized by a party, group, or individual that governs according to religious principles.

ECONOMIC SYSTEMS

Answer: T
Medium
Page: 39

70. In countries where individual goals are given primacy over collective goals, we are more likely to find free market economic systems.

Answer: F
Easy
Page: 39

71. In a pure market economy, all productive activities are owned by the state, as opposed to being privately owned.

Answer: T
Medium
Page: 39

72. In a pure command economy, the goods and services that a country produces, the quantity in which they are produced, and the prices at which they are sold are all planned by the government.

Answer: T
Hard
Page: 40

73. Historically, command economies were found in communist countries where collectivist goals were given priority over individual goals.

Answer: F
Medium
Page: 40

74. Japan and South Korea are frequently cited as examples of command economies.

LEGAL SYSTEM

Answer: F
Easy
Page: 41

75. The legal system of a country is of little importance to international business.

Answer: T
Easy
Page: 41

76. Property rights refer to the bundle of legal rights over the use to which a resource is put and over the use made of any income that may be derived from that resource.

Answer: T
Easy
Page: 43

77. Intellectual property refers to property, such as computer software, a screenplay, or a chemical formula for a new drug, that is the product of intellectual activity.

Answer: F
Medium
Page: 43

78. A copyright grants the inventor of a new product or process exclusive rights to the manufacture, use, or sale of that invention.

Answer: F
Hard
Page: 43

79. The protection of intellectual property rights is very similar from country to country.

Answer: T
Easy
Page: 46

80. Common law is based on tradition, precedent, and custom.

THE DETERMINANTS OF ECONOMIC DEVELOPMENT

Answer: F
Medium
Page: 50

81. The United Nations Quality of Life Index is based on life expectancy, literacy rates, and whether the average income in a particular country is sufficient to meet the basic needs of life.

Answer: T
Easy
Page: 50

82. There is general agreement that innovation is the engine of long-run economic growth.

Answer: T
Medium
Page: 53

83. Privatization refers to the process of selling state-owned enterprises to private investors.

STATES IN TRANSITION

Answer: T
Medium
Page: 61

84. The shift toward a market-based economic system typically entail a number of steps, including deregulation, privatization, and the creation of a legal system to safeguard property rights.

Answer: F
Medium
Page: 61

85. Decentralization involves removing legal restrictions to the free play of markets, the establishment of private enterprises, and the manner in which private enterprise operates.

IMPLICATIONS FOR BUSINESS

Answer: T
Medium
Page: 65

86. In the most general sense, the long-run monetary benefits of doing business in a country are a function of the size of the market, the present wealth of consumers in that market, and the likely future wealth of consumers.

Answer: F
Medium
Page: 66

87. First-mover advantages are the advantages that accrue to the first firms that exit unprofitable markets.

Answer: T
Medium
Page: 67

88. Political risk has been defined as the likelihood that political forces will cause drastic changes in a country's business environment that adversely affect the profit and other goals of a particular business enterprise.

Answer: F
Medium
Page: 68

89. Economic risks might be defined as the likelihood that a trading partner will opportunistically break a contract or expropriate property rights.

Answer: T
Medium
Page: 70

90. The Foreign Corrupt Practices Act is a U.S. law enacted in 1977 that prohibits U.S. companies from making "corrupt" payments to foreign officials for the purpose of obtaining or retaining business.

ESSAY QUESTIONS

Easy
Page: 34

91. What is meant by the term "political system?" What are the two related dimensions by which a political system can be assessed?

Answer: A country's "political system" is its system of government. Political systems can be assessed according to two related dimensions. The first is the degree to which they emphasize collectivism as opposed to individualism. The second dimension is the degree to which they are democratic or totalitarian.

Medium
Page: 35

92. Describe the difference between collectivism and individualism. Are these two ideologies compatible or in direct conflict? Which ideology seems to be gaining ground and which ideology is waning? Is this good news or bad news or international commerce? Explain your answer.

Answer: The term collectivism refers to a political system that stresses the primacy of collective goals over individual goals. The general ideal is that the needs of society as a whole are more important than individual freedoms. As a result, in a collectivist society, an individual's right to do something may be restricted because it runs counter to "the good of the society" or the "common good." Individualism refers to a philosophy that an individual should have freedom in his or her economic and political pursuits. Moreover, individualism stresses that the interests of the individual should take precedence over the interests of the state.

The ideals exposed by individualism and collectivism are in direct conflict with one another. Over the past two decades, collectivism has been waning and individualism has been gaining steam. A wave of democratic ideals and free market economics is currently sweeping away socialism and communism worldwide. Evidence of this can be seen in Eastern Europe and the republics of the former Soviet Union. According to the author of the textbook, this represent good news for international business, since the pro-business and pro-free trade values of individualism create a favorable environment within which international business can thrive.

Medium
Page: 37

93. Draw a distinction between democracy and totalitarianism. Which political system facilitates the development of a free market economic system? Why?

Answer: Democracy and totalitarianism are at different ends of the political spectrum. Democracy refers to a political system in which government is by the people, exercised either directly or through elected representatives. Totalitarianism is a form of government in which one person or political parties exercise absolute control over all spheres of human life, and opposing political parties are prohibited. Most modern democratic states practice what is commonly referred to as representative democracy. In a representative democracy, citizens periodically elect individuals to represent them. There are four major forms of totalitarianism, including communist totalitarianism, theocratic totalitarianism, tribal totalitarianism, and right-wing totalitarianism.

A democratic political system facilitates the development of a free market economy. A democratic system favors the primacy of individual goals over collective goals, which facilitates the development of free markets.

Medium
Page: 39

94. Describe the difference between a pure market economy and a pure command economy. In each type of economy, who decides the goods and services that are produced, the quantities in which they are produced, and the prices that are charged to consumers?

Answer: In a pure market economy all productive activities are privately owned, as opposed to being owned by the state. The goods and services that a country produces, and the quantities in which they are produced, are not planned by anyone. Rather, production is determined by the interaction of supply and demand and signaled to producers through the price system. In a pure command economy, all businesses are state owned. Under these conditions, the goods and services that a country produces, the quantities in which they are produced, and the prices at which they are sold are all planned by the government.

Hard
Page: 43

95. What is intellectual property? What is the philosophy behind intellectual property law? Why is it so important to protect intellectual property rights? Are the laws that protect intellectual property rights fairly consistent across nations, or do they vary widely? Is this a problem?

Answer: Intellectual property refers to property, such as computer software, a screenplay, a musical score, or the chemical formula for a new drug, that is the product of intellectual activity. The philosophy behind intellectual property law is to reward the originator of a new invention, book, musical score, clothes design, and the like for his or her new idea. Without strict intellectual property laws, there would be very little incentive for an individual to work hard to create these types of items. For instance, a person could work very hard and spend huge amounts of money to create a new animated film, and have someone else duplicate the film for the cost of a film duplicating machine and a blank tape.

Unfortunately, the protection of intellectual property rights varies greatly from country to country. This is a problem. Weak laws or the weak enforcement of intellectual property laws in foreign countries encourages the piracy of intellectual property. The world community is addressing this problem, but a satisfactory solution has yet to be found.

Medium
Page: 46

96. What is a contract? What is contract law? Can contract law differ significantly across nations? Is it important for an international business to be familiar with the specifics of the contract law in each of the countries in which it operates?

Answer: A contract is a document that specifies the conditions under which an exchange is to occur, and details the rights and obligations of the parties to a contract. Many business transactions are regulated by some form of contract. Contract law is the body of law that governs contract enforcement. Contact law can differ significantly across countries. It is important for an international business to be familiar with the specifics of the contract law in each of the countries in which it operates. Differences in contract law across countries affects the kind of contracts an international business will want to use to safeguard its position in a particular country should a contact dispute arise.

Easy
Page: 50

97. How important is innovation? Does innovation have a better chance of catching hold in a market economy or a planned economy? Explain your answer.

Answer: There is general agreement that innovation is the engine of long-run economic growth in virtually any country. Innovation has a much better chance of catching hold in a market economy opposed to a planned economy. The individual freedom (and opportunity for personal gain) associated with a market economy (like the economy in the U.S.) creates greater incentives for innovation than either a planned or mixed economy. In a market economy, anyone who has an innovative idea is free to try to develop the idea, and has the potential to reap substantial personal gain. This feature of a market economy provides a powerful incentive for people to work on innovative ideas. In contrast, in a planned economy the state owns all means of production. Consequently there is no incentive or opportunity for entrepreneurial individuals to try to develop valuable new innovations, since it is the state, rather than the individual, that captures all of the gains.

Medium
Page: 61

98. According to our textbook, the shift toward a market-based economic system entails a number of steps. The first step is deregulation, which involves removing legal restrictions to the free play of markets, the establishment of private enterprise, and the manner in which private enterprise operates. What are the remaining two steps, and what do they accomplish?

Answer: The remaining two steps are privatization and the creation of a legal system to safeguard property rights. Privatization involves the sale of state owned property to private individuals or corporations. It is seen as a way of motivating efficiency by putting industry in the hands of private individuals (or corporations) who have a financial incentive to see that the industries succeed. The creation of legal systems to safeguard property rights, which include patents, copyrights, and trademarks, is also important in a market-based economy. Without a legal system that protects property rights, and without the machinery to enforce that system, the incentive to create new products and services and engage in other forms of economic activity is reduced significantly.

Medium
Page: 67

99. What is the difference between political risk, economic risk, and legal risk?

Answer: Political risk is the likelihood that political forces will cause drastic changes in a country's business environment that adversely affect the profit and other goals of a business enterprise. In contrast, economic risk is the likelihood that economic mismanagement will cause drastic changes in a country's business environment that adversely affect the profit and other goals of a business enterprise. Finally, legal risk is the likelihood that a trading partner will opportunistically break a contract or expropriate property rights.

Medium
Page: 69

100. One major ethical dilemma facing firms from Western democracies is whether they should do business in totalitarian countries that routinely violate the human rights of their citizens. What is the principle argument on both sides of this issue? What is your opinion?

Answer: This question is designed to stimulate classroom discussion and/or encourage your students to think about a difficult ethical issue. The two sides to the debate alluded to above are as follows:

Arguments against Western democracies doing business in totalitarian countries: Some people argue that investing in totalitarian countries provides comfort to dictators and can help prop up repressive regimes that abuse basic human rights. Moreover, these critics argue that without the participation of Western investors in their economies, many repressive regimes would collapse and be replaced by more democratically inclined governments.

Arguments in favor of Western democracies doing business in totalitarian countries: In contrast, there are those who argue that investment by a Western firm, by raising the level of economic development of a totalitarian country, can help change it from within. They note that economic well-being and political well-being often go hand-in-hand.

CHAPTER 3

DIFFERENCES IN CULTURE

MULTIPLE-CHOICE QUESTIONS

WHAT IS CULTURE?

Answer: B
Easy
Page: 79

1. A __________ is a system of values and norms that are shared among a group of people and that when taken together constitute a design for living.

   A. fraternity
   B. culture
   C. clique
   D. society

Answer: C
Easy
Page: 79

2. Abstract ideas about what a group believes to be good, right, and desirable are referred to as:

   A. norms
   B. culture
   C. values
   D. philosophies

Answer: D
Easy
Page: 79

3. The social rules and guidelines that prescribe appropriate behavior in public situations are referred to as:

   A. values
   B. cultures
   C. routines
   D. norms

Answer: A
Easy
Page: 79

4. A __________ is a group of people who share a common set of values and norms.

   A. society
   B. cohort
   C. fraternity
   D. country

Answer: D
Medium
Page: 79

5. The two major categories of norms are:

A. routines and values
B. conduct and culture
C. rites and rituals
D. folkways and mores

Answer: A
Easy
Page: 79

6. The routine conventions of everyday life are referred to as __________.

A. folkways
B. mores
C. rites
D. rituals

Answer: D
Hard
Page: 79

7. __________ are social conventions concerning things such as the appropriate dress code in a particular situation, good social manners, eating with the correct utensils, neighborly behavior, and the like.

A. Rites
B. Rituals
C. Mores
D. Folkways

SOCIAL STRUCTURE

Answer: B
Difficult
Page: 81

8. Although there are many different aspects of social structure, two main dimensions stand out when explaining differences between cultures. These are:

A. the degree to which the basic unit of social organization is the group, as opposed to the individual, and the degree to which the basic unit of society is a clique
B. the degree to which the basic unit of social organization is the individual, as opposed to the group, and the degree to which a society is stratified into classes or castes
C. the degree to which the basic unit of social organization is the group, as opposed to the individual, and the degree to which a society is heterogeneous
D. the degree to which the basic unit of social organization is the extended family, and the degree to which the basic unit of society is heterogeneous

Answer: C
Easy
Page: 82

9. A __________ is an association of two or more individuals who have a shared sense of identity and who interact with each other in structured ways on the basis of a common set of expectations about each other's behaviors.

A. society
B. country
C. group
D. assemblage

Answer: D
Hard
Page: 82

10. According to our book, while groups are found in all societies, societies differ according to the degree to which the group is viewed as:

A. the primary means of social mobility
B. the primary means of forming a government
C. the primary means of determining social norms
D. the primary means of social organization

Answer: D
Medium
Page: 82

11. The high level of entrepreneurial activity in the United States can be attributed in part to the high level of emphasis placed on the __________ in the American society.

A. group
B. cadre
C. community
D. individual

Answer: A
Medium
Page: 83

12. In contrast to the Western emphasis on the __________, in many other societies the __________ is the primary unit of social organization.

A. individual, group
B. group, clan
C. coterie, individual
D. clan, group

Answer: B
Medium
Page: 83

13. A central value of the Japanese culture is the importance attached to:

A. individualism
B. group membership
C. personal distinctiveness
D. personal individuality

Answer: C
Easy
Page: 84

14. All societies are stratified on a hierarchical basis into social categories, or:

A. social segments
B. norm based strata
C. social strata
D. norm based associations

Answer: B
Medium
Page: 84

15. The term that refers to the extent to which individuals can move out of the strata into which they are born is referred to as:

A. vertical potential
B. social mobility
C. social potential
D. vertical mobility

Answer: A
Easy
Page: 84

16. The most rigid system of stratification is a:

A. caste system
B. culture
C. community
D. class system

Answer: C
Medium
Page: 84

17. A __________, in which social mobility is possible, is a less rigid form of social stratification than a caste system.

A. community system
B. norm system
C. class system
D. culture system

Answer: A
Medium
Page: 84

18. A caste system is a __________ system of stratification in which social position is determined by the family into which a person is born, and change in that position is usually not possible during an individual's lifetime.

A. closed
B. open
C. malleable
D. flexible

Answer: C
Medium
Page: 84

19. The most rigid system of stratification is a __________ system.

A. degree
B. class
C. caste
D. cross-cultural

Answer: A
Medium
Page: 84

20. Although the number of societies with caste systems has diminished rapidly during the 20th century, one major example still remains. The country of __________ still has four main castes and several thousand subcastes.

A. India
B. Britain
C. China
D. Japan

Answer: D
Medium
Page: 84

21. Historically, British society was divided into three main classes:

A. the higher class, the central class, and the lower class
B. the preferred class, the medium class, and the lower class
C. the topmost class, the central class, and the bottom class
D. the upper class, the middle class, and the working class

Answer: B
Medium
Page: 85

22. __________ refers to a condition where people tend to perceive themselves in terms of their class background, and this shapes their relationships with members of other classes.

A. Social awareness
B. Class consciousness
C. Denominational awareness
D. Category attentiveness

RELIGIOUS AND ETHICAL SYSTEMS

Answer: D
Easy
Page: 86

23. The system of shared beliefs and rituals that are concerned with the realm of the sacred is referred to as:

A. divinity
B. persuasion
C. doctrine
D. religion

Answer: A
Easy
Page: 86

24. __________ systems refer to a set of moral principles, or values, that are used to guide and shape behavior.

A. Ethical
B. Social
C. Norming
D. Class

Answer: D
Medium
Page 86

25. Most of the world's ethical systems are the product of:

A. economic heritage
B. political heritage
C. historical norms
D. religions

Answer: C
Medium
Page: 86

26. The most widely practiced religion in the world is:

A. Islam
B. Hinduism
C. Christianity
D. Buddhism

Answer: B
Easy
Page: 86

27. The vast majority of Christians live in __________.

A. Asia and Australia
B. Europe and the Americas
C. North and South America
D. Eastern Europe and Asia

Answer: D
Hard
Page: 86

28. In 1904, a German sociologist, Max Weber, made a connection between __________ ethics and "the spirit of capitalism" that has since become famous.

A. Catholic
B. Islamic
C. Buddhist
D. Protestant

Answer: B
Hard
Page: 88

29. Which of following pairs of religious beliefs are most likely to lead to economic development and growth?

A. Hinduism and Buddhism
B. Islam and Christianity
C. Christianity and Buddhism
D. Confucianism and Islam

Answer: A
Hard
Page: 88

30. With close to one billion adherents, __________ is the second largest of the world's major religions.

A. Islam
B. Christianity
C. Hinduism
D. Confucianism

Answer: C
Hard
Page: 88

31. Which of the following is not one of the major principles of Islam?

A. honoring and respecting parents
B. respecting the rights of others
C. being pretentious, rather than humble
D. safeguarding the possessions of orphans

Answer: A
Hard
Page: 89

32. The Koran __________ of free enterprise and of earning legitimate profit through trade and commerce.

A. speaks approvingly
B. does not address the issue
C. speaks critically
D. forbids the practice

Answer: C
Medium
Page: 90

33. Islamic countries are likely to be receptive to international business as long as those businesses:

A. employ Islamic people
B. have property in an Islamic nation
C. behave in a manner that is consistent with Islamic ethics
D. adhere to Islamic beliefs

Answer: B
Medium
Page: 90

34. Which of the following religions prohibits the payment or receipt of interest?

A. Christianity
B. Islam
C. Hinduism
D. Confucianism

Answer: C
Medium
Page: 91

35. __________ has approximately 500 million adherents, most of whom are on the Indian subcontinent.

A. Buddhism
B. Confucianism
C. Hinduism
D. Islam

Answer: A
Hard
Page: 92

36. Max Weber, who is famous for expounding on the Protestant work ethic, also argued that the ascetic principles embedded in _________ do not encourage the kind of entrepreneurial activity or pursuit of wealth creation that we find in Protestantism.

A. Hinduism
B. Buddhism
C. Islam
D. Confucianism

Answer: C
Hard
Page: 91

37. Which of the following is the world's oldest major religion?

A. Christianity
B. Islam
C. Hinduism
D. Confucianism

Answer: B
Medium
Page: 92

38. _________ believe there is a moral force in society that requires the acceptance of certain responsibilities, called *dharma*.

A. Muslims
B. Hindus
C. Christians
D. Confucians

Answer: A
Medium
Page: 92

39. The terms *dharma, karma*, and *nirvana* are associated with the _________ religion.

A. Hindu
B. Christian
C. Buddhist
D. Islamic

Answer: D
Medium
Page: 92

40. Buddhists are found primarily in the following areas:

A. South America
B. Western Europe and North America
C. The Middle East and Eastern Africa
D. Central and Southwest Asia, China, Korea, and Japan

Answer: D
Medium
Page: 92

41. __________ was founded in India in the sixth century B.C. by Siddhartha Guatama, an Indian prince who renounced his wealth to pursue an ascetic lifestyle and spiritual perfection.

A. Islam
B. Confucianism
C. Hinduism
D. Buddhism

Answer: C
Medium
Page: 93

42. Individual who follow the teaching of Confucius are found primarily in:

A. The Middle East and Eastern Africa
B. North America and Western Europe
C. China, Korea, and Japan
D. Eastern Europe and the republics of the former Soviet Union

Answer: C
Hard
Page: 93

43. The values of loyalty, reciprocal obligations, and honesty are central to the __________ system of ethics.

A. Buddhist
B. Islamic
C. Confucian
D. Hindu

LANGUAGE

Answer: D
Medium
Page: 94

44. The most widely spoken language in the world is:

A. Spanish
B. German
C. French
D. English

Answer: C
Medium
Page: 94

45. The language of international business is increasingly becoming:

A. Spanish
B. Japanese
C. English
D. French

Answer: D
Medium
Page: 94

46. Based on recent trends in international business, when a Japanese and a German businessperson get together to do business, it is almost certain that they will communicate in:

A. French
B. Japanese
C. German
D. English

CULTURE AND THE WORKPLACE

Answer: D
Easy
Page: 99

47. The most famous study of how culture relates to values in the workplace was undertaken by:

A. Michael Porter
B. George Williams
C. Thomas Peters
D. Geert Hofstede

Answer: A
Medium
Page: 99

48. Geert Hofstede isolated four dimensions that he claimed summarized different cultures. Which of the following is not one of Hofstede's dimensions?

A. capitalistic versus socialistic
B. masculinity versus femininity
C. power distance
D. uncertainty avoidance

Answer: D
Medium
Page: 99

49. In his studies, Hofstede isolated four dimensions that he claimed summarized different cultures. These were:

A. individualism versus collectivism, power distance, tolerant versus intolerant, and aggressive verses passive
B. uncertainty avoidance, masculinity versus femininity, individual versus group oriented, forward versus reserved
C. aggressive versus passive, tolerant versus intolerant, power distance, and individual versus group oriented
D. power distance, individualism versus collectivism, uncertainty avoidance, and masculinity versus femininity

Answer: C
Medium
Page: 99

50. Hofstede's __________ dimension focused on how a society deals with the fact that people are unequal in physical and intellectual capabilities.

A. uncertainty avoidance
B. individualism versus collectivism
C. power distance
D. masculinity versus femininity

Answer: B
Medium
Page: 99

51. Hofstede's __________ dimension focused on the relationship between the individual and his or her fellows.

A. masculinity versus femininity
B. individualism versus collectivism
C. power distance
D. uncertainty avoidance

Answer: C
Medium
Page: 99

52. Hofstede's __________ dimension measured the extent to which different cultures socialized their members into accepting ambiguous situations and tolerating uncertainty.

A. masculinity versus femininity
B. power distance
C. uncertainty avoidance
D. individualism versus collectivism

Answer: D
Medium
Page: 99

53. Which of Hofstede's four dimensions looked at the relationship between gender and work roles?

A. power distance
B. individualism versus collectivism
C. uncertainty avoidance
D. masculinity versus femininity

Answer: B
Hard
Page: 99

54. According to Hofstede's Model, Western nations such as the United States, Canada, and Britain score __________ on the individualism scale and __________ on the power distance scale.

A. high, high
B. high, low
C. low, high
D. low, low

Answer: D
Easy
Page: 99

55. Hofsted's Model assesses:

A. how religious values affect performance in the workplace
B. how language differences affect international business
C. how values affect workplace productivity
D. how culture relates to values in the workplace

Answer: D
Hard
Page: 99

56. According to Hofstede's Model, what country stands out as having a culture with strong uncertainty avoidance and high masculinity?

A. United States
B. Germany
C. China
D. Japan

CULTURAL CHANGE

Answer: A
Medium
Page: 101

57. The Hitachi example in the Management Focus (in Chapter 2) points to two forces that may result in cultural change. These are:

A. economic advancement and globalization
B. political stability and legal reform
C. protection of intellectual property rights, political stability
D. globalization and legal reform

IMPLICATIONS FOR BUSINESS

Answer: A
Easy
Page: 103

58. Ethnocentrism is a belief in the:

A. superiority of one's own ethic group or culture
B. superiority of one's own legal system compared to others
C. superiority of one's own religious beliefs over others
D. superiority of individualism versus collectivism

Answer: C
Medium
Page: 103

59. Acting on the assumption that one's own ethnic group or culture is superior to others is referred to as __________ behavior.

A. individualistic
B. parochial
C. ethnocentric
D. collectivist

Answer: D
Medium
Page: 103

60. Suppose that an international executive from Belgium consistently acted in a manner that indicated that he believed that his ethnic group and culture is superior to any others. If this were the case, the executive would be exhibiting __________ behavior.

A. parochial
B. collectivist
C. patriotic
D. ethnocentric

TRUE-FALSE QUESTIONS

WHAT IS CULTURE?

Answer: T
Easy
Page: 79

61. Culture is a system of values and norms that are shared among a group of people and that when taken together constitute a design for living.

Answer: F
Easy
Page: 79

62. Norms are abstract ideas about what a group believes to be good, right, and desirable.

Answer: T
Easy
Page: 79

63. A society is a group of people who share a common set of values and norms.

Answer: F
Medium
Page: 79

64. Mores are the routine conventions of everyday life.

Answer: F
Medium
Page: 80

65. There is a strict one-to-one correspondence between a society and a nation-state.

Answer: T
Medium
Page: 80

66. Mores are norms that are seen as central to the functioning of a society and to its social life.

SOCIAL STRUCTURE

Answer: T
Easy
Page: 81

67. A society's "social structure" refers to its basic social organization.

Answer: T
Easy
Page: 82

68. A group is an association of two or more individuals who have a shared sense of identity and who interact with each other in structured ways on the basis of a common set of expectations about each other's behaviors.

Answer: F
Medium
Page: 82

69. The value systems of many Western societies place a high emphasis on group achievement.

Answer: F
Hard
Page: 82

70. A recent study of US competitiveness by MIT concluded that U.S. firms are being hurt in the global economy by a failure to place an appropriate amount of emphasis on individual achievement.

Answer: T
Medium
Page: 83

71. In Japan, the social status of an individual is determined as much by the standing of the group to which he or she belongs as by his or her individual performance.

Answer: F
Medium
Page: 84

72. A class system is a closed system of stratification in which social position is determined by the family into which a person is born, and change in that position is usually not possible during an individual's lifetime.

Answer: T
Medium
Page: 85

73. Class consciousness refers to a condition where people tend to perceive themselves in terms of their class background, and this shapes their relationships with members of other classes.

RELIGIOUS AND ETHICAL SYSTEMS

Answer: T
Easy
Page: 86

74. Most of the world's ethical systems are the product of religions.

Answer: T
Easy
Page: 86

75. Ethical systems refer to a set of moral principles, or values, that are used to guide and shape behavior.

Answer: F
Medium
Page: 86

76. Hinduism is the most widely practiced religion in the world.

Answer: T
Medium
Page: 86

77. In 1904 a German sociologist, Max Weber, made a connection between Protestant ethics and "the spirit of capitalism."

Answer: F
Hard
Page: 88

78. With close to 1 billion adherents, Buddhism is the second largest of the world's major religions.

Answer: T
Medium
Page: 89

79. Many of the economic principles of Islam are pro-free enterprise.

Answer: F
Medium
Page: 90

80. The Buddhist religion prohibits the payment or receipt of interest.

Answer: F
Easy
Page: 91

81. Christianity is the world's oldest religion.

LANGUAGE

Answer: T
Hard
Page: 94

82. The most widely spoken language in the world is English, followed by French, Spanish, and Chinese.

Answer: T
Easy
Page: 95

83. Unspoken language refers to nonverbal communication.

CULTURE AND THE WORKPLACE

Answer: F
Medium
Page: 99

84. Probably the most famous study of how religion relates to values in the workplace was undertaken by Geert Hofstede.

Answer: T
Medium
Page: 99

85. Hofstede's power distance dimension focused on how a society deals with the fact that people are unequal in physical and intellectual capabilities.

Answer: F
Medium
Page: 99

86. Hofstede's masculinity versus femininity dimension measured the extent to which different cultures socialized their members into accepting ambiguous situations and tolerating uncertainty.

Answer: T
Hard
Page: 100

87. According to Hofstede's Model, Americans are more individualistic and egalitarian than the Japanese.

CULTURAL CHANGE

Answer: F
Easy
Page: 101

88. Culture tends to be constant over time.

Answer: T
Medium
Page: 101

89. Some observers claim that a major cultural shift is presently occurring in Japan, with a move towards greater individualism.

Answer: T
Easy
Page: 103

90. Ethnocentrism is a belief in the superiority of one's own ethnic group or culture.

ESSAY QUESTIONS

Easy
Page: 79

91. Describe what is meant by the term "culture?" Differentiate between the terms culture, values, and norms.

Answer: Culture can be defined as a system of values and norms that are shared among a group of people and that when taken together constitute a design for living. Values and norms are the underpinnings of culture. Values are abstract ideas about what a group believes to be good, right, and desirable. Put differently, values are shared assumptions about how things ought to be. Norms are the social rules and guidelines that prescribe appropriate behavior in a particular situation.

Medium
Page: 81

92. What are the two dimensions of a society's social structure that stand out as being of particular importance when explaining differences between cultures?

Answer: The first is the degree to which the basic unit of social organization is the individual, as opposed to the group. Western societies tend to emphasize the primacy of the individual, while groups tend to figure much larger in many other societies. The second dimension is the degree to which a society is stratified into classes or castes. Some societies are characterized by a relatively high degree of social stratification and relatively low mobility between strata (e.g., Indian), while other societies are characterized by a low degree of social stratification and high mobility between strata (e.g. American).

Medium
Page: 82

93. In the United States, is there a greater focus on the individual or the group? What are the pluses and minuses of the predominant focus?

Answer: In the United States, the focus is more on the individual than the group. The primary benefit of this approach is that a focus on individual effort tends to facilitate entrepreneurial activity. Entrepreneurial individuals have repeatedly created new products and new ways of doing business in the United States. One could argue that the dynamism of the U.S. economy owes much to the philosophy of individualism. Another benefit of a focus on the individual rather than the group is a high degree of managerial mobility between companies. Because U.S. managers are not as group or company oriented as some of their counterparts around the world, they are typically less reluctant to switch companies.

There are also disadvantages to a focus on the individual rather than the group. Managerial mobility is not always a good thing. While moving from company to company may be good for individual mangers, who are trying to build impressive resumes, it is not necessarily a good thing for American companies. The emphasis on individualism may also make it difficult to build teams within an organization to perform collective tasks. If individuals are always competing with each other on the basis of individual performance, it may prove difficult for them to cooperate.

Medium
Page: 84

94. Describe the concept of social mobility. Does social mobility vary significantly from society to society? Describe the extremes in terms of a society that has low social mobility and a society that has high social mobility. Would you rather live in a society with a high level or a low level of social mobility? Why?

Answer: Social mobility refers to the extent to which individuals can move out of the strata into which they are born. For instance, in a society with a low level of social mobility, it would be very difficult (if not impossible) for someone that is born into a family of laborers to become a manager. Social mobility varies significantly from society to society. The most rigid system of stratification is a caste system. A caste system is a closed system of stratification in which social position is determined by the family into which a person is born, and change in that position is usually not possible during an individual's lifetime. At the other extreme is the American "class" system (i.e. upper class, middle class, and lower-middle class). In this system, class membership is determined mainly by an individual's own efforts and achievements, rather than his or her family heritage. Thus, an individual in American, through effort and achievement, can move smoothly from the lower-middle class (or the working class) to the upper class.

Your students will undoubtedly say that they would rather live in a society with a high level of social mobility. The clear advantage of such a society is that a person's position is determined by his or her own individual effort.

Medium
Page: 85

95. What is meant by the term "class consciousness?" Under what circumstances can class consciousness be bad?

Answer: The term class consciousness refers to a condition where people tend to perceive themselves in terms of their class background, and this shapes their relationships with members of other classes. Class consciousness can be bad if it leads to hostility and animosity between classes. For example, if the "upper-class" in a society (in terms of economic stature) tries to dominate the "lower-class," it can lead to hostility and a mutual antagonism between the classes. This typically makes it difficult to achieve cooperation between management and labor, if the "upper-class" is typically in management and the "lower-class" constitutes the majority of the laborers.

Medium
Page: 86

96. What is meant by the Protestant work ethic? What impact has the Protestant work ethic had on the emergence of modern day capitalism?

Answer: In 1904 a German sociologist, named Max Weber, made a connection between Protestant ethics and "the spirit of capitalism." Weber drew this conclusion by observing that, in Western Europe, the business leaders and owners of capital were overwhelmingly Protestant. This relationship led Weber to conclude that there was a link between Protestantism and the emergence of modern capitalism. Weber argued that Protestant ethics emphasized the importance of hard work and wealth creation, which are the essential components of capitalism. Thus, Weber coined the term "Protestant work ethic" to denote the tendency on the part of Protestants to work hard and accumulate wealth, which are the underpinnings of capitalism.

Medium
Page: 86

97. What are some of the similarities between Islam and Christianity as they related to the practice of business?

Answer: Having the same roots, Islam and Christianity share many similarities regarding the conduct of business. Many of the economic principles of Islam are pro free enterprise and hostile to socialist ideals. In both Islamic and Christian societies, it is appropriate to earn a profit through trade and commerce, as long as the profit is justly earned and not based on the exploitation of others. In addition, the principles of honesty, respect for the rights of others, and dealings justly and equitable with others are found in both religions.

Hard
Page: 99

98. Hofstede isolated four dimensions that he claimed characterized the cultures of different countries. Briefly describe each of Hofstede's four dimensions. Should Hofstede's dimensions be used by managers to determine how cultures differ and what that might mean for management practices?

Answer: Hostede's four dimension are: power distance, individualism versus collectivism, uncertainty avoidance, and masculinity versus femininity. Each of these dimensions is briefly described below.

Power Distance: This dimension focuses on how a society deals with the fact that people are unequal in physical and intellectual capabilities.

According to Hofstede, high power distance cultures are found in countries that let inequalities grow over time into inequalities of power and wealth. Low power distance cultures are found in societies that try to play down such inequalities as much as possible.

Individualism versus Collectivism: This dimension focuses on the relationship between the individual and his or her fellows. In individualistic societies, the ties between individuals are loose and individual achievement and freedom are highly valued. In societies where collectivism is emphasized, the ties between individuals are tight.

Uncertainty Avoidance: This dimension measures the extent to which different cultures socialize their members into accepting ambiguous situations and tolerating uncertainty. Members of high uncertainty avoidance cultures place a premium on job security, career patterns, retirement benefits, and so on. Lower uncertainty avoidance cultures are characterized by a greater readiness to take risks and less emotional resistance to change.

Masculinity versus Femininity: Finally, this dimension looks at the relationship between gender and work roles. In masculine cultures, sex roles are sharply differentiated and traditional "masculine values," such as achievement and the effective exercise of power, determines cultural ideals. If feminine cultures, sex roles are less sharply distinguished, and little differentiation is made between men and women in the same job.

Hofstede used these dimensions to develop charts that provided descriptive information about cultures. These charts were intended to be used by managers to understand the dynamics of different cultures.

As articulated in the textbook, Hofstede's model has some weaknesses, and should not be used as the sole determinant of how one interfaces with individuals from other cultures. On the other hand, Hofstede's model is a tool that can provide a manager insight that he or she might not otherwise have relative to cultural issues.

Medium
Page: 103

99. What is ethnocentric behavior? Is ethnocentrism a desirable or an undesirable attribute for the manager of an international firm?

Answer: Ethnocentrism is a belief in the superiority of one's own ethnic group or culture. Often, this leads to behavior that reflects a disregard or contempt for the cultures of other countries. Ethnocentric behavior is not a desirable attribute for the manager of an international firm.

International managers must have a healthy respect for one another and a balanced perspective.

Hard
Page: 104

100. In the case of Japan, how does culture influence its national advantage?

Answer: It can be argued that the culture of modern day Japan lowers the costs of doing business in that country, relative to the costs of doing business in most western nations. Japanese culture emphasizes group affiliation, loyalty, reciprocal obligations, honesty, and education, all of which may boost the competitiveness of Japanese companies. The emphasis on group affiliation and loyalty encourages individuals to identify strongly with the companies in which they work. In turn, this tends to foster an ethic of hard work and cooperation between management and labor "for the good of the company." Similarly, the concepts of reciprocal obligations and honesty help foster an atmosphere of trust between companies and their suppliers. In turn, this encourages them to enter into long-term relationships with each other to work on factors such as inventory reduction, quality control, and joint design - all of which have been shown to improve the competitiveness of an organization. In addition, the availability of a pool of highly skilled labor, and particularly engineers, has undoubtedly helped Japanese enterprises develop a number of cost reducing process innovations that have boosted their productivity. Thus, cultural factors may help explain the competitive advantage enjoyed by many Japanese businesses in international markets.

CHAPTER 4

INTERNATIONAL TRADE THEORY

MULTIPLE-CHOICE QUESTIONS

AN OVERVIEW OF TRADE THEORY

Answer: A
Easy
Page: 120

1. Propagated in the 16th and 17th centuries, __________ advocates that countries should simultaneously encourage exports and discourage imports.

A. mercantilism
B. collectivism
C. isolationism
D. ethnocentrism

Answer: D
Easy
Page: 120

2. Adam Smith advanced the theory of:

A. mercantilism
B. ethnocentrism
C. similar opportunity
D. absolute advantage

Answer: D
Easy
Page: 120

3. __________ occurs when a government does not attempt to influence through quotas or duties what its citizens can buy from another country or what they can produce and sell to another country.

A. Clear commerce
B. Unencumbered commerce
C. Unrestrained exchange
D. Free trade

Answer: B
Medium
Page: 120

4. __________ argued that the invisible hand of the market mechanism, rather than government policy, should determine what a country imports and what it exports.

A. Geert Hofstede
B. Adam Smith
C. Michael Porter
D. David Ricardo

Answer: A
Medium
Page: 121

5. The theory of comparative advantage, which is based on the work of English economist __________, is described in our textbook as the intellectual basis of the modern argument for unrestricted free trade.

A. David Ricardo
B. Bertil Ohlin
C. Raymond Vernon
D. Geert Hofstede

Answer: B
Medium
Page: 122

6. One early response to the failure of the Heckscher-Olin theory to explain the observed pattern of international trade was the:

A. theory of rising costs
B. product life-cycle theory
C. theory of comparative advantage
D. theory of cultural constraints

Answer: C
Medium
Page: 122

7. Which of the following selections correctly matches a scholar with the theory that he or she proposed?

A. Adam Smith / Comparative Advantage
B. David Ricardo / New Trade
C. Raymond Vernon / Product Life Cycle
D. Eli Heckscher / Absolute Advantage

Answer: C
Medium
Page: 123

8. The __________ theory stresses that in some cases countries specialize in the production and export of particular products not because of underlying differences in factor endowments, but because in certain industries the world market can support only a limited number of firms.

A. product life-cycle
B. Heckscher-Olin
C. new trade
D. limited potential

Answer: B
Hard
Page: 123

9. Which of the following theories argues that the observed pattern of trade between nations may in part be due to the ability of firms to capture first-mover advantages?

A. Heckscher-Ohlin
B. new trade
C. comparative advantage
D. product life-cycle

Answer: D
Medium
Page: 123

10. The theory of __________, developed by Michael Porter, focuses on the importance of country factors such as domestic demand and domestic rivalry in explaining a nation's dominance in the production and export of particular products.

A. new trade
B. absolute advantage
C. comparative advantage
D. national competitive advantage

Answer: D
Hard
Page: 123

11. Which of the following scholars (or teams of scholars) is not associated with the theory that follows his name?

A. Michael Porter / National Competitive Advantage
B. Adam Smith / Absolute Advantage
C. David Ricardo / Comparative Advantage
D. Eli Heckscher and Bertil Ohlin / Product Life-Cycle

Answer: A
Medium
Page: 123

12. The theory of national competitive advantage was developed by:

A. Michael Porter
B. Paul Krugman
C. Adam Smith
D. David Ricardo

Answer: B
Hard
Page: 124

13. Which of the following two theories justify some limited and selective government intervention to support the development of certain export-oriented industries?

A. the theory of national competitive advantage and the Heckscher-Ohlin theory
B. the new trade theory and the theory of national competitive advantage
C. the Heckscher-Ohlin theory and the theory of comparative advantage
D. the product life-cycle theory and the theory of absolute advantage

MERCANTILISM

Answer: A
Easy
Page: 124

14. The first theory of international trade emerged in England in the mid-16th century. Referred to as __________, its principal assertion was that gold and silver were the mainstays of national wealth and essential to vigorous commerce.

A. mercantilism
B. collectivism
C. economic conservatism
D. capitalism

Answer: B
Medium
Page: 124

15. The main tenant of mercantilism was that it is in a country's best interests to maintain:

A. a trade deficit
B. a trade surplus
C. a trade balance
D. a strict policy of no foreign trade

Answer: B
Hard
Page: 124

16. Which of the following is not consistent with the central beliefs of mercantilism?

A. government should intervene to achieve a surplus in the balance of trade
B. policies should be put in place to minimize exports and maximize imports
C. imports should be limited by tariffs and quotas
D. exports should be subsidized

Answer: A
Medium
Page: 124

17. The flaw with mercantilism was that it viewed trade as a:

A. zero-sum game
B. threat to a government's independence
C. economic necessity
D. non essential economic activity

Answer: C
Easy
Page: 124

18. A __________ is one in which a gain by one country results in a loss by another.

A. unbalanced scorecard
B. positive-sum game
C. zero-sum game
D. quid pro quo transfer

Answer: B
Easy
Page: 124

19. A situation in which all countries can benefit, even if some benefit more than others is called a:

A. balanced scorecard
B. positive-sum game
C. zero-sum game
D. near-equivalent game

ABSOLUTE ADVANTAGE

Answer: D
Easy
Page: 125

20. In his 1776 landmark book *The Wealth of Nations*, __________ attacked the mercantilist assumption that trade is a zero-sum game.

A. David Ricardo
B. Michael Porter
C. Bertil Ohlin
D. Adam Smith

Answer: A
Medium
Page: 125

21. In his 1776 landmark book __________, Adam Smith attacked the mercantilist assumption that trade is a zero-sum game.

A. *The Wealth of Nations*
B. *Free Trade and Mercantilism*
C. *The Folly of Mercantilism*
D. *The Free Trade Advocate*

Answer: C
Medium
Page: 125

22. According to Smith, countries should specialize in the production of goods for which they have an __________, and then trade these goods for the goods produced by other countries.

A. approximate advantage
B. proportionate advantage
C. absolute advantage
D. comparative advantage

Answer: B
Medium
Page: 128

23. In his 1817 book entitled *Principles of Political Economy*, David Ricardo introduced the theory of:

A. proportionate advantage
B. comparative advantage
C. absolute advantage
D. approximate advantage

Answer: D
Medium
Page: 128

24. According to Ricardo's theory of __________, it makes sense for a country to specialize in the production of those goods that it produces most efficiently and to buy the goods that it products less efficiently from other countries, even if this means buying goods from other countries that it could produce more efficiently itself.

A. pertinent advantage
B. absolute advantage
C. competitive advantage
D. comparative advantage

Answer: A
Hard
Page: 130

25. The basic message of the theory of comparative advantage is that:

A. potential world production is greater with unrestricted free trade than it is with restricted trade
B. potential world production is not significantly affected by trade policy
C. potential world production is greater with restricted trade
D. it makes sense for a country to specialize in the production of those goods that it produces most efficiently and to buy the goods that it produces less efficiently from other countries, unless this means buying goods from other countries that it could produce more efficiently itself

Answer: A
Medium
Page: 130

26. Ricardo's theory of comparative advantage suggests that consumers in all nations can consume more if there are:

A. no trade restrictions
B. severe trade restrictions
C. trade restrictions on services only
D. trade restrictions on manufactured goods only

Answer: C
Easy
Page: 131

27. __________ returns to specializing occur when more units of resources are required to produce each additional unit.

A. Sinking
B. Lagging
C. Diminishing
D. Constant

Answer: D
Medium
Page: 131

28. __________ returns to specialization occur when the resources required to produce a good are assumed to remain constant no matter where it is on a country's production possibility frontier.

A. Diminishing
B. Static
C. Dynamic
D. Constant

HECKSCHER-OHLIN THEORY

Answer: B
Medium
Page: 133

29. Swedish economists' __________ advanced a theory of trade that argued that comparative advantage arises from differences in national factor endowments.

A. Durbin and Coles
B. Hecksher and Ohlin
C. Mouton and Penn
D. Rivette and Delhomme

Answer: A
Medium
Page: 134

30. The __________ theory predicts that countries will export those goods that make intensive use of those factors that are locally abundant, while importing goods that make intensive use of factors that are locally scarce.

A. Heckscher-Olin
B. Smith-Ricardo
C. Krugman-Porter
D. factor endowments

Answer: C
Medium
Page: 134

31. The Heckscher-Olin theory argues that the pattern of international trade is determined by differences in:

A. productivity
B. political interests
C. factor endowments
D. national priorities

Answer: A
Hard
Page: 134

32. According to the textbook, most economists prefer the Heckscher-Ohlin theory to Ricardo's theory of comparative advantage because of two factors. These are:

A. it makes fewer simplifying assumptions and it has been subjected to many empirical tests
B. it has been subjected to many empirical tests and it has stood the test of time
C. it makes fewer simplifying assumptions and it has been acknowledged by the World Trade Organization as the better of the two theories
D. it has been acknowledged as the better of the two theories by the United Nations, and it has stood the test of time

Answer: B
Medium
Page: 134

33. Contrary to what the Heckscher-Ohlin theory would predict, the United States has been a primary importer rather than an exporter of capital goods. This apparent contradiction is known as the _________ paradox.

A. Theler
B. Leontief
C. Cormier
D. Ricardo

THE PRODUCT LIFE-CYCLE THEORY

Answer: A
Easy
Page: 135

34. __________ initially proposed the product life-cycle theory in the mid-1960s.

A. Raymond Vernon
B. Bertil Ohlin
C. David Ricardo
D. Michael Porter

Answer: D
Easy
Page: 135

35. Raymond Vernon initially proposed the __________ in the mid-1960s.

A. new trade theory
B. theory of comparative advantage theory
C. theory of national competitive advantage theory
D. product life-cycle theory

Answer: D
Medium
Page: 135

36. Which theory of international trade suggests that the production of products is likely to switch from advanced countries to developing countries over time?

A. new trade
B. comparative advantage
C. Hecksher-Ohlin
D. product life-cycle

Answer: D
Medium
Page: 135

37. Vernon's product life-cycle theory was based on the observation that for most of the 20th century a very large proportion of the world's new products had been developed by U.S. firms and sold first in the __________ market.

A. Japanese
B. Western European
C. Eastern European
D. U.S.

THE NEW TRADE THEORY

Answer: B
Medium
Page: 137

38. The __________ argues that in many industries, because of substantial economies of scale, there are increasing returns to specialization.

A. product life-cycle
B. new trade theory
C. Heckscher-Ohlin theory
D. theory of the comparative advantage

Answer: D
Medium
Page: 137

39. The __________ theory argues that due to the presence of substantial scale economies, world demand will support only a few firms in many industries.

A. product life-cycle
B. national competitive advantage
C. absolute advantage
D. new trade

Answer: D
Hard
Page: 137

40. What theory of international trade directly explains why there are only two-three producers of airliners in the world today?

A. product life-cycle
B. comparative advantage
C. absolute advantage
D. new trade

Answer: A
Easy
Page: 138

41. The economic and strategic advantages that accrue to early entrants in an industry are called:

A. first-mover advantages
B. initial-class advantages
C. early-entrant advantages
D. first-stage benefits

Answer: D
Hard
Page: 138

42. The new trade theorists argue that the United States leads in exports of commercial jet aircraft not because it is better endowed with the factors of production required to manufacture aircraft, but because:

A. U.S. built commercial jet aircraft have the best safety record
B. the U.S. commercial jet aircraft industry has a lower wage rate than foreign competitors
C. the World Trade Organization has given preferential treatment to the U.S. commercial jet aircraft industry
D. two of the first movers in the industry were U.S. firms

Answer: C
Hard
Page: 138

43. New trade theorists stress the role of the following three variables in giving a firm first-mover advantages?

A. availability of capital, entrepreneurship, and favorable tax rates
B. entrepreneurship, innovation, and favorable foreign exchange rates
C. luck, entrepreneurship, and innovation
D. modernization, luck, and the availability of capital

NATIONAL COMPETITIVE ADVANTAGE: PORTER'S DIAMOND

Answer: C
Medium
Page: 139

44. In 1990, Michael Porter published the results of an intensive research effort that attempted to determine why some nations succeed and others fail in international competition. The name of the book was:

A. *The Comparable Advantage of Domestic and Global Markets*
B. *The Wealth of Nations*
C. *The Competitive Advantage of Nations*
D. *The Absolute Advantage of Nations*

Answer: B
Hard
Page: 139

45. In his book *The Competitive Advantage of Nations*, Porter's thesis was that four broad attributes of a nation shape the environment in which local firms compete, and that these attributes promote or impede the creation of competitive advantage. Which of the following is not one of these attributes?

A. factor endowments
B. customs
C. firm strategy, structure, and rivalry
D. related and supporting industries

Answer: A
Medium
Page: 139

46. The focus of Porter's theory of national competitive advantage is to:

A. explain why a nation achieves international success in a particular industry
B. identify which industries should be targeted for government subsidies
C. understand the role of government in making its industries competitive
D. show why a country may import products that it could produce for itself

Answer: C
Medium
Page: 139

47. What theory attempts to explain why Japan is strong in automobiles, Switzerland in precision instruments and pharmaceuticals, and Germany in chemicals?

A. absolute advantage
B. comparative advantage
C. national competitive advantage
D. new trade theory

Answer: B
Medium
Page: 140

48. Porter visually depicted the four broad attributes that shape the competitive advantage of a nation as a:

A. square
B. diamond
C. rectangle
D. sphere

Answer: C
Medium
Page: 140

49. In his study dealing with the competitive advantage of nations, Porter argued that in regard to factor endowments, __________ factors are the most significant for competitive advantage.

A. standard
B. complementary
C. advanced
D. basic

Answer: A
Medium
Page: 140

50. In his study dealing with the competitive advantage of nations, Porter argued that a nation's firms gain competitive advantage if their domestic consumers are both __________ and __________.

A. sophisticated, demanding
B. exacting, unpretentious
C. unpretentious, passive
D. modest, passive

Answer: C
Hard
Page: 140

51. What, according to Porter's theory of national competitive advantage, is the relationship between basic and advanced factors?

A. basic factors are more important than advanced factors
B. if a country has advanced factors, then basic factors are not important
C. the level of basic factors can influence the development of advanced factors
D. if a country has basic factors, then advanced factors are not important

Answer: A
Hard
Page: 141

52. Which of the following theorists argued that successful industries within a country tend to be grouped into "clusters" of related industries?

A. Porter
B. Heckscher
C. Vernon
D. Smith

Answer: B
Hard
Page: 141

53. In his study, Porter observed that there is a predominance of __________ on the top-management teams of German and Japanese firms.

A. marketing specialists
B. engineers
C. accountants
D. lawyers

Answer: A
Hard
Page: 141

54. In his study, Porter observed that there are a disproportionate number of people with finance backgrounds on the top management teams of many __________ industries.

A. United States
B. Japanese
C. German
D. Chinese

Answer: D
Medium
Page: 141

55. According to Porter's theory of national competitive advantage, domestic firm rivalry:

A. stifles innovation
B. lowers profits and competitiveness
C. leads to a short term financial emphasis
D. should be vigorous to create better international competitors

Answer: D
Medium
Page: 142

56. In sum, Porter concludes that the degree to which a nation is likely to achieve international success in a certain industry is a function of the combined impact of factor endowments, domestic demand conditions, related and supporting industries, and:

A. domestic wage rates
B. membership in the World Trade Organization
C. availability of capital
D. firms strategy, structure, and rivalry

Answer: A
Medium
Page: 141

57. Porter's "diamond" of the determinants of national competitive advantage includes factor endowments, related and supporting industries, firm strategy, structure and rivalry, and:

A. demand conditions
B. membership in the World Trade Organization
C. domestic wage rates
D. government support

Answer: C
Medium
Page: 142

58. If Porter is correct, we would expect his model to predict:

A. currency exchange rates
B. membership in the World Trade Organization
C. the pattern of international trade
D. factor endowments

IMPLICATIONS FOR BUSINESS

Answer: C
Medium
Page: 144

59. According to the new trade theory, firms that establish a __________ advantage with regard to the production of a particular new product may subsequently dominate global trade in that product.

A. initial-class
B. early entrant
C. first-mover
D. initial-entrant

Answer: A
Hard
Page: 144

60. According to our textbook, in recent years, __________ firms, rather than their European or North American competitors, seem to have undertaken the vast investments and years of losses required to build a first-mover advantage.

A. Japanese
B. South Korean
C. Chinese
D. Australian

TRUE-FALSE QUESTIONS

AN OVERVIEW OF TRADE THEORY

Answer: T
Easy
Page: 120

61. Free trade occurs when a government does not attempt to influence through quotas or duties what its citizens can buy from another country or what they can produce and sell to another country.

Answer: F
Medium
Page: 120

62. David Ricardo argued that the invisible hand of the market mechanism, rather than government policy, should determine what a country imports and what it exports.

Answer: F
Hard
Page: 121

63. According to our textbook, Adam Smith's theory of absolute advantage is the intellectual basis of the modern argument for unrestricted free trade.

Answer: T
Easy
Page: 122

64. The product life-cycle theory suggests that early in their life cycle, most new products are produced in and exported from the country in which they were developed.

MERCANTILISM

Answer: F
Easy
Page: 124

65. The main tenant of mercantilism was that it is in a country's best interest to maintain a trade deficit, to import more than its exports.

Answer: T
Medium
Page: 124

66. The flaw with mercantilism was that it viewed trade as a zero-sum game.

ABSOLUTE ADVANTAGE

Answer: T
Medium
Page: 125

67. In his 1776 landmark book *The Wealth of Nations*, Adam Smith attacked the mercantilist assumption that trade is a zero-sum game.

Answer: T
Medium
Page: 125

68. According to Adam Smith, countries should specialize in the production of goods for which they have an absolute advantage and then trade these good for the goods produced by other countries.

Answer: F
Medium
Page: 125

69. Through the theory of absolute advantage, Adam Smith proved that trade is a zero-sum game.

COMPARATIVE ADVANTAGE

Answer: F
Medium
Page: 128

70. According to Ricardo's theory of comparative advantage, it makes sense for a country to specialize in the production of those goods that it produces most efficiently and to buy the goods that it produces less efficiently from other countries, unless it can produce those goods more efficiently itself.

Answer: T
Medium
Page: 130

71. The basic message of the theory of comparative advantage is that potential world production is greater with unrestricted free trade then it is with restricted trade.

Answer: F
Hard
Page: 130

72. To a lesser degree than the theory of absolute advantage, the theory of comparative advantage suggests that trade is a positive-sum game in which all gain.

Answer: T
Medium
Page: 131

73. By constant returns to specialization, we mean that the units of resources required to produce a good are assumed to remain constant no matter where one is on a country's production possibility frontier (PPF).

HECKSHER-OHLIN THEORY

Answer: T
Easy
Page: 134

74. Swedish economists Eli Heckscher and Bertil Ohlin argued that comparative advantage arises from differences in national factor endowments.

Answer: T
Medium
Page: 134

75. The Heckscher-Ohlin theory predicts that countries will export those goods that make intensive use of those factors that are locally abundant, while importing goods that make intensive use of factors that are locally scarce.

Answer: F
Hard
Page: 134

76. Using the theory of comparative advantage, Ricardo postulated that since the United States was relatively abundant in capital compared to other nations, the United States would be an exporter of capital-intensive goods and an importer of labor-intensive goods.

Answer: F
Medium
Page: 134

77. According to our textbook, the Heckscher-Ohlin theory is an excellent predictor of real-world international trade patterns.

THE PRODUCT-LIFE CYCLE THEORY

Answer: T
Easy
Page: 135

78. Raymond Vernon initially proposed the product life-cycle theory in the mid-1960s.

Answer: F
Medium
Page: 135

79. Vernon's product life-cycle theory was based on the observation that for most of the 20th century, only a small proportion of the world's new products were developed by U.S. firms and almost none were sold initially in the United States.

Answer: T
Hard
Page: 137

80. According to our textbook, the product life-cycle theory has only limited relevance in the modern world.

THE NEW TRADE THEORY

Answer: F
Medium
Page: 138

81. The product life-cycle theorists argue that countries may export certain products simply because they have a firm that was an early entrant into an industry that will support only a few firms because of substantial economies of scale.

Answer: T
Easy
Page: 138

82. The notion of first-mover advantages is associated with the new trade theory.

Answer: T
Medium
Page: 138

83. New trade theorists stress the role of luck, entrepreneurship, and innovation in giving a firm first-mover advantages.

NATIONAL COMPETITIVE ADVANTAGE: PORTER'S DIAMOND

Answer: F
Medium
Page: 138

84. In 1990, Michael Porter of the Harvard Business School published the results of an intensive research effort that attempted to determine why some nations succeed and others fail in international competition. The name of the book was *The Comparative Advantage of Trade and Globalization.*

Answer: F
Hard
Page: 140

85. In the context of factor endowments, Porter argued that basic factors are the most significant for competitive advantage.

Answer: T
Hard
Page: 140

86. In Porter's study of national competitive advantage, he argued that a nations firms' gain competitive advantage if their domestic consumers are sophisticated and demanding.

Answer: T
Easy
Page: 140

87. Porter depicted his four attributes of competitive advantage pictorially as a diamond.

Answer: T
Medium
Page: 141

88. In sum, Porter concluded that the degree to which a nation is likely to achieve international success in a certain industry is a function of the combined impact of factor endowments, domestic demand conditions, related and supporting industries, and the availability of capital.

IMPLICATIONS FOR BUSINESS

Answer: F
Medium
Page: 144

89. According to the theory of comparative advantage, firms that establish a first-mover advantage in the production of a new product may dominate global trade in that product.

Answer: T
Hard
Page: 145

90. Porter's theory of national competitive advantage suggests that it is in a firm's best interests to upgrade advanced factors of production.

ESSAY QUESTIONS

Easy
Page: 120

91. When does free trade occur?

Answer: Free trade occurs when a government does not attempt to influence through quotas or duties what its citizens can buy from another country or what they can produce and sell to another country.

Medium
Page: 120

92. Describe Adam Smith's concept of absolute advantage.

Answer: According to Smith, countries should specialize in the production of goods for which they have an absolute advantage and then trade those goods for the goods produced by other countries. For instance, during Smith's time, England had an absolute advantage in the production of textiles, and France had an absolute advantage in the production of wine. According to the concept of absolute advantage, it then only makes sense for England to produce textiles (and export them to France), and France to produce wine (and export it to England). Smith's basic argument, therefore, was that a country should never produce goods at home that it can buy at a lower cost from other countries. Moreover, Smith argued that by specializing in the production of goods in which each has an absolute advantage, both countries benefit by engaging in trade.

Medium
Page: 122

93. Describe the central tenant of the product life-cycle theory.

Answer: Proposed by Raymond Vernon, the product life-cycle theory suggest that early in their life cycle, most new products are produced in an exported from the country in which they were developed. As a new product becomes widely accepted internationally, production starts in other countries. As a result, the theory suggests, the product may ultimately be exported back to the country of its innovation.

Hard
Page: 123

94. Describe the new trade theory. How does the new trade theory help us understand why the United States is dominant in the world market for commercial aircraft exports?

Answer: The new trade theory stresses that in some cases countries specialize in the production and export of particular products not because of underlying differences in factor endowments, but because in certain industries, the world market can support only a limited number of firms. In such industries, firms that enter the market first build a competitive advantage that is difficult to challenge. Thus, the observed pattern of trade between nations may in part be due to the ability of firms to capture first-mover advantages.

This theory helps us understand why the United States is dominant in the world market for commercial aircraft exports. American firms such as Boeing were first movers in the world market in the commercial aircraft industry. As a result, Boeing and to a lesser extent other American firms built a competitive advantage that has subsequently been difficult for firms from countries with equally favorable factor endowments to challenge.

Medium
Page: 124

95. Describe the concept of mercantilism. What did the mercantilist doctrine advocate in terms of the role of government in international trade? What type of policies did the mercantilists recommend to their governments?

Answer: The main tenant of mercantilism, which emerged in England in the mid-16th century, was that it was in a country's best interest to maintain a trade surplus. By doing so, a country would accumulate gold and silver, and increase its national wealth and prestige. The mercantilist doctrine advocated government intervention to achieve a surplus in the balance of trade. The mercantilists saw no virtue in a large volume of trade. Rather, they recommended to their governments to limit imports by tariffs and quotas and stimulate exports through subsidies.

Hard
Page: 125

96. Most doctors, if they needed to, could type their own letters and memos on a typewriter or word processor, and deliver them to the post office. Yet, most doctors, and other professions, hire a typist to do these tasks. Using theories of international trade, explain why a doctor would hire a typist to type his letters and memos, even if he could do it himself. If a particular doctor could type faster than the fastest typist, explain why he still might hire a typist to type his letters and memos. Again, use what you have learned from international trade theory in answering this question.

Answer: Doctors have a specialized skill in the area of medicine. As a result, they have an absolute advantage in this area, and can likely earn more money by spending more time seeing extra patients than it costs them to hire a typist. Thus they can benefit from performing those tasks where they have an absolute advantage and letting others that specialize in typing provide those services. Even if a doctor had an absolute advantage in medicine and typing, he would still have a comparative advantage only in medicine. The doctor is *comparatively* more efficient in the practice of medicine than he is in typing. As a result, it makes sense for him to focus on medicine, and pay a typist to do his typing.

Easy
Page: 131

97. Define the concept of diminishing returns to specialization. Provide an example of this concept.

Answer: Diminishing returns to specialization suggests that the more of a good a country produces, the greater the units of resources required to produce each additional unit of the item. For example, Canada is a major producer of wheat. However, if Canada tries to constantly push its wheat production up, at some point it will be producing wheat in the northern tundra or the western rain forests, and the wheat output per acre or per hour of labor will fall.

Medium
Page: 133

98. Describe the Heckscher-Ohlin theory of international trade. Is the Heckscher-Olin theory consistent with the notion of free trade? Why or why not?

Answer: The Heckscher-Ohlin theory predicts that countries will export those goods that make intensive use of those factors that are locally abundant, while importing goods that make intensive use of factors that are locally scarce. Thus, the Heckscher-Ohlin theory attempts to explain the pattern of international trade that we see in the world economy. The Heckscher-Ohlin theory is consistent with the notion of free trade. It also has commonsense appeal, and there are many examples of international commerce that are supportive of the theory.

Easy
Page: 138

99. Describe what is meant by first-mover advantages?

Answer: First mover advantages are the economic and strategic advantages that accrue to early entrants into an industry. Because they are able to gain economies of scale, early entrants may get a lock on the world market that discourages subsequent entry. In other words, the ability of first-movers to reap economies of scale creates a barrier to entry. In the commercial aircraft industry, for example, the fact that Boeing and Airbus are already in the industry and have achieved substantial economies of scale effectively discourages new entrants.

Medium
Page: 139

100. In an extensive study that was published in a book entitled *The Competitive Advantage of Nations*, Michael Porter concluded that four broad attributes of a nation shape the environment in which local firms compete, and that these attributes promote or impede the creation of competitive advantage. Identify and describe the four attributes advanced by Porter. What did Porter conclude from his analysis?

Answer: The four attributes identified by Porter are as follows:

Factor Endowments: A nation's position in factors of production such as skilled labor or the infrastructure necessary to compete in a given industry.

Demand Conditions: The nature of home demand for the industry's product or service.

Related or Supporting Industries: The presence or absence in a nation of supplier industries and related industries that are internationally competitive.

Firm Strategy, Structure, and Rivalry: The conditions in the nation governing how companies are created, organized, and managed and the nature of domestic rivalry.

Porter speaks of these four attributes as constituting the diamond. He argues that firms are most likely to succeed in industries or industry segments where the diamond is most favorable.

CHAPTER 5

THE POLITICAL ECONOMY OF INTERNATIONAL TRADE

MULTIPLE-CHOICE QUESTIONS

INSTRUMENTS OF TRADE POLICY

Answer: C
Easy
Page: 153

1. A __________ is a tax levied on imports.

   A. subsidy
   B. quota
   C. tariff
   D. special assessment

Answer: A
Easy
Page: 153

2. According to our textbook, __________ are the oldest and simplest instrument of trade policy.

   A. tariffs
   B. local content requirements
   C. subsidies
   D. quotas

Answer: C
Easy
Page: 153

3. A tariff is a tax levied on:

   A. exports
   B. products that the World Trade Organization has determined are being overproduced worldwide
   C. imports
   D. products that the World Trade Organization has determined are potentially dangerous or hazardous

Answer: A
Medium
Page: 153

4. Tariffs fall into two categories. These are:

   A. specific tariffs and ad valorem tariffs
   B. global tariffs and domestic tariffs
   C. general tariffs and specific tariffs
   D. flexible tariffs and ad valorem tariffs

Answer: D
Easy
Page: 153

5. Tariffs that are levied as a fixed charge for each unit of a good imported are referred to as __________ tariffs.

A. ad valorem
B. flexible
C. general
D. specific

Answer: A
Easy
Page: 153

6. __________ tariffs are levied as a proportion of the value of the imported good.

A. Ad Valorem
B. Specific
C. Flexible
D. General

Answer: D
Medium
Page: 153

7. An example of a(n) __________ tariff is the 25 percent tariff the American government placed on imported light trucks in the late 1980s.

A. Global
B. Specific
C. special circumstance
D. ad valorem

Answer: A
Medium
Page: 153

8. According to our textbook, tariffs benefit the following two groups.

A. government and producers
B. consumers and trade associations
C. government and consumers
D. producers and consumers

Answer: C
Medium
Page: 153

9. According to our textbook, the biggest losers as the result of tariffs are:

A. producers
B. trade associations
C. consumers
D. governments

Answer: D
Hard
Page: 153

10. According to our textbook, tariffs are unambiguously:

A. anti-producer and pro-consumer
B. anti-producer and anti-consumer
C. pro-consumer and pro-producer
D. pro-producer and anti-consumer

Answer: C
Easy
Page: 154

11. A __________ is a government payment to a domestic producer.

A. tariff
B. quota
C. subsidy
D. duty

Answer: B
Hard
Page: 154

12. By lowering costs, subsidies help domestic producers in the following two ways.

A. they help lower domestic tax rates, and they help domestic producers gain export markets
B. they help domestic producers compete against low-cost foreign imports, and they help domestic producers gain export markets
C. they help domestic producers attract lower cost labor from abroad, and they help lower domestic tax rates
D. they help lower tariff rates, and they help domestic producers gain export markets

Answer: A
Medium
Page: 154

13. The main gains from subsidies accrue to __________, whose international competitiveness is increased as a result.

A. domestic producers
B. global competitors
C. importers
D. special consortiums of domestic and international businesses

Answer: B
Hard
Page: 154

14. Advocates of strategic trade policy favor the use of __________ to help domestic firms achieve a dominant position in those industries where economies of scale are important and the world market is not large enough to profitably support more than a few firms (e.g. aerospace, semiconductors).

A. quotas
B. subsidies
C. tariffs
D. duties

Answer: A
Easy
Page: 155

15. A __________ is a direct restriction on the quantity of some good that may be imported into a country.

A. import quota
B. import duty
C. subsidy
D. tariff

Answer: B
Medium
Page: 155

16. A quota on trade imposed by an exporting country, typically at the request of the importing country's government, is referred to as a:

A. refereed export restraint
B. voluntary export restraint
C. involuntary import restraint
D. trade reconciliation

Answer: C
Hard
Page: 155

17. One of the most famous examples of a __________ is the limitation on auto exports to the United States enforced by Japanese automobile producers in 1981.

A. trade reconciliation
B. involuntary import restraint
C. voluntary export restraint
D. refereed export restraint

Answer: D
Medium
Page: 156

18. Foreign producers typically agree to voluntary export restrictions because:

A. they are required to by the World Trade Organization
B. they can divert their exports to other countries and charge more for their products
C. their manufacturing capacity is limited
D. they fear far more damaging punitive tariffs or import quotas might follow if they do not

Answer: A
Easy
Page: 156

19. A __________ calls for some specific fraction of a good to be produced domestically.

A. local content requirement
B. subsidy
C. ad valorem tariff
D. local duty

Answer: C
Medium
Page: 156

20. If Boeing won an order to sell 50 of its new Boeing 777 airplanes to China, but the Chinese government stipulated that 20 percent of the component parts of the 777s that it purchased must be produced in China, that stipulation would be an example of a:

A. ad valorem content requirement
B. specific content requirement
C. local content requirement
D. ad hoc content requirement

Answer: A
Medium
Page: 156

21. For a domestic producer of component parts, local content requirements provide protection in the same way an import quota does:

A. by limiting foreign competition
B. by increasing tariffs
C. by eliminating foreign competition
D. by encouraging foreign competition

Answer: B
Easy
Page: 156

22. In the context of international trade, __________ is variously defined as selling goods in a foreign market at below their costs of production, or as selling goods in a foreign market at below their "fair" market value.

A. subsidizing
B. dumping
C. slicing
D. slashing

Answer: C
Medium
Page:156

23. An alleged example of __________occurred in 1997, when two Korean manufacturers of semiconductors, LG Semicon and Hyundai Electronics, were accused of selling dynamic random access memory chips in the US market at below their costs of production.

A. slashing
B. subsidizing
C. dumping
D. slicing

Answer: D
Easy
Page: 157

24. Bureaucratic rules that are designed to make it difficult for imports to enter a country are referred to as:

A. situational trade policies
B. ad valorem trade policies
C. supplemental trade policies
D. administrative trade policies

THE CASE FOR GOVERNMENT INTERVENTION

Answer: A
Easy
Page: 157

25. In general, there are two types of arguments for government intervention in international trade. These are:

    A. political and economic
    B. judicial and sociocultural
    C. political and judicial
    D. sociological and economic

Answer: B
Medium
Page: 158

26. Perhaps the most common political argument for government intervention into the free flow of trade is that:

    A. it is necessary to maintain domestic economic stability
    B. it is necessary for protecting jobs and industries from foreign competition
    C. it protects national pride
    D. politicians and their constituents tend to think that domestically produced products are superior to products produced in another country

Answer: C
Hard
Page: 160

27. The __________ allows Americans to sue foreign firms that use Cuban property confiscated from them after the 1959 revolution.

    A. Frederick-Helms Act
    B. Perkins-Dole
    C. Helms-Burton Act
    D. D'Amato-Perkins

Answer: B
Easy
Page: 161

28. The __________ argument is by far the oldest economic argument for government intervention into the free flow of trade.

    A. mature industry
    B. infant industry
    C. declining industry
    D. proprietary industry

Answer: C
Hard
Page: 161

29. According to the __________ argument, many developing countries have a potential comparative advantage in manufacturing, but new manufacturing industries there cannot initially compete with well-established industries in developed countries. To allow manufacturing to get a toehold, the argument is that governments should temporarily support new industries (with tariffs, quotas, and subsidies) until they have grown strong enough to meet international competition.

A. proprietary industry
B. strategic trade policy
C. infant industry
D. emerging industry

Answer: A
Medium
Page: 161

30. The infant industry argument has been recognized as a legitimate reason for protectionism by the:

A. World Trade Organization
B. United Nations
C. North Atlantic Treaty Organization
D. Organization of American and Asian Exporters

Answer: A
Medium
Page: 162

31. According to the strategic trade policy argument, a government should use subsidies to:

A. support promising firms in emerging industries
B. support established firms in key industries
C. support the import of goods that a country cannot product domestically
D. support the export of agricultural products

Answer: B
Hard
Page: 162

32. An important component of __________ is that it might pay governments to intervene in an industry if it helps domestic firms overcome the barriers to entry created by foreign firms that have already reaped first-mover advantages.

A. tactical trade policy
B. strategic trade policy
C. administrative trade policy
D. comparative trade policy

Answer: D
Medium
Page: 163

33. MIT Professor __________ argues that strategic trade policy aimed at establishing domestic firms in a dominant position in a global industry are beggar-thy-neighbor policies that boost national income at the expense of other countries.

A. Geert Hofstede
B. David Ricardo
C. Michael Porter
D. Paul Krugman

Answer: C
Hard
Page: 163

34. According to our textbook, Paul Krugman, a professor at MIT, predicts that a country that attempts to use strategic trade policy to establish a domestic firm (or firms) in a dominant position in a global industry will probably:

A. succeed fairly smoothly
B. be viewed favorably in the international community
C. provoke retaliation
D. be successful if the policy is in force for at least three years

DEVELOPMENTS OF THE WORLD TRADING SYSTEM

Answer: C
Medium
Page: 164

35. Free trade as a government policy was first officially embraced by Great Britain in 1846, when the British Parliament repealed the:

A. steel laws
B. coal laws
C. corn laws
D. apparel laws

Answer: D
Hard
Page: 164

36. The Corn Laws:

A. were repealed after record harvests in Britain
B. were repealed after a stinging speech in parliament by David Ricardo where he outlined the theory of comparative advantage
C. were enacted by the U.S. government after defeating Britain in the War of Independence
D. placed a high tariff on corn imported into Britain

Answer: A
Hard
Page: 165

37 Aimed at avoiding rising unemployment by protecting domestic industry and diverting consumer demand away from foreign products, the __________ tariff erected an enormous wall of tariff barriers.

A. Smott-Hawley
B. Smith-Krugman
C. Heckscher-Ohlin
D. Porter-Ricardo

Answer: C
Medium
Page: 165

38 The General Agreements on Tariffs and Trade (GATT) was established in:

A. 1867
B. 1901
C. 1947
D. 1963

Answer: A
Easy
Page: 165

39. The __________ was a multilateral agreement whose objective was to liberalize trade by eliminating tariffs, subsidies, import quotas, and the like.

A. General Agreement on Trade and Tariffs
B. United Nations Charter on Free Trade
C. World Agreement on Trade and Free Commerce
D. Multinational Agreement on Globalization

Answer: D
Medium
Page: 165

40. The latest round of the GATT Agreement, referred to as the __________, was launched in 1986 and completed in December 1993.

A. Luxembourg Round
B. Paris Round
C. Geneva Round
D. Uruguay Round

Answer: D
Medium
Page: 165

41. In its early years, GATT was by most measures:

A. very unsuccessful
B. slightly unsuccessful
C. slightly successful
D. very successful

Answer: B
Hard
Page: 166

42. During the 1980s and early 1990s, the world trading system erected by the GATT began to come under strain as pressures for greater protectionism increased around the world. The reasons behind this strain included all of the following except:

A. many countries found ways to get around GATT regulations
B. increased use of VERs by U.S. exporters
C. the persistent trade deficit in the U.S.
D. the economic success of Japan

Answer: A
Medium
Page: 166

43. One of the best known examples of __________ is the agreement between the United States and Japan, under which Japanese producers promised to limit their auto imports to the United States as a way of defusing growing trade tensions.

A. voluntary export restraints
B. ad valorem tariffs
C. subsidies
D. import quotas

Answer: C
Medium
Page: 167

44. Against the background of rising pressures for protectionism, in 1986 the members of the GATT embarked upon their eighth round of negotiations to reduce tariffs, the:

A. Brussels Round
B. South American Round
C. Uruguay Round
D. Washington Round

Answer: D
Hard
Page: 167

45. Which of the following was not one of the objectives of the member countries going into the Uruguay Round of the GATT agreement?

A. to extend GATT rules to cover trade in services
B. to write rules governing the protection of intellectual property
C. to reduce agricultural subsidies
D. to extend GATT rules to cover trade in manufactured goods

Answer: D
Hard
Page: 167

46. The Uruguay Round of the GATT agreement lasted for:

A. 11 months
B. three years
C. five years
D. seven years

Answer: A
Hard
Page: 167

47. Which of the following statement was not a component of the Uruguay Round agreement?

A. agricultural subsidies will be substantially increased
B. a World Trade Organization will be created to implement the GATT Agreement
C. barriers on trade in textiles will be significantly reduced over 10 years
D. tariffs on industrial goods will be reduced by more than one-third

Answer: C
Easy
Page: 167

48. The World Trade Organization was created by the __________ of the GATT negations.

A. Brussels Round
B. Italian Round
C. Uruguay Round
D. Cyprus Round

Answer: B
Medium
Page: 167

49. As a result of the Uruguay Round agreement, the __________ was created to arbitrate trade disputes and monitor the trade policies of member countries.

A. International Trade Authority
B. World Trade Organization
C. Global Commerce Authority
D. United Trade Authority

Answer: B
Easy
Page: 167

50. In the context of GATT, the acronym WTO stands for:

A. World Trade Outlook
B. World Trade Organization
C. Western Trade Alliance
D. World Technology Outlook

Answer: C
Hard
Page: 168

51. What was the effect of the Uruguay Round Agreement on industrial tariffs?

A. easier access to world markets for exports of industrial goods; higher prices for consumers
B. harder access to world markets for exports of industrial goods; higher prices for consumers
C. easier access to world markets for exporters of industrial goods; lower prices for consumers
D. none

Answer: B
Medium
Page: 168

52. What is the main effect of the Uruguay Round Agreement on agricultural products?

A. consumers will face higher prices
B. farm subsidies will be reduced
C. inefficient producers will be better off
D. nothing - the Uruguay Round failed to make progress on this issue because European farmers threatened to boycott GATT if reforms were approved

Answer: D
Medium
Page: 169

53. The primary role of the World Trade Organization is to:

A. act as a mediator in trade disputes
B. set tariff levels that must be followed by all member countries
C. provide export development assistance loans to developing countries
D. monitor compliance with regulations and arbitrate trade disputes

IMPLICATIONS FOR BUSINESS

Answer: C
Easy
Page: 173

54. Trade barriers __________ the costs of exporting products to a country.

A. lower
B. have no effect on
C. raise
D. eliminate

Answer: D
Medium
Page: 173

55. The rapid expansion of Japanese automaking capacity in the U.S. during the 1980s was a direct result of __________ export restraints placed on the number of Japanese built automobiles that were entering U.S. markets.

A. statutory
B. legal
C. mandatory
D. voluntary

Answer: B
Medium
Page: 173

56. __________ may limit a firm's ability to serve a country from locations outside of that country.

A. Statutory export restraints
B. Voluntary export restraints
C. Mandatory export restraints
D. Legal export restraints

Answer: C
Hard
Page: 174

57. According to our textbook, government intervention in trade policy is unlikely to be well-executed for the following reason:

A. inexperience
B. the costs association with intervention
C. the impact of special interest groups
D. because of the high turnover of officials in government agencies

Answer: A
Easy
Page: 175

58. According to our textbook, most economists would probably argue that the best interests of international business are served by a _________ to international trade

A. free stance
B. "hands-off" stance
C. protectionism stance
D. laissez-faire stance

Answer: D
Medium
Page: 175

59. _________ has brought great advantages to firms that have exploited it and to consumers who benefit from the resulting lower prices.

A. Protectionism
B. A laissez-fair international attitude towards trade
C. A "hands-off" attitude on the part of the WTO towards trade issues
D. Free trade

Answer: C
Medium
Page: 175

60. According to our textbook, business probably has _________ from government efforts to open protected markets to imports and foreign direct investment than from government efforts to support current domestic industries in a manner consistent with the recommendations of strategic trade policy.

A. felt little impact
B. slightly more to gain
C. much more to gain
D. much more to lose

TRUE-FALSE QUESTIONS

INSTRUMENTS OF TRADE POLICY

Answer: F
Easy
Page: 153

61. A subsidy is a tax levied on imports.

Answer: T
Easy
Page: 153

62. Specific tariffs are levied as a fixed charge for each unit of a good imported.

Answer: F
Medium
Page: 153

63. A tariff of $3.00 per barrel on imported oil is an example of an ad valorem tariff.

Answer: T
Easy
Page: 153

64. Ad volorem tariffs are levied as a proportion of the value of an imported good.

Answer: T
Easy
Page: 153

65. A tariff raises the cost of imported products relative to domestic products.

Answer: F
Medium
Page: 163

66. Tariffs are unambiguously pro-consumer and anti-producer.

Answer: T
Easy
Page: 154

67. A subsidy is a government payment to a domestic producer.

Answer: T
Medium
Page: 154

68. The main gains from subsidies accrue to domestic producers, whose international competitiveness in increased as a result.

Answer: F
Medium
Page: 154

69. According to the author of our textbook, most subsidies are extremely successful at increasing the international competitiveness of domestic producers.

Answer: T
Easy
Page: 155

70. An import quota is a direct restriction on the quantity of some good that may be imported into a country.

Answer: F
Hard
Page: 155

71. A voluntary export restraint is a quota on trade imposed by the importing country, typically at the request of the exporting country's government.

Answer: T
Medium
Page: 156

72. For a domestic producer of component parts, local content requirements provide protection in the same was an import quota does: by limiting foreign competition.

Answer: T
Medium
Page: 156

73. In the context of international trade, dumping is variously defined as selling goods in a foreign market at below their costs of production, or as selling goods in a foreign market at below their "fair" market value.

Answer: F
Medium
Page: 157

74. Administrative trade policies are bureaucratic rules designed to make it difficult for domestic firms to export products to foreign markets.

THE CASE FOR GOVERNMENT INTERVENTION

Answer: T
Easy
Page: 158

75. The most common political argument for government intervention into international trade policy is that it is necessary for protecting jobs and industries from foreign competition.

Answer: T
Hard
Page: 160

76. The Helms-Burton Act allows American firms to sue foreign firms that use Cuban property confiscated from them after the 1959 revolution.

Answer: F
Easy
Page: 161

77. The infant industry argument is one of the newest arguments for government intervention into international trade.

Answer: T
Medium
Page: 161

78. According to the infant industry argument, governments should temporarily support new industries (with tariffs, import quotas, and subsidies) until they have grown strong enough to meet international competition.

Answer: F
Medium
Page: 162

79. According to the strategic trade policy argument, a government should use local content requirements to support promising firms in emerging industries.

DEVELOPMENTS OF THE WORLD TRADING SYSTEM

Answer: F
Madium
Page: 164

80. Free trade as a government policy was first officially embraced by Great Britain in 1846, when the British Parliament repealed the Textile Laws.

Answer: T
Easy
Page: 165

81. The General Agreement on Trade and Tariffs (GATT) was established in 1947.

Answer: T
Medium
Page: 165

82. During the 1980s and 1990s, the world trading system erected by the GATT began to come under strain as pressures for greater protectionism increased around the world.

Answer: F
Easy
Page: 167

83. The most recent round of negotiations within the auspices of the GATT Agreement was referred to as the Paris Round.

Answer: T
Hard
Page: 167

84. One of the provisions of the Uruguay Round agreement was that GATT rules are to be extended to protect patents, copyrights, and trademarks.

Answer: F
Medium
Page: 167

85. One of the disappointing outcomes of the Uruguay Round was the lack of progress on reducing agricultural subsidies.

Answer: T
Medium
Page: 170

86. The Uruguay Round of GATT negotiations extended global trading rules to cover services.

Answer: T
Easy
Page: 169

87. According to our textbook, the world is better off with a GATT deal than without it.

IMPLICATIONS FOR BUSINESS

Answer: T
Easy
Page: 173

88. Trade barriers constrain a firm's ability to disperse its productive activities to the countries where they can be performed most efficiently.

Answer: F
Medium
Page: 175

89. Most economists would probably argue that the best interests of international business are served by a laissez-faire stance.

ESSAY QUESTIONS

Easy
Page: 153

90. What is a tariff? Describe the difference between specific tariffs and ad valorem tariffs.

Answer: A tariff is a tax levied on imports. Specific tariffs are levied as a fixed charge for each unit of a good imported (for example, $500 for each automobile). Ad valorem tariffs are levied as a proportion of the value of the imported good. An example of an ad valorem tariff is the 25 percent tariff that the U.S. government placed on imported light trucks (including pickup trucks, four-wheel-drive vehicles, and minivans) in the late 1980s.

Medium
Page: 153

91. Who gains and who losses from the imposition of a tariff on an imported good? How can it be determined whether the net gain from the tariff exceeds the net loss?

Answer: The government gains, because the tariff increases government revenues. Domestic producers gain, because the tariff gives them some protection against foreign competitors by increasing the cost of imported foreign goods. Consumers lose because they must pay more for certain imports. Whether the gains to the government and domestic producers exceeds the loss to consumers depends on various factors such as the amount of the tariff, the importance of the imported good to domestic consumers, the number of jobs saved in the protected industry, and so on.

Medium
Page: 154

92. What is a subsidy? Provide some examples of the forms that subsidies take. How do subsidies help domestic producers?

Answer: A subsidy is a government payment to a domestic producer. Subsidies take many forms including cash grants, low-interest loans, tax breaks, and government equity participation in domestic firms. By lowering costs, subsidies help domestic producers in two ways: they help them compete against low-cost foreign imports and they help them gain export markets.

Easy
Page: 155

93. What is an import quota? How are import quota's typically enforced?

Answer: An import quota is a direct restriction on the quantity of some good that may be imported into a country. The restriction is normally enforced by issuing import licenses to a group of individuals or firms. For example, the United States has a quota on imports of cheese. The only firms allowed to import cheese are certain trading companies, each of which is allocated the right to import a maximum number of pounds of cheese each year. In some cases, the right to sell is given directly to the governments of exporting countries. This is the case for sugar and textile imports in the United States.

Medium
Page: 155

94. What is a voluntary export restraint? Can countries use voluntary export restraints to avoid trade retaliation? Explain your answer.

A voluntary export restraint is a "voluntary" quota on trade imposed by the exporting company (on itself) typically at the request of the importing country's government. One of the most famous examples is the limitation on auto exports to the United States enforced by the Japanese automobile producers in 1981. In response to direct pressure from the U.S. government, this voluntary export restraint limited Japanese automobile imports to no more than 1.68 million vehicles per year.

Clearly, voluntary export restraints can be used to "head off" higher tariffs, more restrictive formal quotas, and other forms of trade retaliation.

Medium
Page: 157

95. What are administrative trade policies? Are these trade policies deliberately designed to restrict the flow of imports into a country, or do they simply reflect the complexity of the bureaucracies in many foreign countries? Provide at least one example of an "administrative trade policy."

Answer: Administrative trade policies are bureaucratic rules that are almost always deliberately designed to restrict the flow of a particular import into a country. For instance, a country may design some administrative rule that makes it totally impractical for a foreign company to import a particular product into its country. An example that is provided in the textbook is tulip bulbs. The Netherlands exports tulip bulbs to almost every country of the world except Japan. The reason is that Japanese customs inspectors insist on checking every tulip bulb by cutting it vertically down the middle, which in effect ruins the bulb. Other example are equally as compelling. For example, a country might insist that every VCR that is imported into the country be thoroughly tested to make sure that it will not subject the user to an "electric shock." If it took several weeks for these tests to be completed, it would be very difficult to make money importing VCRs into this country.

Obviously, these types of administrative trade policies are informal tariffs and are designed to block specific imports from entering a country.

Hard
Page: 158

96. What are the principle political and economic arguments for government intervention into international trade? Please describe these arguments. In your opinion, which set of arguments are the most compelling?

Answer: *Political Arguments:* The political arguments cover a range of issues, including protecting jobs, protecting industries deemed important for national security, and retaliating against unfair foreign competition. In regard to protecting jobs, this is the most common political argument for government intervention. For example, the Japanese quotas on rice imports are aimed at protecting jobs in that country's agricultural sector. In terms of protecting industries deemed important for national security, countries sometimes argue that it is necessary to protect certain industries (like aerospace, steel, advanced electronics, etc.) because they are important for national security. Finally, in regard to retaliating against foreign competition, some people argue that governments should use the threat to intervene in trade policy as a bargaining tool to help open foreign markets and force trading partners to "play by the rules of the game."

Economic arguments: The economic arguments in favor of government intervention include the infant industry argument and strategic trade policy. The infant industry argument is most often used by developing countries. According to this argument, many developing countries have a potential comparative advantage in manufacturing, but new manufacturing industries there can not initially compete with well-established industries in developed countries. To allow manufacturing to get a toehold, the argument is that governments should temporarily support new industries (with tariffs, import quotas, and subsidies) until they have grown strong enough to meet international standards. The strategy trade policy argument is more complex, but basically argues that governments should use their trade policies to help certain domestic firms dominate their global industries and gain first-mover advantages, and that it might pay government to intervene in an industry if it helps domestic firms overcome the barriers to entry created by foreign firms that have already reaped first-mover advantages.

The author of the textbook clearly believes that the economic arguments for government intervention into international trade are the most compelling. This question presents an interesting and engaging topic for classroom discussion.

Hard
Page: 165

97. During the 1980s and early 1990s, the world trading system erected by the GATT began to come under strain as pressures for greater protectionism increased around the world. Three main reasons caused the rise in such pressures during the 1980s. Identify these reasons.

Answer: First, the economic success of Japan strained the world trading system. Second, the world's trading system was further strained by the persistent trade deficit in the world's largest economy, the United States. Finally, many countries found ways to get around GATT regulations. For example, bilateral voluntary export restraints circumvented GATT agreements because neither the importing country nor the exporting country complained to the GATT bureaucracy in Geneva - and without a complaint, the GATT bureaucracy could do nothing.

Medium
Page: 167

98. The World Trade Organization (WTO) was created by the recently completed Uruguay Round of the GATT negotiations. According to the textbook, has the WTO gotten off to a good start or a poor start? Do you believe that the WTO will be effective in the long run? Why or why not?

Answer: According to the textbook, the early life of the WTO suggests that its policing and enforcement mechanisms are having a positive effect. Countries are using the WTO to settle trade disputes, which represents an important vote of confidence in the organization's dispute resolution procedures. So far, the users of the system have included both developed and developing countries, which is also a promising development. In addition, some powerful developed countries, including the United States, have been willing to accept WTO ruling that have gone against them, which attests to the organization's legitimacy.

The second part of this question – do you believe that the WTO will be effective in the long run – is designed to provide a forum for classroom discussion and/or ask your students to "think" about the role of an organization like the WTO in settling international commerce disputes.

Medium
Page: 173

99. Given that the gains to projectionist policies usually accrue to the producers, why shouldn't an industry lobby its government for protection from imports?

Answer: Free trade has brought great advantages to the firms that have exploited it, and to consumers who benefit from the resulting lower prices. Given the danger of retaliatory action, business firms that lobby their governments to engage in protectionism must realize that by doing so they may be denying themselves the opportunity to build a competitive advantage by constructing a globally dispersed production system. Moreover, by encouraging their government to engage in protectionism, their own activities and sales overseas may be put in jeopardy if foreign governments retaliate.

CHAPTER 6

FOREIGN DIRECT INVESTMENT

MULTIPLE-CHOICE QUESTIONS

INTRODUCTION

Answer: A
Easy
Page: 182

1. __________ occurs when a firm invests directly in facilities to produce and/or market a product in a foreign country.

A. Foreign direct investment
B. Cross-boarder international investment
C. International capital investment
D. Reciprocal foreign investment

Answer: A
Hard
Page: 182

2. According to the U.S. Department of Commerce, FDI occurs whenever an U.S. citizen, organization, or affiliated group takes an interest of __________ or more in a foreign business entity.

A. 10 percent
B. 20 percent
C. 33.3 percent
D. 50 percent
E. more than 50 percent

Answer: C
Easy
Page: 182

3. In the context of international trade, FDI is an acronym that stands for:

A. Federation of Direct Investors
B. Federal Diversification Initiative
C. Foreign Direct Investment
D. Formal Direct Internationalization

Answer: B
Easy
Page: 182

4. A __________ is a company that conducts business in more than one country.

A. international conglomerate
B. multinational enterprise
C. synergistic enterprise
D. cross-cultural enterprise

Answer: A
Easy
Page: 182

5. A multinational enterprise is defined as a country that operates in:

A. more than one country
B. at least three countries
C. at least five countries
D. at least seven countries

Answer: D
Medium
Page: 182

6. The investment by individuals, firms, or public bodies in foreign financial instruments is referred to as:

A. foreign direct investment
B. foreign indirect investment
C. foreign securities enactment
D. foreign portfolio investment

Answer: A
Medium
Page: 182

7. According to our textbook, firms often view exports and FDI as:

A. substitutes for each other
B. complementary to one another
C. unequal to one another
D. mutually exclusive

Answer: C
Medium
Page: 182

8. In return for licensing one of its products to a foreign firm, the licensor:

A. gets preferential trade treatment from the country of the licensee
B. gets a special subsidy from the country of the licensee
C. collects a royalty fee on every unit the licensee sells
D. gets a one time payment from the licensee

Answer: C
Medium
Page: 182

9. _________ foreign direct investment is FDI in the same industry as a firm operates in at home.

A. Correspondent
B. Synergistic
C. Horizontal
D. Complementary

Answer: A
Medium
Page: 182

10. _________ foreign direct investment is FDI in an industry that provides inputs for a firm's domestic operations, or it may be FDI in an industry abroad that sells the outputs of a firm's domestic operations.

A. Vertical
B. Synergistic
C. Horizontal
D. Correspondent

Answer: C
Medium
Page: 182

11. Which of the following is not an example of a FDI?

A. U.S. based IBM deciding to build a new computer manufacturing facility in Scotland
B. U.S. based Hewlett-Packard buying a German software company from it's Swiss owner
C. U.S. based General Electric buying a 25% stake from Electrolux in Electrolux's U.S. plant
D. Sony's purchase of CBS records and Columbia Pictures from U.S. parents

FOREIGN DIRECT INVESTMENT IN THE WORLD ECONOMY

Answer: A
Medium
Page: 183

12. The __________ of foreign direct investment refers to the amount of FDI undertaken over a given period (normally a year). The __________ of foreign direct investment refers to the total accumulated value of foreign-owned assets at any time.

A. flow, stock
B. portfolio, current
C. stock, flow
D. stockpile, portfolio

Answer: D
Easy
Page: 183

13. The __________ of FDI refers to the total amount of FDI undertaken over a given time period (normally a year).

A. stock
B. register
C. portfolio
D. flow

Answer: B
Easy
Page: 183

14. The __________ of FDI refers to the total accumulated value of foreign-owned assets at a given time.

A. portfolio
B. stock
C. flow
D. register

Answer: A
Hard
Page: 183

15. Which of the following two statements accurately reflects the trend in foreign direct investment over the past 20 years?

A. there has been a rapid increase in the total volume of FDI undertaken, and there has been a change in the importance of various countries as recipients for FDI
B. there has been a rapid increase in the total volume of FDI undertaken, and the countries that have been instrumental as recipients of FDI have remained the same
C. there has been a rapid decrease in the total volume of FDI undertaken, and there has been a change in the importance of various countries as recipients for FDI
D. there has been a rapid decrease in the total volume of FDI undertaken, and the countries that have been instrumental as recipients of FDI have remained the same

Answer: C
Hard
Page: 183

16. As a result of the strong FDI flow, by 1998 the global stock of FDI exceeded:

A. $ 800 billion
B. $ 1.5 trillion
C. $ 4.0 trillion
D. $ 5.5 trillion

Answer: C
Medium
Page: 183

17. The past 20 years has seen a marked increase:

A. the flow but not the stock of foreign direct investment
B. the stock but not the flow of foreign direct investment
C. both the flow and stock of foreign direct investment
D. neither the flow nor the stock of foreign direct investment

Answer: A
Medium
Page: 184

18. FDI is growing more rapidly than:

A. world trade and world output
B. world trade but not world output
C. neither world trade nor world output
D. world output but not world trade

Answer: D
Medium
Page: 184

19. Which of the following factors has not contributed to the increase in FDI over the past several years?

A. businesses still fear protectionist pressures
B. political and economic changes that have been occurring in many of the world's developing nations
C. the globalization of the world economy
D. shifts towards socialist and communist political institutions

Answer: C
Easy
Page: 185

20. The country that accounts for the largest share of FDI inflows is:

A. Japan
B. China
C. United States
D. Great Britain

Answer: B
Medium
Page: 187

21. Which of the following is not a reason that FDI inflows have increased in recent years in Mexico and Brazil?

A. privatization
B. protectionist policies
C. the liberalization of regulations governing FDI
D. the growing importance of regional free trade areas

Answer: B
Easy
Page: 188

22. The total amount of capital invested in factories, stores, office buildings, and the like is referred to as:

A. total long-term capital placement
B. gross fixed capital formation
C. absolute fixed capital placement
D. total long-term capital formation

Answer: B
Hard
Page: 188

23. In general, FDI accounts for between __________ of worldwide gross fixed capital formation.

A. 1 and 3.4 percent
B. 3 and 5.4 percent
C. 4 and 6.2 percent
D. 6 and 7.8 percent

Answer: A
Medium
Page: 189

24. Compared to the amount of FDI inflows in other industrialized nations, the amount of FDI that comes into Japan can be characterized as:

A. extremely low
B. slightly low
C. slightly high
D. extremely high

HORIZONTAL FOREIGN DIRECT INVESTMENT

Answer: B
Hard
Page: 190

25. Other things being equal, FDI is __________ and __________ compared to exporting or licensing.

A. inexpensive, risk adverse
A. expensive, risky
C. expensive, risk adverse
D. inexpensive, risky

Answer: C
Medium
Page: 190

26. Compared to exporting and licensing, FDI is expensive because:

A. of high tariffs
B. of the high cost of labor in most countries
C. a firm must bear the costs of establishing production facilities in a foreign country or of acquiring a foreign enterprise
D. of high tax rates worldwide

Answer: C
Medium
Page: 191

27. When transportation costs are added to production costs, it becomes unprofitable to ship some products over a large distance. This is particularly true of products that have a:

A. high value-to-weight ratio
B. moderate value-to-weight ratio
C. low value-to-weight ratio
D. extremely high value-to-weight ratio

Answer: D
Medium
Page: 191

28. For which product is exporting likely to be the most feasible?

A. cement
B. gatorade
C. coal
D. diamonds

Answer: B
Medium
Page: 191

29. For products with a __________, the attractiveness of exporting, relative to FDI or licensing, decreases.

A. high value-to-weight ratio
B. low value-to-weight ratio
C. extremely high value-to-weight ratio
D. moderate value-to-weight ratio

Answer: A
Medium
Page: 191

30. For products with a __________, transportation costs have little impact on the relative attractiveness of exporting, licensing, and FDI.

A. high value-to-weight ratio
B. low value-to-weight ratio
C. extremely low value-to-weight ratio
D. moderate value-to-weight ratio

Answer: D
Easy
Page: 191

31. Factors that inhibit markets from working perfectly are referred to as:

A. global imperfections
B. international deficits
C. global flaws
D. market imperfections

Answer: B
Medium
Page: 191

32. The __________ explanation of FDI is the one favored by most economists.

A. product life-cycle
B. market imperfections
C. value-to-weight
D. economic anomaly

Answer: C
Medium
Page: 191

33. In the international business literature, the marketing imperfection approach to FDI is typically referred to as:

A. globalization theory
B. international commerce theory
C. internalization theory
D. economic anomaly theory

Answer: B
Hard
Page: 191

34. With regard to horizontal FDI, market imperfections arise in two circumstances. These are:

A. when tariff rates are high, and when import quotas are restrictive
B. when there are impediments to the free flow of products between nations, and when there are impediments to the sale of know-how
C. when import quotas are restrictive, and when there are impediments to the sale of know-how
D. when tariff rates are high, and when there are impediments to the free flow of products between nations

Answer: A
Medium
Page: 191

35. Impediments to the free flow of products between nations decrease the profitability of __________, relative to __________.

A. exporting, FDI and licensing
B. licensing, FDI and exporting
C. FDI, exporting and licensing
D. exporting and licensing, FDI

Answer: B
Hard
Page: 191

36. The __________ explanation predicts that FDI will be preferred whenever there are impediments that make both exporting and the sale of know-how difficult and/or expensive.

A. product life-cycle
B. market imperfections
C. value-to-weight
D. economic anomaly

Answer: B
Medium
Page: 191

37. According to our textbook, __________ are the main source of impediments to the free flow of products between nations.

A. multinational corporations
B. governments
C. trade associations
D. international trade organizations

Answer: A
Hard
Page: 192

38. For a company to favor FDI, the following two conditions must hold:

A. transportation costs and/or impediments to exporting must rule out exporting as an option, and there must be some reason the company cannot sell its know-how to foreign producers
B. tariffs rates must be very low (or nonexistent), and import quotas must be very low (or nonexistent)
C. transportation costs and/or impediments to exporting must rule out exporting as an option, and import quotas must be very low (or nonexistent)
D. there must be some reason the company cannot sell its know-how to foreign producers, and tariff rates must be very low (or nonexistent)

Answer: D
Hard
Page: 192

39. According to economic theory, there are three reasons the market does not always work well as a mechanism for selling know-how. Which of the following is not one of these reasons?

A. licensing may result in a firm's giving away its know-how to a potential foreign competitor
B. licensing does not give a firm the tight control over manufacturing, marketing, and strategy in a foreign country that may be required to profitably exploit its advantage in know-how
C. a firm's know-how may not be amenable to licensing
D. uncertainties in tariff rates make licensing unattractive, particularly if tariff rates go up

Answer: D
Medium
Page: 192

40. Which of the following is not a condition that would lead a firm towards licensing?

A. high transportation costs
B. know-how is amenable to licensing
C. tight control over foreign operations is not required
D. know-how cannot be protected by a contract

Answer: C
Easy
Page: 193

41. An __________ is an industry composed of a limited number of large firms (i.e. an industry in which four firms control 80 percent of a domestic market).

A. syndicate
B. cartel
C. oligopoly
D. monopoly

Answer: A
Easy
Page: 193

42. An industry composed of a limited number of large firms (i.e. in which four firms control 80 percent of the domestic market) is referred to as an:

A. oligopoly
B. cartel
C. syndicate
D. monopoly

Answer: B
Medium
Page: 193

43. Which of the following theories (or ideas) is associated with the work of F.T. Knickerbocker?

A. foreign direct investment
B. oligopoly
C. product life-cycle
D. globalization

Answer: D
Medium
Page: 195

44. __________ arises when two or more enterprises encounter each other in different regional markets, national markets, or industries.

A. Multilateral competition
B. Diamond competition
C. Diagonal competition
D. Multipoint competition

Answer: C
Medium
Page: 195

45. __________ argued that firms undertake FDI at particular stages in the life cycle of a product that they have pioneered.

A. Knickerbocker
B. Porter
C. Vernon
D. Dunning

Answer: A
Medium
Page: 196

46. British economist __________ argued that location-specific advantages can help explain the nature and direction of FDI.

A. John Dunning
B. Michael Porter
C. F.T. Knickerbocker
D. Raymond Vernon

Answer: C
Medium
Page: 196

47. Advantages that arise from using resource endowments or assets that are tied to a particular location and that a firm finds valuable to combine with its own unique assets are referred to as:

A. geographic-specific preferences
B. unique-geographic advantages
C. location-specific advantages
D. region-specific advantages

Answer: A
Medium
Page: 196

48. By __________, Dunning means the advantages that arise from utilizing resource endowments or assets that are tied to a particular foreign location and that a firm finds valuable to combine with its own unique assets.

A. location-specific advantages
B. locale-specific preferences
C. unique-geographic advantages
D. geographic-specific preferences

Answer: D
Easy
Page: 196

49. According to __________, firms undertake FDI to exploit resource endowments or assets that are location specific.

A. Porter
B. Smith
C. Vernon
D. Dunning

Answer: D
Medium
Page: 196

50. Knowledge spillovers that occur when companies in the same industry locate in the same area are referred to as:

A. inward overflows
B. cognitive overflows
C. concentric overflows
D. externalities

VERTICAL FOREIGN DIRECT INVESTMENT

Answer: C
Medium
Page: 197

51. Historically, most backward vertical FDI has been in:

A. services industries
B. agriculture
C. extractive industries
D. manufacturing

Answer: C
Medium
Page: 197

52. __________ FDI is FDI into an industry abroad that sells the outputs of a firm's domestic production processes.

A. Forward horizontal
B. Backward vertical
C. Forward vertical
D. Backward horizontal

Answer: B
Medium
Page: 197

53. __________ FDI is FDI into an industry abroad that provides inputs for a firm's domestic production processes.

A. Forward horizontal
B. Backward vertical
C. Forward vertical
D. Backward horizontal

Answer: A
Hard
Page: 197

54. According to economic theory, by __________ integrating __________ to gain control over the source of raw material, a firm can raise entry barriers and shut new competitors out of an industry.

A. vertically, backward
B. horizontally, forward
C. horizontally, backward
D. vertically, forward

IMPLICATIONS FOR BUSINESS

Answer: C
Medium
Page: 199

55. The location-specific advantages argument association with John Dunning helps explain the __________ of FDI, both with regard to horizontal and vertical FDI.

A. intensity
B. significance
C. direction
D. longevity

Answer: A
Hard
Page: 200

56. Licensing tends to be more common in:

A. fragmented, low-technology industries in which globally dispersed manufacturing is not an option
B. consolidated, high-technology industries in which globally dispersed manufacturing is an attractive option
C. fragmented, high-technology industries in which globally dispersed manufacturing is an attractive option
D. consolidated, low-technology industries in which globally dispersed manufacturing is not an option

Answer: D
Medium
Page: 200

57. __________ is essentially the service-industry version of licensing - although it normally involves much longer-term commitments than licensing.

A. FDI
B. Exporting
C. Outsourcing
D. Franchising

Answer: B
Medium
Page: 201

58. McDonalds has expanded into foreign markets primarily through:

A. exporting
B. franchising
C. FDI
D. licensing

Answer: B
Hard
Page: 201

59. The __________ points out that vertical FDI may be a way of building barriers to entry into an industry.

A. product life-cycle approach
B. strategic behavior approach
C. location-specific advantages
D. market imperfections

Answer: D
Hard
Page: 201

60. The __________ approach points to the importance of investments in specialized assets and imperfections in the market for know-how as factors that increase the relative attractiveness of vertical FDI.

A. strategic behavior
B. product life-cycle
C. location-specific advantages
D. market imperfections

TRUE-FALSE QUESTIONS

INTRODUCTION

Answer: T
Easy
Page: 182

61. Foreign direct investment occurs when a firm invests directly in facilities to produce and/or market a product in a foreign country.

Answer: T
Easy
Page: 182

62. Once a firm undertakes FDI it becomes a multinational enterprise.

Answer: F
Hard
Page: 182

63. Foreign portfolio investment involves taking a significant equity stake in a foreign business entity.

Answer: F
Medium
Page: 182

64. Vertical foreign direct investment is FDI in the same industry as a firm operates in at home.

Answer: F
Medium
Page: 183

65. Horizontal foreign direct investment is FDI in an industry that provides inputs for a firm's domestic operations, or it may be FDI in an industry abroad that sells the outputs of a firm's domestic operations.

FOREIGN DIRECT INVESTMENT IN THE WORLD ECONOMY

Answer: T
Easy
Page: 183

66. The flow of FDI refers to the amount of FDI undertaken over a given time period (normally a year).

Answer: T
Easy
Page: 183

67. The stock of FDI refers to the total accumulated value of foreign-owned assets at any given time.

Answer: F
Medium
Page: 183

68. During the past 20 years, there has been a marked increase in the flow of FDI, and a marked decrease in the stock of FDI.

Answer: F
Hard
Page: 183

69. As a result of the strong flow of FDI in recent years, by 1998 the global stock of FDI exceeded $10 trillion.

Answer: T
Medium
Page: 184

70. FDI is growing more rapidly than world trade and world output.

Answer: F
Medium
Page: 185

71. In recent years, there has been a decline of FDI into the developing nations of the world.

Answer: T
Easy
Page: 188

72. Gross fixed capital formation summarizes the total amount of capital invested in factories, stores, office buildings, and the like.

Answer: T
Hard
Page: 188

73. In general, FDI accounts for between 3 percent and 5.4 percent of worldwide gross fixed capital formation.

Answer: F
Medium
Page: 189

74. To the extent that capital inflows allow a country to achieve higher future growth rates, countries such as Japan and South Korea are really helping themselves by adopting restrictive regulations with regard to FDI inflows.

Answer: T
Easy
Page: 189

75. Since World War II, the United States has traditionally been by far the largest source country for FDI.

HORIZONTAL FOREIGN DIRECT INVESTMENT

Answer: T
Easy
Page: 190

76. Horizontal FDI is FDI in the same industry abroad as a firm operates at home.

Answer: F
Medium
Page: 190

77. Other things being equal, FDI is inexpensive and risk-adverse compared to exporting or licensing.

Answer: T
Medium
Page: 190

78. FDI is expensive because a firm must bear the costs of establishing production facilities in a foreign country or of acquiring a foreign enterprise.

Answer: F
Medium
Page: 191

79. Exporting is an attractive option for products that have a low value-to-weight ratio.

Answer: T
Easy
Page: 191

80. Market imperfections are factors that inhibit markets from working perfectly.

Answer: F
Medium
Page: 191

81. International trade organizations are the main source of impediments to the free flow of products between nations.

Answer: F
Medium
Page: 193

82. An oligopoly in an industry composed of a high number of large firms (typically four or more).

Answer: T
Easy
Page: 195

83. Multipoint competition arises when two or more enterprises encounter each other in different regional markets, national markets, or industries.

Answer: T
Medium
Page: 195

84. Raymond Vernon, the originator of the product life-cycle theory, has argued that firms undertake FDI at particular stages in the life cycle of a product they have pioneered.

Answer: F
Medium
Page: 196

85. The British economist John Dunning has argued that location specific advantages can help explain the nature and direction of licensing.

VERTICAL FOREIGN DIRECT INVESTMENT

Answer: T
Medium
Page: 197

86. Forward vertical FDI is FDI into an industry abroad that sells the outputs of a firm's domestic production processes.

Answer: F
Hard
Page: 197

87. According to economic theory, by vertically integrating backward to gain control over the source of raw material, a firm can lower entry barriers and shut new competition out of an industry.

IMPLICATIONS FOR BUSINESS

Answer: T
Medium
Page: 199

88. The locations-specific advantages argument associated with John Dunning helps explain the direction of FDI, both with regard to horizontal and vertical FDI

Answer: F
Medium
Page: 199

89. Licensing is an attractive option when a firm needs tight control over a foreign entity to maximize its market share and earnings in the foreign entity's country.

Answer: T
Medium
Page: 201

90. With franchising, the firm licenses its brand name to a foreign firm in return for a percentage of the franchisee's profits.

ESSAY QUESTIONS

Easy
Page: 182

91. What is meant by the term Foreign Direct Investment? Describe the difference between the flow of foreign direct investment and the stock of foreign direct investment.

Answer: Foreign direct investment (FDI) occurs when a firm invests directly in new facilities to produce and/or market a product in a foreign country. To be more precise, the U.S. Department of Commerce describes FDI as follows: FDI occurs whenever a U.S. citizen, organization, or affiliated group takes an interest of 10 percent or more in a foreign business entity.

The flow of foreign direct investment refers to the amount of FDI undertaken over a given period (normally a year). The stock of foreign direct investment refers to the total accumulated value of foreign-owned assets at a given time.

Easy
Page: 182

92. How does vertical FDI differ from horizontal FDI?

Answer: Horizontal FDI involves investing internationally in the same industry in which a firm operates domestically. Vertical FDI involves investing in an industry that provides inputs for a firm's domestic operations, or it may be FDI in an industry abroad that sells the outputs of a firm's domestic production.

Medium
Page: 183

93. Is FDI growing or waning worldwide? Is FDI growing more rapidly or less rapidly than world trade and world output? Explain your answer.

Answer: FDI is growing worldwide. The average yearly outflow of FDI increased from about $25 billion in 1975 to a record $430 billion in 1998. FDI is growing more rapidly than world trade and world output for several reasons. First, despite the general decline in trade barriers that we have witnessed over the past 30 years, business firms' still fear protectionist pressures. In light of this, business executives see FDI as a way of circumventing future trade barriers. Second, must of the recent increase in FDI is being driven by the dramatic political and economic changes that have been occurring in many of the world's developing nations. The general shift towards democratic political institutions and free market economies has encouraged FDI. Finally, the globalization of the world economy is having a positive impact on the volume of FDI. Firms such as General Motors and Sony now see the whole world as their market, and they are undertaking FDI in an attempt to make sure they have a significant presence in every region of the world.

Medium
Page: 190

94. Despite its advantages, FDI has been described as an "expensive" and "risky" international growth strategy. Other things being equal, why is FDI expensive and risky? Compare the risks involved with FDI to the risks involved with exporting and licensing.

Answer: FDI is expensive because a firm must bear the costs of establishing production facilities in a foreign country or of acquiring a foreign enterprise. FDI is risky because of the problems associated with doing business in another culture where the "rules of the game" may be very different. As a result, relative to firms native to a culture, there is a greater probability that a firm undertaking FDI in a foreign culture will make costly mistakes due to ignorance. When a firm exports, it need not bear the costs of FDI, and the risks associated with selling abroad can be reduced by using a native sales agent. Similarly, when a firm licenses its know-how, it need not bear the costs or risks of FDI, since there are born by the native firm that licenses the know-how.

Medium
Page: 191

95. How do transportation costs affect the attractiveness of exporting?

Answer: When transportation costs are added to production costs, it becomes unprofitable to shift some products over a long distance. This is particularly true of products that have a low value-to-weight ratio and can be produced at almost any location (e.g., cement, soft drinks, beer, etc.). For such products, relative to either FDI or licensing, the attractiveness of exporting decreases. For products with a high value-to-weight ratio, however, transport costs are normally a very minor component of total landed costs (e.g. jewelry, medical equipment, computer chips). In such cases, transportation costs have little impact on the attractiveness of exporting.

Hard
Page: 192

96. Name three reasons that licensing may not be an attractive option.

Answer: First, licensing may result in a firm's giving away its know-how to a potential foreign competitor. There are many documented cases of where licensees learned how to produce a product from its licensor, and quickly exited the licensing agreement and started producing a similar product on its own. Second, licensing does not give a firm the tight control over manufacturing, marketing, and strategy in a foreign country that may be required to profitably exploit its advantage in know-how. With licensing, control over production, marketing, and strategy is granted to a licensee in return for a royalty fee. However, for both strategic and operational reasons, a firm may want to retain control over these functions. Third, a firm's know-how may not be amenable to licensing. This is particularly true of management and marketing know-how.

Medium
Page: 193

97. According to the work of F.T. Knickerbocker, why do firms undertake horizontal FDI? What is the major deficiency with this theory?

Answer: According to Knickerbocker's "follow the leader" theory, firms undertake horizontal FDI when another firms in their industry has already done so. Hence they also invest overseas in order to keep from being locked out of other markets or to keep tabs on their international competitors. What this theory does not explain is why the first firm takes the action that the other firms subsequently imitative.

Medium
Page: 195

98. According to Raymond Vernon's product life-cycle theory, at what stages in a product's life cycle is FDI likely to take place and in what types of countries?

Answer: According to Vernon's product life-cycle theory, firms will invest in industrialized countries when demand in those countries is sufficient to support local production. They subsequently shift production to developing countries when product standardization and market saturation give rise to price competition and cost pressures. Investment in developing countries, where labor costs are lower, is seen as the best way to reduce costs.

Hard
Page: 196

99. Describe what is meant by the eclectic paradigm? Who is its principle champion? Does this paradigm make sense as a rationale for FDI?

Answer: The principle champion of the eclectic paradigm is British economist John Dunning. Dunning argues that in addition to other factors, location-specific advantages are also of considerable importance in explaining both the rationale for and the direction of foreign direct investment. By location-specific advantages, Dunning means the advantages that arise from utilizing resource endowments or assets that are tied to a particular foreign location and that a firm finds valuable to combine with its own unique assets. Dunning accepts the arguments of internationalization theory, that it is difficult for a firm to license its own unique capabilities and know-how. Therefore, he argues that combining location-specific assets or resource endowments and the firm's own unique capabilities often requires FDI in production facilities.

This paradigm does make sense as a rationale for FDI. For example, as described in the text, an obvious example of Dunning's arguments is natural resources, such as oil and other minerals, which are specific to certain locations. Dunning suggests that to exploit such foreign resources a firm must undertake FDI. Many U.S. oil companies have done this. They have had to invest in refineries in the areas of the world where the oil is located in order to combine their technological and managerial capabilities with this valuable location-specific resource. Another example is California's Silicon Valley, where a substantial portion of the world's R&D in terms of computer technology is taking place. It might make sense for a foreign producer of computer chips to locate their R&D facility in the Silicon Valley to be near this community of computer chip researchers and manufacturers.

Medium
Page: 197

100. Describe the difference between forward vertical FDI and backward vertical FDI. Provide an example of each type of vertical FDI.

Answer: Backward vertical FDI is FDI in an industry abroad that provides inputs for a firm's domestic production process. For example, Exxon might buy oil-producing capacity in the Middle East that is used to refine into gasoline that is sold in the U.S. Forward vertical FDI is FDI into an industry abroad that sells the outputs of a firm's domestic production processes. For example, GM has either acquired or built a number of car dealerships in Europe that sell U.S. produced GM cars.

CHAPTER 7

THE POLITICAL ECONOMY OF FOREIGN DIRECT INVESTMENT

MULTIPLE-CHOICE QUESTIONS

INTRODUCTION

Answer: A
Medium
Page: 208

1. In recent years, the Japanese government has:

A. pressured many Japanese firms to undertake FDI
B. pressured many Japanese firms to reduce their FDI
C. has not pressured its firms to increase or decrease their level of FDI
D. pressured many Japanese firms to terminate their FDI

Answer: C
Medium
Page: 208

2. The Japanese government sees __________ as a substitute for exporting and thus as a way of reducing Japan's politically embarrassing balance of payments surplus.

A. licensing
B. franchising
C. foreign direct investment
D. loaning money offshore

Answer: B
Medium
Page: 208

3. In recent years the Japanese government has pressured many Japanese firms to undertake FDI in order to:

A. improve its trade balance
B. reduce its balance of payments surplus
C. find lower cost labor
D. put pressure on Japanese bankers to provide funds internationally

Answer: A
Easy
Page: 208

4. Historically, one important determinant of a government's policy toward FDI has been its:

A. political ideology
B. sociocultural ideology
C. legal ideology
D. economic ideology

POLITICAL IDEOLOGY AND FOREIGN DIRECT INVESTMENT

Answer: B
Easy
Page: 209

5. The __________ view traces its roots to Marxist political and economic theory.

   A. pragmatic
   B. radical
   C. free market
   D. conservative

Answer: C
Medium
Page: 208

6. Radical writers argue that the multinational enterprise is an instrument of:

   A. economic oppression
   B. conservative suppression
   C. imperialist domination
   D. free market expansionism

Answer: D
Medium
Page: 208

7. According to the __________ view, FDI by the MNEs of advanced capitalist nations keeps the less developed countries of the world relatively backward and dependent on advanced capitalist nations for investment, jobs, and technology.

   A. imperialist
   B. conservative
   C. free market
   D. radical

Answer: C
Hard
Page: 209

8. From __________, the radical view was very influential in the world economy.

   A. 1880 until the 1920s
   B. 1910 until 1945
   C. 1945 until the 1980s
   D. 1980 until the mid 1990s

Answer: D
Medium
Page: 209

9. Which of the following is not one of the reasons that by the end of the 1980s, the radical position was in retreat almost everywhere in the world.

A. the collapse of communism in Eastern Europe
B. the generally abysmal economic performance of those countries that embraced the radical position, and a growing belief by many of these countries that FDI can be an importance source of technology and jobs and can stimulate economic growth
C. the strong economic performance of those developing countries that embraced capitalism rather than radical ideology
D. lobbying efforts on the part of the United Nations in favor of FDI

Answer: A
Easy
Page: 209

10. The free market view traces its roots to classical economics and the international trade theories of Adam Smith and:

A. David Ricardo
B. Raymond Vernon
C. Michael Porter
D. Eli Heckscher

Answer: D
Medium
Page: 209

11. The free market view argues that international production should be distributed among countries according to the theory of:

A. absolute advantage
B. national competitive advantage
C. product life-cycle
D. comparative advantage

Answer: C
Medium
Page: 209

12. The __________ view traces its roots to classical economics and the international trade theories of Adam Smith and David Ricardo.

A. radical
B. conservative
C. free market
D. pragmatic

Answer: B
Medium
Page: 209

13. Within the free market framework, the MNE is:

A. an instrument that oppresses developing nations
B. an instrument for dispersing the production of goods and services to the most efficient locations around the globe
C. an instrument that fails to distinguish between efficient locations and inefficient locations for the production of goods and services around the world
D. an extension of the policies of industrialized nations

Answer: A
Easy
Page: 210

14. In recent years, the __________ view has been ascendant worldwide, spurring a global move toward the removal or restrictions on inward and outward foreign direct investment.

A. free market
B. pragmatic
C. radical
D. conservative

Answer: C
Medium
Page: 211

15. In practice, many countries have adopted neither a radical policy nor a free market policy toward FDI, but instead a policy that can best be described as:

A. inward protectionism
B. utilitarian nationalism
C. pragmatic nationalism
D. utilitarian protectionism

Answer: A
Medium
Page: 211

16. The pragmatic nationalist view is that FDI has:

A. both benefits and costs
B. benefits and essentially no costs
C. costs and essentially no benefits
D. no benefits or costs

Answer: D
Medium
Page: 211

17. "FDI should be allowed only if the benefits outweigh the costs" is the view espoused by which policy?

A. radical
B. free market
C. conservative
D. pragmatic nationalism

Answer: D
Hard
Page: 211

18. Japan's approach to trade is most closely aligned with:

A. the radical view
B. the free market view
C. the dogmatic view
D. pragmatic nationalism

Answer: B
Medium
Page: 212

19. A distinctive aspect of __________ is the tendency to aggressively court FDI believed to be in the national interest by, for example, offering subsidies to foreign MNEs in the form of tax breaks or grants.

A. the dogmatic view
B. pragmatic nationalism
C. the radical view
D. the conservative view

Answer: B
Hard
Page: 212

20. Which statement best describes the current trend among countries with respect to their ideological position towards FDI?

A. restrictive protectionism is replacing dogmatic nationalism as the dominant view
B. there is a movement away from the radical position and towards the free market view
C. countries that have had the most pure free market view are now moving more towards a dogmatic realism approach
D. there is an overall movement away from the free market view, with more countries adopting the radical view

Answer: C
Hard
Page: 212

21. The volume of FDI worldwide has been:

A. declining twice as fast as the growth in world trade
B. just keeping pace with the growth in world trade
C. growing twice as fast as the growth in world trade
D. stagnate, compared to the significant growth in world trade

THE BENEFITS OF FDI TO HOST COUNTRIES

Answer: C
Easy
Page: 213

22. A __________ country is one that is on the receiving end of FDI.

A. residence
B. home
C. host
D. global

Answer: B
Easy
Page: 213

23. A country that Is on the receiving end of FDI is referred to as the:

A. global country
B. host country
C. home country
D. residence country

Answer: D
Easy
Page: 213

24. A __________ country is one that is on the receiving end of foreign direct investment. A __________ country is a source country for foreign direct investment.

A. residence, global
B. global, residence
C. home, host
D. host, home

Answer: D
Medium
Page: 213

25. Which of the following is not one of the four main benefits of FDI for a host country?

A. the resource-transfer effect
B. the employment effect
C. the balance-of-payments effect
D. the political stability effect

Answer: C
Hard
Page: 213

26. The four main benefits of FDI for a host country are:

A. the cultural awareness effect, the political stability effect, the sociocultural effect, and the resource transfer effect
B. the balance-of-payments effects, the cultural awareness effect, the accounting effect, and the currency exchange effect
C. the resource transfer effect, the employment effect, the balance-of-payments effect, and the effect on competition and economic growth
D. the capital transfer effect, the technology effect, the currency exchange effect, and the employment effect

Answer: D
Medium
Page: 213

27. The four main benefits of FDI for a host country are the resource-transfer effect, the effect on competition and economic growth, the balance-of-payments effect, and the:

A. cultural awareness effect
B. political stability effect
C. technology effect
D. employment effect

Answer: A
Easy
Page: 213

28. "FDI can make a positive contribution to a host country by supplying capital, technology, and management skills that would not otherwise be available." This statement best describes the:

A. resource transfer effect
B. employment effect
C. market imperfections effect
D. balance of payments effect

Answer: C
Medium
Page: 213

29. The Japanese government has insisted in the past that technology be transferred to Japan through __________, rather than FDI.

A. franchising
B. exporting
C. licensing
D. diplomatic channels

Answer: B
Medium
Page: 214

30. According to our textbook, beneficial __________ arise when local personnel who are trained to occupy managerial, financial, and technical posts in the subsidiary of a foreign MNE leave the firms and help to establish indigenous firms.

A. residual effects
B. spin-off effects
C. remainder effects
D. surplus effects

Answer: A
Medium
Page: 214

31. The beneficial employment effects claimed for FDI is that it:

A. brings jobs to a host country that would otherwise not be created there
B. raises wage rates in the host country
C. leads to the construction of job training facilities
D. raises wage rates in the home country

Answer: B
Easy
Page: 215

32. A country's __________ keep track of both its payments to and its receipts from other countries.

A. ledger of accounts
B. balance-of-payments accounts
C. checks and balances accounts
D. financial integrity accounts

Answer: D
Medium
Page: 216

33. Balance-of-payment accounts are divided into two main sections. These are:

A. the liquid account and the permanent account
B. the current account and the reserve account
C. the open account and the reserve account
D. the current account and the capital account

Answer: A
Medium
Page: 216

34. When a German consumer purchases a Canadian chain saw, this transaction is recorded as a:

A. debit on the German current account
B. credit on the Canadian current account
C. debit on the German capital account
D. credit on the Canadian capital account

Answer: D
Medium
Page: 216

35. When a Japanese firm purchases stock in a U.S. company, the transaction enters the U.S. balance of payments as a:

A. debit on the capital account
B. credit on the current account
C. debit on the current account
D. credit on the capital account

Answer: C
Easy
Page: 216

36. The basic principle of balance-of-payments accounting is:

A. single-entry bookkeeping
B. capital accounting
C. double-entry bookkeeping
D. triple-entry accounting

Answer: C
Medium
Page: 216

37. In the context of balance-of-payment accounts, the __________ account records transactions that pertain to merchandise trade, services, and investment income.

A. liquid
B. open
C. current
D. capital

Answer: A
Hard
Page: 216

38. In the context of balance-of-payment accounts, a current account deficit occurs:

A. when a country imports more goods, services, and income than it exports
B. when capital expenditures run over budget
C. when current assets are less then current liabilities in a country's financial reserves
D. when a country exports more goods, services, and income than it imports

Answer: D
Medium
Page: 216

39. In the context of balance-of-payment accounts, a __________ occurs when a country exports more goods, services, and income than it imports.

A. open account surplus
B. liquidity account excess
C. capital account excess
D. current account surplus

Answer: C
Medium
Page: 216

40. When a Japanese firm purchases stock in a U.S. company, the transaction enters the U.S. balance of payments as a credit on the:

A. current account
B. open account
C. capital account
D. intermediate account

Answer: B
Medium
Page: 216

41. When capital flows out of the United States, it enters the __________ account as a __________.

A. capital, credit
B. capital, debit
C. current, credit
D. current, debit

Answer: B
Easy
Page: 217

42. Economic theory tells us that the efficient functioning of markets depends on an adequate level of __________ between producers.

A. cooperation
B. competition
C. synergy
D. antagonism

Answer: C
Medium
Page: 217

43. By increasing consumer choice, foreign direct investment can help to increase the level of competition in national markets, thereby:

A. driving down prices and decreasing the economic welfare of consumers
B. increasing prices and increasing the economic welfare of consumers
C. driving down prices and increasing the economic welfare of consumers
D. increasing prices and decreasing the economic welfare of consumers

THE COST OF FDI TO HOST COUNTRIES

Answer: B
Medium
Page: 218

44. Which of the following is not one of the three main costs of FDI for a host country?

A. possible adverse effects on competition within the host country
B. a decrease in employment
C. adverse effects on the balance of payments
D. the perceived loss of national sovereignty and autonomy

Answer: D
Hard
Page: 218

45. Three main costs of inward FDI concern host countries. These are:

A. the employment effect, the perceived loss of national sovereignty and autonomy, and the resource transfer effect
B. the possible adverse effects of FDI on competition within the host country, the resource transfer effect, and the perceived loss of national sovereignty and autonomy
C. the resource transfer effect, the employment effect, and the possible adverse effects of FDI on competition within the host country
D. the possible adverse effects of FDI on competition within the host country, adverse effects on the balance of payments, and the perceived loss of national sovereignty and autonomy

Answer: A
Medium
Page: 218

46. Three main costs of FDI concern host countries. They arise from possible adverse effects on competition within the host nation, adverse effects on the balance of payments, and:

A. the perceived loss of national sovereignty and autonomy
B. possible increases in unemployment in the host country
C. possible increases in inflation in the host country
D. the perceived loss of economic power

THE BENEFITS AND COSTS OF FDI TO HOME COUNTRIES

Answer: D
Medium
Page: 220

47. Which of the following is not one of the benefits of FDI to the home country?

A. positive impact on balance-of-payments
B. positive employment effects
C. reverse resource-transfer effect
D. negative interest rates effect

Answer: A
Easy
Page: 221

48. The term __________ refers to FDI undertaken to serve the home market.

A. offshore production
B. overseas outsourcing
C. cross-boarder production
D. overseas throughput

GOVERNMENT POLICY INSTRUMENTS AND FDI

Answer: D
Easy
Page: 221

49. Which of the following is not a policy designed to encourage FDI?

A. foreign risk insurancc
B. capital assistance
C. tax incentives
D. the manipulation of tax rules to try to encourage investment at home

Answer: A
Medium
Page: 221

50. Many investor nations now have government-backed insurance programs to cover major types of foreign investment risk. The types of risks insurable through these programs include the risks of expropriation, war losses, and:

A. the inability to transfer profits back home
B. currency devaluation
C. strategic business errors
D. embargo

Answer: C
Medium
Page: 221

51. In the context of international trade, double taxation refers to:

A. many countries have tax rates double that of the U.S. and other industrialized countries
B. taxes are collected twice a year in many foreign countries
C. taxation on foreign income in both the host country and the home country
D. in many foreign countries, FDI is taxed at triple the normal rate

Answer: C
Easy
Page: 222

52. As a way of encouraging inward FDI, many countries offer incentives to foreign firms to:

A. export to their country
B. sell franchises in their country
C. invest in their country
D. license their products and services in their country

Answer: A
Medium
Page: 222

53. To encourage inward FDI, many countries offer incentives to foreign firms to invest in their country. Such incentives take many forms, but the most common are tax concessions, grants or subsidies, and:

A. low-interest loans
B. cash payments
C. free housing for the company's employees
D. free facilities for the company's operations

Answer: C
Medium
Page: 222

54. Host governments use a wide range of controls to restrict FDI in one way or another. The two most common are:

A. geographic restraints and earnings restraints
B. capital restraints and income restraints
C. ownership restraints and performance restraints
D. earnings restraints and geographic restraints

Answer: C
Hard
Page: 222

55. In Sweden, FDI is not permitted in the areas of tobacco and mining. This is an example of a __________ that is intended to restrict inward FDI.

A. performance restraint
B. capital restraint
C. ownership restraint
D. selection restraint

Answer: A
Medium
Page: 223

56. The most common performance requirements that are intended to restrict inward FDI are related to local content, exports, technology transfer, and:

A. local participation in top management
B. expatriation of earnings
C. product offerings
D. service offerings

Answer: B
Medium
Page: 223

57. Until recently there has been no consistent involvement by multinational institutions in the governing of FDI. This is now changing rapidly with the formation of the __________ in 1995.

A. International FDI Monitoring Commission
B. World Trade Organization
C. United Nations Commission on FDI
D. International Trade Authority

Answer: A
Medium
Page: 223

58. In the area of FDI, the thrust of the World Trade Organization's efforts has been to:

A. push for the liberalization of regulations governing FDI
B. push of the tightening of regulations governing FDI
C. push for the elimination of all regulations governing FDI
D. push for the elimination of FDI

Answer: B
Medium
Page: 223

59. Under the auspices of the __________, two extensive multinational agreements were reached in 1997 to liberalize trade in telecommunications and financial services.

A. International Manufacturing and Services Monitoring Commission
B. World Trade Organization
C. United Nations Commission on Services in International Trade
D. International Trade Authority

Answer: A
Hard
Page: 223

60. The __________ is a Paris-based intergovernmental organization of "wealthy" nations whose purpose is to provide its 29 member states with a forum in which governments can compare their experiences, discuss the problems they share, and seek solutions that can then be applied within their own national contexts.

A. Organization for Economic Cooperation and Development
B. Forum of Advanced and Developed Nations
C. Organization of Leading Industrial Nations
D. North Atlantic, American, and Asian Forum for Cooperation

TRUE-FALSE QUESTIONS

INTRODUCTION

Answer: F
Easy
Page: 208

61. In recent years, the Japanese government has pressured many Japanese firms to cut back on their FDI.

Answer: T
Medium
Page: 208

62. The Japanese government sees FDI as a substitute for exporting and thus as a way of reducing Japan's politically embarrassing balance of payments surplus.

Answer: F
Medium
Page: 208

63. To a greater or lesser degree, the officials of many governments tend to be free market advocates who weigh the benefits and costs of FDI and typically lean in favor of liberal FDI policies.

POLITICAL IDEOLOGY AND FOREIGN DIRECT INVESTMENT

Answer: T
Easy
Page: 208

64. Advocates of the radical view argue that the multinational enterprise is an instrument of imperialist domination.

Answer: F
Medium
Page: 208

65. Advocates of pragmatic nationalism see the MNE as a tool for exploiting host countries to the exclusive benefit of their capitalist-imperialist home countries.

Answer: T
Easy
Page: 209

66. The free market view traces its roots to classical economics and the international trade theories of Adam Smith and David Ricardo.

Answer: F
Medium
Page: 210

67. In recent years, the free market view has been on the decline worldwide, spurring a global move toward more stringent restrictions on inward and outward foreign direct investment.

Answer: T
Easy
Page: 211

68. In practice, many countries have adopted neither a radical policy nor a free market policy toward FDI, but instead a policy that can best be described as pragmatic nationalism.

Answer: F
Easy
Page: 211

69. According to the radical view, FDI should be allowed only if the benefits outweigh the costs.

THE BENEFITS OF FDI TO HOST COUNTRIES

Answer: T
Medium
Page: 213

70. The four main benefits of FDI for a host country include the resource-transfer effect, the employment effect, the balance-of payments effect, and the effect on competition and economic growth.

Answer: T
Medium
Page: 214

71. The beneficial employment effect claimed for FDI is that it brings jobs to a host country that would otherwise not be created there.

Answer: F
Easy
Page: 215

72. A country's checks-and-balances accounts keep tract of both its payments to and its receipts from other countries.

Answer: F
Medium
Page: 216

73. Balance-of-payments accounts are divided into two main sections: the liquid account and the permanent account.

Answer: T
Hard
Page: 217

74. If a U.S. citizen owns a share of a Finnish company and receives a dividend payment of $5, that payment shows up on the U.S. current account as the receipt of $5 of investment income.

THE COSTS OF FDI TO HOST COUNTRIES

Answer: T
Medium
Page: 218

75. The three main costs of FDI that concern host countries are: possible adverse effects on competition within the host country, adverse effects on the balance of payments, and the perceived loss of national sovereignty and autonomy.

Answer: T
Easy
Page: 219

76. Many host governments worry that FDI is accompanied by some loss of economic independence.

THE BENEFITS AND COSTS OF FDI IN HOME COUNTRIES

Answer: F
Medium
Page: 220

77. One of the benefits of FDI to home countries identified in our textbook is the negative interest rates effect.

Answer: T
Medium
Page: 220

78. Two of the advantages of FDI to home countries are positive employment effects and positive impact on balance-of-payments.

GOVERNMENT POLICY INSTRUMENTS AND FDI

Answer: T
Medium
Page: 221

79. One way that home countries encourage outward FDI is through government-backed insurance programs to cover major types of foreign investment risk.

Answer: F
Medium
Page: 221

80. In the context of international trade double taxation refers to fact that in many foreign countries, FDI is taxed at double the domestic rate

Answer: T
Medium
Page: 222

81. It is Increasingly common for governments to offer incentives to foreign firms to invest in their countries.

Answer: F
Medium
Page: 222

82. Host governments use a wide range of controls to restrict FDI in one way or another. The two most common are ownership restraints and geographic restraints.

Answer: T
Hard
Page: 222

83. Ownership restraints seem to be based on the idea that local owners can help to maximize the resource-transfer and employment benefits of FDI for the host country.

Answer: T
Medium
Page: 223

84. The most common performance requirements are related to local content, exports, technology transfer, and local participation in top management.

Answer: F
Medium
Page: 223

85. Historically, there has been substantial involvement by multinational institutions in the governing of FDI.

Answer: F
Medium
Page: 223

86. The World Trade Organization has taken a "hands-off" policy in regard to regulations governing FDI.

IMPLICATIONS FOR BUSINESS

Answer: F
Easy
Page: 224

87. The objective of any negotiation is to reach an agreement that benefits the weaker of the two parties.

Answer: F
Hard
Page: 224

88. The negotiation process has been characterized as occurring within the context of "the four CS": common interests, conflicting interests, compromise, and chain of effects.

Answer: T
Easy
Page: 225

89. The outcome of any negotiated agreement depends on the relative bargaining power of both parties.

Answer: T
Hard
Page: 226

90. From the perspective of a firm negotiating in terms of an investment with a host government, the firm's bargaining power is high when the host government places a high value on what the firms has to offer, the number of comparable alternatives open to the firm is great, and the firm has a long time in which to complete the negotiations.

ESSAY QUESTIONS

Easy
Page: 208

91. According to the radical view, what is the effect of FDI on developing countries?

Answer: According to the radical view, FDI by MNEs of advanced capitalist nations keeps the less developed countries of the world relatively backward and dependent upon advanced capitalist nations for investment, jobs, and technology. Taken to the extreme, this suggests that no country under any circumstance should every permit foreign corporations to undertake FDI, since FDI in not an instrument of economic development, but instead of economic domination.

Medium
Page: 209

92. According to the free market view, what is the role of MNEs in FDI and the world economy?

Answer: The free market view argues that international production should be distributed among different countries according to the theory of comparative advantage - countries should specialize in the production of those goods and services that they can produce most efficiently. The MNE is thus an instrument for dispersing the production of goods and services to those locations around the globe where they can be produced most efficiently. Viewed this way, FDI by the MNE can be seen as a way of increasing the overall efficiency of the world economy.

Medium
Page: 211

93. Describe the pragmatic nationalism approach to FDI. What criteria would a pragmatic nationalist use to determine if FDI should be allowed in his or her country?

Answer: The pragmatic nationalist view is that FDI has both benefits and costs. FDI can benefit a host country by bringing capital, skills, technology, and jobs, but those benefits often come at a cost. When profits are produced by a foreign company rather than a domestic company, the profits from that investment go abroad. Many countries are also concerned that a foreign-owned manufacturing plant may import many components from its home country, which has a negative implication for the host country's balance-of-payments position.

Countries that adopt a pragmatic stance pursue policies designed to maximize the national benefits and minimize the national costs. According to this view, FDI should be allowed only if the benefits outweigh the costs.

Hard
Page: 213

94. Describe the four main benefits of inward FDI (i.e. FDI coming into a country from foreign sources) for the host country? Are these benefits compelling?

Answer: The four main benefits of FDI for the host country are the resources-transfer effect, the employment effect, and the balance-of-payments effect, and the effect on competition and economic growth. These potential benefits are explained in more detail below.

The Resource-Transfer Effect: FDI can make a positive contribution to a host country by supplying capital, technology, and management resources that would otherwise not be available. The provision of these skills by a multinational company (through FDI) may boost a country's intellectual capital and economic growth rate.

The Employment Effects: The beneficial employment effects claimed for FDI is that foreign direct investment brings jobs to a host country that would otherwise not be created there. For instance, the Japanese auto factories in the United States have provided thousands of jobs for U.S. workers.

The Balance-of-Payment Effects: The effect of FDI on a country's balance-of-payments account in an important policy issue for most host governments. Governments typically like to see a balance-of-payments surplus rather than a deficit. There are two ways that FDI can help a host country experience a balance-of-payments surplus. First, if the FDI is a substitute for imports of goods or services, it can improve a country's balance of payments. For example, the Japanese auto plants in the U.S. produce cars that act as "substitutes" for Japanese imports. Second, FDI may result in an increase in exports. A portion of the goods and services that are produced as a result of FDI may be exported to other countries.

The Effects on Competition and Economic Growth: Economic theory tells us that the efficient functioning of markets depends on an adequate level of competition between producers. By increasing consumer choice, foreign direct investment can help to increase the level of competition in national markets, thereby driving down prices and increasing the economic welfare of consumers

These arguments are compelling, but must be weighed against the costs of FDI. The arguments against FDI include: the possible adverse effects of FDI on competition within the host nation, adverse effects on the balance-of-payments, and the perceived loss of national sovereignty and autonomy.

Medium
Page: 214

95. Explain the employment effects of FDI on both the host and the home country.

Answer: From a host country's perspective, there are positive employment effects from both the direct hiring of people by the foreign firm and the indirect job creation in firms that supply and service the new employer. More important than the number of jobs created by direct and indirect effects of the new employer, however, is the net effect of the new employer on overall employment. If some domestic firms go out of business because of the more efficient MNE, then some or all of the job gains may be offset by the loss of other jobs.

From a home country's perspective, there can be negative effects on employment if jobs are essentially exported overseas. But there can also be positive effects on the domestic suppliers of the overseas operation. A company might also expand the number of people that it employs in its headquarters facility at home to provide administrative oversight to an overseas location.

Medium
Page: 215

96. What are a country's balance of payments accounts? Describe the difference between a current account and a capital account.

Answer: A country's balance-of-payments accounts keep track of both its payments to and its receipts from other countries. A summary copy of the U.S. balance-of-payments accounts for 1995 is given in Table 7.2 in the textbook.

Balance-of-payment accounts are divided into two main sections: the current account and the capital account. The current account records transactions that pertain to three categories. The first category, merchandise trade, refers to the export of import of goods. The second category is the export or import of services. The third category, investment income, refers to income from foreign investments and payments that have to be made to foreigners investing in a country. In contrast, the capital account records transactions that involve the purchase or sale of assets.

Easy
Page: 219

97. How could FDI affect the national sovereignty of a host country?

Answer: Many host governments worry that FDI is accompanies by some loss of economic independence. The concern is that key decisions that can affect the host country's economy will be made by a foreign partner that has no real commitment to the host country, and over which the host country's government has no real control.

Medium
Page: 220

98. Describe how a "reverse resource transfer effect" can benefit a home country and the parent MNE.

Answer: Reverse resource transfer benefits arise when the home country MNE learns valuable skills or technology from its exposure to foreign markets that can subsequently be transferred back to the home country. Through its exposure to a foreign market, a MNE can learn about superior management techniques or superior product and process technologies, and then transfer these back to the home country, with a commensurate beneficial effect on the parent company's success in its home market and the home country's economic growth.

Medium
Page: 224

99. How does a potential host government's attitude toward FDI affect a company's willingness to engage in FDI in that country? Should a host government's attitude toward FDI be a major consideration when making a FDI decision? Why?

Answer: A host government's attitude toward FDI should be an important variable in making decisions about where to locate foreign production facilities and where to make a FDI. According to the author of the textbook, other things being equal, investing in countries that have permissive policies toward FDI is clearly preferable to investing in countries that resist FDI.

However, this issue is not straightforward. Many countries have a rather businesslike stance toward FDI. In such cases, a firm considering FDI usually must negotiate the specific terms of the investment with the host government. Such negotiations typically center on two issues. First, if the host country is trying to attract FDI, the negotiations will typically focus on the kind of incentives the host government is prepared to offer the foreign firm and what the firm will commit in exchange. On the other hand, if the host government is leery of FDI, the central issue is likely to be the concessions the firm will make to be allowed to go forward with its project.

Medium
Page: 224

100. What is the principal objective of any negotiation? Why is negotiation characterized as both an art and a science?

Answer: the objective of any negotiation is to reach an agreement that benefits both parties. Negotiation is both an art and a science. The science of it requires analyzing the relative bargaining strengths of each party and the different strategic options available to each party and assessing how the other party might respond to various bargaining ploys. The art of negotiation incorporates "interpersonal skills, the ability to convince and be convinced, the ability to employ a basketful of bargaining ploys, and the wisdom to know when and how to use them.

CHAPTER 8

REGIONAL ECONOMIC INTEGRATION

MULTIPLE-CHOICE QUESTIONS

INTRODUCTION

Answer: A
Easy
Page: 232

1. An agreement between countries in a geographic region to reduce tariff and nontarrif barriers to the free flow of goods, services, and factors of production between each other is referred to as:

   A. regional economic integration
   B. cross-cultural economic integration
   C. geographic economic-political integration
   D. cross-cultural economic-political integration

Answer: B
Easy
Page: 232

2. By __________, we mean agreements among countries in a geographic region to reduce, and ultimately remove, tariff and nontariff barriers to the free flow of goods, services, and factors of production between each other.

   A. geographic economic-political integration
   B. regional economic integration
   C. cross-cultural economic integration
   D. cross-cultural economic-political integration

Answer: D
Hard
Page: 232

3. In the five years between 1992 and 1996, __________ regional trade agreements were reported to the World Trade Organization.

   A. 12
   B. 33
   C. 51
   D. 77

Answer: B
Medium
Page: 232

4. Nowhere has the movement toward regional integration been more successful than in:

   A. North America
   B. Europe
   C. South America
   D. Asia

Answer: D
Easy
Page: 232

5. The following three countries recently implemented the North American Free Trade Agreement (NAFTA).

A. Panama, Mexico, and the United States
B. Canada, Brazil, and the United States
C. United States, Argentina, and Mexico
D. Canada, Mexico, and the United States

Answer: B
Hard
Page: 232

6. The free trade area known as MERCOSUR consists of the following four countries:

A. Chile, Mexico, Columbia, and Paraguay
B. Argentina, Brazil, Paraguay, and Uruguay
C. Chile, Brazil, Uruguay, and Columbia
D. Mexico, Columbia, Paraguay, and Uruguay

LEVELS OF ECONOMIC INTEGRATION

Answer: C
Hard
Page: 233

7. Which of the following selections accurately depicts the levels of economic integration from least integrated to most integrated?

A. economic union, common market, full political union, customs union, and free trade area
B. common market, economic union, full political union, free trade area, and customs union
C. free trade area, customs union, common market, economic union, and full political union
D. full political union, free trade area, common market, customs union, and economic union

Answer: A
Hard
Page: 233

8. Which of the following selections accurately depicts the levels of economic integration from most integrated to least integration?

A. full political union, economic union, common market, customs union, and free trade area
B. free trade area, common market, customs union, full political union, and economic union
C. common market, economic union, full political union, customs union, and free trade area
D. economic union, common market, full political union, free trade area, and customs union

Answer: A
Medium
Page: 233

9. In a free trade area:

A. barriers to the trade of goods and services among member nations are removed
B. a common currency is adopted
C. a single parliament determines political and foreign policy
D. a common external trade policy is adopted

Answer: D
Medium
Page: 233

10. The European Free Trade Association (EFTA) is the most enduring __________ in the world.

A. economic union
B. common market
C. customs union
D. free trade area

Answer: D
Hard
Page: 233

11. The European Free Trade Association currently includes the following four countries:

A. Sweden, Iceland, Ireland, and Wales
B. Iceland, Sweden, Liechtenstein, and Switzerland
C. Wales, Great Britain, Sweden, and Finland
D. Norway, Iceland, Liechtenstein, and Switzerland

Answer: B
Medium
Page: 234

12. A __________ eliminates trade barriers between member countries and adopts a common external trade policy.

A. tariff-free union
B. customs union
C. free trade area
D. global union

Answer: B
Medium
Page: 234

13. Like a customs union, the theoretically ideal __________ has no barriers to trade between member countries and a common external trade policy.

A. free trade area
B. common market
C. tariff union
D. external market

Answer: C
Easy
Page: 234

14. The EU is currently a:

A. free trade area
B. customs union
C. common market
D. economic union

Answer: A
Medium
Page: 234

15. Which of the following is not an attribute of a common market?

A. harmonization of the member countries' tax rates
B. there are no restrictions on the cross-border flow of capital between member nations
C. there is no restriction on immigration between member nations
D. factors of production are allowed to move freely between member nations

Answer: A
Medium
Page: 234

16. Which of the following is not an attribute of an economic union?

A. political union
B. common currency
C. harmonization of members' tax rates
D. free flow of products and factors of production between member countries

Answer: C
Medium
Page: 235

17. The __________, which is playing an ever more important role in the EU, has been directly elected by citizens of the EU countries since the late 1970s.

A. European Congress
B. European Trade Commission
C. European Parliament
D. European Ministry

THE CASE FOR REGIONAL INTEGRATION

Answer: A
Medium
Page: 235

18. Economic theories suggest that free trade and investment is a positive-sum game, in which:

A. all participating countries stand to gain
B. more participating countries gain than lose
C. at lease one participating country gains
D. more than 50 percent of the participating countries gain

Answer: C
Medium
Page: 235

19. Because many governments have accepted part or all of the case for intervention, unrestricted free trade and FDI have proved to be:

A. a goal that should be realized soon
B. a goal that there is no rationale for
C. only an ideal
D. a reality

Answer: B
Hard
Page: 236

20. The European Community (which was the forerunner of the EU) was established in:

A. 1945
B. 1957
C. 1966
D. 1979

Answer: A
Medium
Page: 236

21. The two main reasons that have made economic integration difficult to achieve are:

A. cost and concerns over national sovereignty
B. employment effects and concerns over immigration
C. concerns over national sovereignty and concerns over immigration
D. cost and concerns over economic stability

Answer: D
Medium
Page: 236

22. The two main reasons that have made economic integration difficult to achieve are cost and:

A. concerns over economic stability
B. concerns over the safety of travel from one nation to another
C. concerns over immigration
D. concerns over national sovereignty

Answer: B
Medium
Page: 236

23. In the context of regional trade integration, concerns about __________ arise because close economic integration demands that countries give up some degree of their control over such key policy issues as monetary policy, fiscal policy, and trade policy.

A. cost
B. national sovereignty
C. financial stability
D. cultural uniformity

Answer: D
Medium
Page: 236

24. The strongest holdout opposing a common currency in the EU is:

A. France
B. Germany
C. Spain
D. Britain

THE CASE AGAINST REGIONAL INTEGRATION

Answer: A
Easy
Page: 237

25. __________ occurs when high-cost domestic producers are replaced by low-cost producers within the free trade area.

A. Trade creation
B. Trade diversion
C. Trade alteration
D. Trade qualification

Answer: C
Easy
Page: 237

26. __________ occurs when lower-cost external suppliers are replaced by higher-cost suppliers within the free trade area.

A. Trade detour
B. Trade alternation
C. Trade diversion
D. Trade creation

Answer: C
Medium
Page: 237

27. __________ occurs when high-cost domestic producers are replaced by low-cost producers within the free trade area. In contrast, __________ occurs when lower-cost external suppliers are replaced by higher-cost suppliers within the free trade area.

A. Trade diversion, trade creation
B. Trade alteration, trade qualification
C. Trade creation, trade diversion
D. Trade qualification, trade alteration

Answer: B
Hard
Page: 237

28. WTO rules allow free trade areas to be formed only if:

A. the countries are geographically contiguous to one another
B. the members set tariffs that are not higher or more restrictive to outsiders than the ones previously in effect
C. the members agree to prohibit trade creation
D. the members agree to prohibit trade diversion

REGIONAL ECONOMIC INTEGRATION IN EUROPE

Answer: A
Medium
Page: 237

29. There are two trade blocs in Europe. These are:

A. European Union and the European Free Trade Association
B. European Federation and the European Trade Association
C. North Atlantic Trade Block and the European Union
D. European Federation and the North Atlantic Trade Block

Answer: C
Medium
Page: 237

30. Of the two trade blocks in Europe, the _________ is by far the more significant, not just in terms of membership, but also in terms of economic and political influence in the world economy.

A. European Free Trade Association
B. North Atlantic Trade Block
C. European Union
D. European Federation

Answer: B
Hard
Page: 238

31. The original forerunner of the EU, the _________, was formed in 1951 by Belgium, France, West Germany, Italy, Luxembourg, and the Netherlands.

A. European Market
B. European Coal and Steel Community
C. European War Reconstruction Union
D. European Agricultural, Textiles, and Energy Union

Answer: C
Medium
Page: 238

32. In 1994, the European Community became the European Union following the ratification of the:

A. World Trade Organization Charter
B. Luxembourg Treaty
C. Maastricht Treaty
D. Berlin Conference on Trade

Answer: D
Hard
Page: 239

33. The economic policies of the EU are formulated and implemented by a complex and still-evolving political structure. The five main institutions in this structure are the:

A. European Parliament, the Court of Justice, the Council of Technology, the Council of Labor, and the Council of Natural Resources
B. Council of Labor, the Council of Technology, the Ministry of Justice, the European Council, and the European Commission
C. European Commission, the Council of Agricultural, the Council of Trade, the Ministry of Justice, and the Council of Labor
D. European Council, the Council of Ministers, the European Commission, the European Parliament, and the Court of Justice

Answer: A
Medium
Page: 239

34. The __________ is composed of the heads of state of the EU's member nations and the president of the European Commission.

A. European Council
B. Council of Ministers
C. European Commission
D. European Parliament

Answer: C
Medium
Page: 240

35. The __________ is responsible for proposing EU legislation, implementing it, and monitoring compliance with EU laws by member states.

A. European Parliament
B. Council of Ministers
C. European Commission
D. European Council

Answer: B
Medium
Page: 241

36. The members of the European Parliament are:

A. appointed by the heads of state of the member nations
B. directly elected by the populations of the member states
C. appointed by the President of the European Union
D. appointed by a 15 member bipartisan commission

Answer: B
Medium
Page: 241

37. The purpose of the __________ was to have a single market in place by December 31, 1992.

A. North Atlantic Sovereignty Act
B. Single European Act
C. European Primacy Act
D. European Sovereignty Act

Answer: C
Medium
Page: 242

38. Who or what was the Delores Commission named after?

A. the Delores region of Luxembourg where the EU is headquartered
B. the Delores region of France, which borders Germany, Luxembourg, and Belgium
C. Jacques Delors, president of the EC
D. Henrique Delors, an early champion of regional integration in Europe

Answer: D
Medium
Page: 243

39. To signify the importance of the Single European Act, the European Community decided to change its name to the __________ once the act took place.

A. Common Market
B. European Federation
C. Federation of Free Europe
D. European Union

REGIONAL ECONOMIC INTEGRATION IN THE AMERICAS

Answer: A
Easy
Page: 247

40. In 1988 the governments of the United States and Canada agreed to enter into a __________, which went into effect on January 1, 1989.

A. free trade agreement
B. economic union
C. common market
D. full political union

Answer: D
Easy
Page: 248

41. The trade agreement entered into by Canada, the United States, and Mexico is referred to as the:

A. North American Common Market
B. North American Free Trade Zone
C. North American Economic Union
D. North American Free Trade Agreement

Answer: C
Easy
Page: 248

42. The agreement that is designed to abolish within 10 years tariffs on 99 percent of the goods traded between Mexico, Canada, and the United States is called the:

A. American Federation
B. North American Common Market
C. North American Free Trade Agreement
D. North Atlantic Trade Federation

Answer: D
Medium
Page: 248

43. According to our textbook, one likely short-term effect of NAFTA will be that many U.S. and Canadian firms will move some production to Mexico to take advantage of:

A. stricter pollution regulations
B. a higher skilled labor force
C. lower interest rates
D. lower labor costs

Answer: B
Medium
Page: 248

44. The principle argument of those that opposed NAFTA centered around the fear that ratification would result in:

A. higher interest rates in the U.S.
B. many Canadian and U.S. jobs transferred to Mexico
C. the move towards a common currency for NAFTA member nations
D. retaliation from the European Union

Answer: A
Hard
Page: 249

45. According to our textbook, the first year after NAFTA became a reality turned out to be:

A. a largely positive experience for all three countries
B. a largely negative experience for all three countries
C. a largely positive experience for Mexico, and a largely negative experience for the U.S. and Canada
D. a largely positive experience for the U.S. and Canada, and a largely negative experience Mexico

Answer: C
Medium
Page: 249

46. The early euphoria over NAFTA was snuffed out in December 1994 when the __________ was shaken by a financial crisis.

A. Canadian economy
B. U.S. economy
C. Mexican economy
D. entire North American region

Answer: C
Hard
Page: 250

47. The Andean Pact was formed in 1969 when __________ signed the Cartagena Agreement.

A. Bolivia, Chile, Argentina, French Guiana, and Venezuela
B. Brazil, Venezuela, Argentinia, and Peru
C. Bolivia, Chile, Ecuador, Colombia, and Peru
D. Argentina, Chile, Ecuador, Columbia, and Guyana

Answer: D
Hard
Page: 251

48. The initial principles of the Andean Pact included all of the following except:

A. internal tariff reduction program
B. common external tariff
C. transportation policy
D. common currency among member nations

Answer: B
Medium
Page: 251

49. MERCOSUR originated in 1988 as a free trade pact between:

A. Venezuela and Columbia
B. Brazil and Argentina
C. Mexico and Brazil
D. Peru and Columbia

Answer: C
Medium
Page: 251

50. Brazil is a member of:

A. Andean Pact
B. NAFTA
C. MERCOSUR
D. CARICOM

Answer: A
Medium
Page: 251

51. MERCOSUR originated in 1998 as a(n) __________ between Brazil and Argentina.

A. free trade pact
B. customs union
C. common market
D. economic union

Answer: C
Hard
Page: 251

52. Currently, the four member states of MERCOSUR include:

A. Columbia, Chile, Brazil, and Paraguay
B. Argentina, Mexico, Chile, and Brazil
C. Brazil, Argentina, Paraguay, and Uruguay
D. Peru, Chile, Brazil, and Mexico

Answer: D
Hard
Page: 251

53. Which of the following countries is not a member of MERCOSUR?

A. Peru
B. Chile
C. Brazil
D. Mexico

Answer: B
Hard
Page: 252

54. In the early 1960s, Costa Rica, El Salvador, Guatemala, Honduras, and Nicaragua attempted to set up a Central America __________.

A. free trade area
B. common market
C. customs union
D. economic union

REGIONAL ECNOMIC INTEGRATION ELSEWHERE

Answer: A
Hard
Page: 253

55. Formed in 1967, __________ includes Brunei, Indonesia, Laos, Malaysia, Myanmar, Philippines, Singapore, Thailand, and Vietnam.

A. ASEAN
B. Pacific Rim Trade Association
C. Southeast-Asia Trade Union
D. APEC

Answer: C
Hard
Page: 253

56. Which of the following countries is not a member of ASEAN?

A. Philippines
B. Singapore
C. Japan
D. Thailand

Answer: D
Medium
Page: 253

57. Asia Pacific Economic Cooperation (APEC) was founded in 1990 at the suggestion of:

A. United States
B. Japan
C. South Korea
D. Australia

Answer: A
Hard
Page: 253

58. The stated aim of APEC is to increase multilateral cooperation in view of:

A. the economic rise of the Pacific nations and the growing interdependence within the region
B. the economic rise of Western Europe and the growing interdependence within the region
C. the economic rise of South America and the growing interdependence within the region
D. the economic rise of Asia and the growing interdependence within the region

IMPLICATIONS FOR BUSINESS

Answer: A
Medium
Page: 253

59. According to our textbook, the most significant developments in regional economic integration are occurring in:

A. EU, NAFTA, and MERCOSUR
B. EFTA, the Andean Pact, and ASEAN
C. APEC, EU, and ASEAN
D. MERCOSUR, EFTA, and ASEAN

Answer: B
Medium
Page: 254

60. The term "Fortress Europe" refers to:

A. the military prowess of European nations
B. the perception that the European Union is designed to protect the European continent from the import of foreign produced goods
C. the unwillingness of European nations to consider forming trade relationships
D. the economic stability of the European continent

TRUE-FALSE QUESTIONS

INTRODUCTION

Answer: F
Easy
Page: 232

61. The last decade has witnessed an unprecedented decline in the number of regional trade agreement around the world.

Answer: T
Medium
Page: 232

62. Nowhere has the movement toward regional economic integration been more successful than in Europe.

LEVELS OF ECONOMIC INTEGRATION

Answer: F
Hard
Page: 233

63. From least integrated to most integrated, the levels of economic integration are: free trade area, common market, customs union, economic union, and full political union.

Answer: T
Medium
Page: 233

64. In a free trade area, all barriers to the trade of goods and services among member countries are removed.

Answer: F
Medium
Page: 233

65. The most enduring free trade area in the world is the European Union.

Answer: T
Medium
Page: 234

66. A customs union eliminates trade barriers between member countries and adopts a common external trade policy.

Answer: F
Medium
Page: 234

67. A common market entails even closer economic integration and cooperation than an economic union.

THE CASE FOR REGIONAL INTEGRATION

Answer: T
Easy
Page: 235

68. Economic theories suggest that free trade and investment is a positive-sum game, in which all participating countries stand to gain.

Answer: T
Medium
Page: 235

69. Because many governments have accepted part or all of the case for intervention, unrestricted free trade and FDI have proved to be only an ideal.

THE CASE AGAINST REGIONAL INTEGRATION

Answer: F
Medium
Page: 237

70. Trade diversion occurs when high-cost domestic producers are replaced by low-cost producers within the free trade area.

Answer: F
Medium
Page: 237

71. Trade creation occurs when lower-cost external suppliers are replaced by higher-cost suppliers with the free trade area.

REGIONAL ECONOMI INTEGRATION IN EUROPE

Answer: T
Medium
Page: 237

72. Europe has two trade blocs - the European Union and the European Free Trade Association.

Answer: F
Hard
Page: 238

73. The original forerunner of the EU, the European Textiles and Agricultural Community, was formed in 1951 by Belgium, France, West Germany, Italy, Luxembourg, and the Netherlands.

Answer: T
Hard
Page: 239

74. The five main institutions of the EU are the European Council, the Council of Ministers, the European Commission, the European Parliament, and the Court of Justice.

Answer: F
Medium
Page: 239

75. The European Commission is composed of the heads of state of the EU's member nations and the president of the European Council.

Answer: T
Medium
Page: 240

76. The European Commission is responsible for proposing EU legislation, implementing it, and monitoring compliance with EU laws by member states.

Answer: F
Medium
Page: 241

77. The European Parliament, which now has about 630 members, is appointed by the European Commission.

Answer: T
Medium
Page: 241

78. The Single European Act committed the EC countries to work toward establishment of a single market by December 31, 1992.

REGIONAL ECONOMIC INTEGRATION IN THE AMERICAS

Answer: T
Easy
Page: 248

79. The North American Free Trade Agreement includes Canada, the United States, and Mexico.

Answer: F
Medium
Page: 248

80. One likely short-term effect of NAFTA will be that many Canadian firms and US firms will move some production to Mexico to take advantage of stricter environmental laws.

Answer: T
Medium
Page: 249

81. The first year after NAFTA turned out to be a largely positive experience for all three countries.

Answer: T
Medium
Page: 249

82. The early euphoria over NAFTA was snuffed out in December 1994 when the Mexican economy was shaken by a financial crisis.

Answer: F
Medium
Page: 250

83. The MERCOSUR Pact was formed in 1969 when Bolivia, Chile, Ecuador, Columbia, and Peru signed the Cartagena Agreement.

Answer: F
Hard
Page: 250

84. The Adrean Pact was largely based on the EU model, but has been much more successful at achieving its stated goals.

Answer: T
Medium
Page: 251

85. MERCOSUR originated in 1988 as a free trade pact between Brazil and Argentina.

Answer: T
Hard
Page: 252

86. In the early 1960s, Costa Rica, El Salvador, Guatemala, Honduras, and Nicaragua attempted to set up a Central American common market.

REGIONAL ECONOMIC INTEGRATION ELSEWHERE

Answer: T
Hard
Page: 253

87. Formed in 1967, ASEAN includes Brunei, Indonesia, Laos, Malaysia, Myanmar, Philippines, Singapore, Thailand, and Vietnam.

Answer: F
Medium
Page: 253

88. Asia Pacific Economic Cooperation was founded in 1990 at the suggestion of Japan.

Answer: T
Hard
Page: 253

89. The stated aim of APEC is to increase multilateral cooperation in view of the economic rise of the Pacific nations and the growing interdependence within the region.

IMPLICAITONS FOR BUSINESS

Answer: T
Medium
Page: 254

90. Currently the most significant developments in regional economic integration are occurring in the EU, NAFTA, and MERCOSUR group.

ESSAY QUESTIONS

Easy
Page: 232

91. Describe the concept of regional economic integration. Do you believe that regional economic integration is a good thing? Explain your answer.

Answer: Regional economic integration refers to agreements made by groups of countries in geographic regions to reduce, and ultimately remove, tariff and nontariff barriers to the free flow of goods, services, and factors of production between each other. The North American Free Trade Agreement, which is an agreement between the United States, Mexico, and Canada to reduce and eliminate tariffs between the three countries, is an example of regional economic integration.

Ask your students to comment on whether regional economic integration is a good thing. In general, the observers of international trade believe that regional economic integration is a positive development. Countries that have participated in regional trade agreements have typically experienced nontrival gains in trade from other member countries. In addition, as predicted by the theory of comparative advantage (explained in Chapter 4), there should be a substantial net gain from regional trade agreements.

Easy
Page: 233

92. Describe the difference between a free trade area and a common market?

Answer: In a free trade area all barriers to the trade of goods and services among member countries are removed. In a common market, the factors of production are also allowed to move freely between member countries and a common external trade policy is adopted. In addition, in a common market, labor and capital are free to move because there are no restrictions on immigration, emigration, or cross-border flows of capital between member nations.

Medium
Page: 233

93. Please briefly explain the following forms of economic integration: free trade area, customs union, common market, economic union, and full political union. Provide an example of each form of economic integration.

Answer: *Free Trade Area*: In a free trade area, all barriers to the trade of goods and services among member countries are removed. In a theoretically ideal free trade area, no discriminatory tariffs, quotas, subsidies, or administrative impediments are allowed to distort trade between member nations. Each country, however, is allowed to determine its own trade policies with regard to nonmembers. The European Free Trade Association, involving Norway, Iceland, and Switzerland, is an example of a free trade area.

Customs Union: A customs union eliminates trade barriers between member countries and adopts a common external policy. The Andean Pack, which involves Bolivia, Columbia, Ecuador, and Peru, is an example of a customs union.

Common Market: A common market eliminates trade barriers between member countries and adopts a common external policy. In addition, factors of production are also allowed to move freely between member countries. Thus, labor and capital are free to move, as there are no restrictions on immigration, emigration, or cross-border flows of capital between members. Hence, a much closer union is envisaged in a common market than a customs union. The European Union is currently a common market, although its goal is full economic union.

Economic Union: An economic union eliminates trade barriers between members nations, adopts a common external policy, and permits factors of production to move freely between member countries. In addition, a full economic union requires a common currency, harmonization of the member countries' tax rates, and a common monetary and fiscal policy. There are no true economic unions in the world today.

Political Union: A political union is the bringing together of two or more previously separate countries into essentially one country. As a result, all of the components of an economic union would apply, in addition to the political coupling of the countries involved. The United States is an example of a political union, in which previously separate "states" combined into one country. If Puerto Rico ever becomes the 51st state, the political coupling of the present United States with Puerto Rico would be an example of a political union

Medium
Page: 236

94. Describe the political case for intervention. Did political considerations have any role in the formation of the EU? Why or why not?

Answer: The political case for integration has two main points: (1) By linking neighboring economies and making them increasingly dependent on each other, incentives are created for political cooperation between the neighboring stages. In turn, the potential for violent conflict between the states is reduced; (2) By linking countries together, they have greater clout and are politically much stronger in dealing with other nations.

These considerations were instrumental in the establishment of the EU. Europe had suffered through two world wars in the first half of the century, and the desire for unity was high. In addition, many Europeans felt that after World War II the European nation-states were no longer large enough to hold their own in world markets and world politics. The need for a united Europe to deal with the U.S. on one side and the former Soviet Union on the other loomed large in the minds of the EC's founders.

Hard
Page: 236

95. What are the primary impediments to integration? Are these impediments difficult to overcome? Explain your answer.

Answer: Even though there may be a clear rationale for economic integration, there are two impediments that make integration difficult in many cases. First, although economic integration typically benefits the majority of the people in a country, certain groups may lose. For example, according to the author of the textbook, as a result of the 1994 establishment of NAFTA some Canadian and U.S. workers in such industries as textiles, which employ low-cost, low-skilled labor, will lose their jobs as Canadian and U.S. firms move their production to Mexico. As a result, even though the population as a whole may gain as a result of an agreement like NAFTA, these individuals may lose. If these individuals have enough political clout, they may be able to stop a NAFTA type agreement.

The second impediment to integration arises from concerns over national sovereignty. For example, for a full economic union to become a reality, the countries involved have to establish a common currency. The citizens of many countries view their currencies as symbols of national sovereignty and pride. As a result, the desire to maintain a sovereign currency may prohibit a country from joining an economic union. Similar examples prevent countries from entering into all of the forms of regional integration.

In many cases, these impediments to integration are very difficult to overcome. For instance, it is very easy to sympathize with someone who might lose their job as the result of a trade agreement. Similarly, many people become very intransigent on issues involving national sovereignty, which make some forms of regional integration almost impossible to achieve.

Medium
Page: 237

96. Define trade creation and trade diversion with respect to regional economic integration. Given that integration can both create and divert trade, under what circumstances will regional integration be in the best interest of the world economy?

Answer: Trade creation occurs when high-cost domestic producers are replaced by low-cost producers within the free trade area. It may also occur when higher-cost external producers are replaced by lower-cost external producers with the free trade area. Trade diversion occurs when lower-cost external suppliers are replaced by higher-cost suppliers within the free trade area. A regional free trade agreement will benefit the world only if the amount of trade it creates exceeds the amount it diverts.

Medium
Page: 244

97. From the standpoint of business and international trade, what are the advantages of a single currency within a trade block (like the EU)?

Answer: The gains to business from a single currency arise from decreased exchange costs and reduced risk of disruption from unexpected variations in the value of different currencies. A single currency would also help firms reduce administrative costs, as fewer resources would be required for accounting, treasury management, and the like. Finally, a single currency would make it difficult for companies to charge different prices in different countries in the trade block.

Medium
Page: 246

98. What is meant by the term "Fortress Europe?" Is this term fair, or is it an exaggeration?

Answer: There are presently two trade blocks in Europe: the European Union (EU) and the European Free Trade Association (EFTA). The EFTA has three members, including Norway, Iceland, and Switzerland. The European Union has 15 members, with more countries trying to get in. The fear on the part of non-European nations is that as regional integration in Europe continues to spread and deepen, the European countries will become more dependent upon one another and more protectionist in terms of their trade practices with other parts of the world. Thus, the term "Fortress Europe."

It is too early to tell whether this characterization is fair or not. What is particularly worrisome to Asia and the West, is that the EU, in particular, might increase external protection as weaker members attempt to offset their loss of protection against other EU countries by arguing for limitations on outside competition.

Medium
Page: 247

99. Describe the arguments for and against the North American Free Trade Agreement (NAFTA). In your opinion, is the recent ratification of NAFTA a positive development or a negative development for the citizens of the countries involved?

Answer: This question is designed to provide a forum for classroom discussion and/or to ask students' to think about the pluses and minuses of the NAFTA. In general, the proponents of NAFTA have argued that NAFTA should be seen as an opportunity to create an enlarged and more efficient productive based for the entire North American region. The proponents concede that some lower-income jobs will move from the United States and Canada to Mexico. However, they argue that in the end, this will benefit all three countries involved because the movement of jobs to Mexico will create employment and economic growth, and as Mexico's economy grows the demand for U.S. and Canadian products in Mexico will increase. In addition, the international competitiveness of U.S. and Canadian firms that move production to Mexico to take advantage of lower labor costs will be enhanced, enabling them to better compete against Asian and European rivals.

Those that oppose NAFTA claim that U.S. and Canadian citizens will lose their jobs in alarming numbers as low-income positions are moved to Mexico to take advantage of lower wage rates. To date, the movement of jobs from the U.S. and Canada has not reached the numbers that NAFTA's critics envisioned. Environmentalists have also voiced concerns about NAFTA. Because Mexico has more lenient environmental protection laws than either the U.S. or Canada, there is a concern that U.S. and Canadian firms will relocate to Mexico to avoid the cost of protecting the environment. Finally, there is continued opposition in Mexico to NAFTA from those who fear a loss of national sovereignty. Mexican critics fear that NAFTA will allow their country to be dominated by U.S. and Canadian multinationals, and use Mexico as a low-cost assembly site, while keeping their higher-paying jobs in their own countries.

Hard
Page: 251

100. Who are the member nations of MERCOSUR? Describe the expanding objectives of MERCOSUR.

Answer: MERCOSUR originated in 1988 as a free trade pact between Brazil and Argentina. Encouraged by early success, the pact was expanded in march 1990 to include Paraguay and Uruguay. The objectives of MERCOSUR are to perfect their free trade area and move toward a full customs union. Also, the four member states of MERCOSUR have now formally committed themselves to establishing a wider free trade area, the South American Free Trade Area (SAFTA). The goal is to bring other South American countries into the agreement, including the nations of the Andean Pact, and to have internal free trade for not less than 80 percent of goods produced in the region by 2005.

CHAPTER 9

THE FOREIGN EXCHANGE MARKET

MULTIPLE-CHOICE QUESTIONS

INTRODUCTION

Answer: A
Easy
Page: 278

1. The __________ is a market for converting the currency of one country into that of another.

   A. foreign exchange market
   B. cross-cultural interchange
   C. financial barter market
   D. monetary replacement market

Answer: B
Easy
Page: 278

2. A __________ is simply the rate at which one currency is converted into another.

   A. resale rate
   B. exchange rate
   C. barter rate
   D. replacement rate

Answer: C
Medium
Page: 278

3. Without the __________ market, international trade and international investment on the scale that we see today would be impossible.

   A. monetary replacement
   B. financial barter
   C. foreign exchange
   D. foreign resale

Answer: D
Medium
Page: 278

4. One function of the foreign exchange market is to provide some insurance against the risks that arise from changes in exchange rates, commonly referred to as:

   A. commerce uncertainty
   B. global jeopardy
   C. foreign market hazard
   D. foreign exchange risk

THE FUNCTIONS OF THE FOREIGN EXCHANGE MARKET

Answer: D
Medium
Page: 279

5. The foreign exchange market serves two main functions. These are:

A. collect duties on imported products and convert the currency of one country into the currency of another
B. insure companies against foreign exchange risk and set interest rates charged to foreign investors
C. collect duties on imported products and set interest rates charged to foreign investors
D. convert the currency of one country into the currency of another and provide some insurance against foreign exchange risk

Answer: C
Medium
Page: 279

6. The two main functions of the foreign exchange market is to convert the currency of one country into the currency of another and:

A. collect duties on imported products
B. set interest rates charged to foreign investors
C. provide some insurance against foreign exchange risk
D. arbitrate disputes between trade partners

Answer: C
Easy
Page: 279

7. Which of the following correctly matches a country with its currency?

A. Japan, franc
B. Germany, yen
C. Great Britain, pound
D. France, deutsche mark

Answer: C
Easy
Page: 279

8. The __________ helps us to compare the relative prices of goods and services in different countries.

A. interest rate
B. customs rate
C. exchange rate
D. tariff rate

Answer: C
Medium
Page: 280

9. Which of the following is not one of the four mains uses that international businesses have for the foreign exchange markets?

A. international businesses use foreign exchange markets when they must pay a foreign company for its products or services in its country's currency
B. international businesses use foreign exchange markets when they have spare cash that they wish to investment for short terms in money markets
C. international businesses use foreign exchange markets in determining domestic wage rates
D. currency speculation

Answer: A
Medium
Page: 280

10. Currency speculation typically involves:

A. the short term movement of funds from one currency to another in the hopes of profiting from shifts in exchange rates
B. the permanent movement of funds from one currency to another in the hopes of profiting from long-term investment in a particular currency
C. the simultaneous purchase of currencies from several countries in hopes of profiting from increasing economic prosperity
D. the liquidation of currency in favor of precious metals as a hedge against inflation

Answer: C
Easy
Page: 280

11. When two parties agree to exchange currency and execute the deal immediately, the transaction is referred to as a:

A. point-in-time exchange
B. temporal exchange
C. spot exchange
D. forward exchange

Answer: A
Medium
Page: 281

12. The __________ is the rate at which a foreign exchange dealer converts one currency into another currency on a particular day.

A. spot exchange rate
B. forward exchange rate
C. target exchange rate
D. statutory exchange rate

Answer: C
Medium
Page: 281

13. The value of a currency is determined by:

A. the World Trade Organization
B. a consortium of international traders
C. the interaction between the demand and supply of that currency relative to the demand and supply of other currencies
D. negotiations between the central banks of the leading five industrial powers of the world

Answer: C
Medium
Page: 282

14. A __________ exchange occurs when two parties agree to exchange currency and execute the deal at some specific date in the future.

A. spot
B. hedge
C. forward
D. reverse

Answer: B
Medium
Page: 282

15. For most major currencies, __________ are quoted for 30 days, 90 days, and 180 days into the future.

A. spot exchange rates
B. forward exchange rates
C. target exchange rates
D. statutory exchange rates

Answer: D
Medium
Page: 282

16. An exchange in which two parties agree to exchange currency and execute the deal at some specific date in the future is called a:

A. hedge exchange
B. statutory exchange
C. spot exchange
D. forward exchange

Answer: B
Medium
Page: 282

17. A __________ is the simultaneous purchase and sale of a given amount of foreign exchange for two different value dates.

A. monetary barter
B. currency swap
C. currency exchange
D. liquid trade

Answer: D
Medium
Page: 285

18. Firms engage in currency swaps in an effort to protect themselves against:

A. international monetary regulators
B. excess taxes
C. arbitrary penalties
D. foreign exchange risk

THE NATURE OF FOREIGN EXCHANGE MARKET

Answer: B
Hard
Page: 285

19. The most important trading centers for the foreign exchange market are in:

A. San Francisco, Tokyo, and Brussels
B. London, New York, and Tokyo
C. New York, Paris, and Singapore
D. Tokyo, Paris, and New York

Answer: D
Hard
Page: 285

20. The largest trading center in the foreign exchange market is:

A. Hong Kong
B. Tokyo
C. New York
D. London

Answer: D
Medium
Page: 286

21. In reference to the foreign exchange market, what is meant by the cliché "the market never sleeps."

A. foreign exchange rates are very sensitive to economic indicators (i.e. interest rate fluctuations, employment rates, etc.) and continually incorporate all relevant information into exchange rates
B. market tickers around the world are continually being updated by around the clock computer systems
C. currency traders are known to work long hours, and often work 24-hour shifts at their respective exchanges
D. there is no time during every 24-hour period that a foreign exchange market is not open at some location in the world

Answer: A
Easy
Page: 286

22. The process of buying a currency low and selling it high is referred to as:

A. arbitrage
B. skimming
C. situational exchange
D. opportunism

Answer: C
Medium
Page: 286

23. According to our textbook, although a foreign exchange transaction can in theory involved any two currencies, most transactions involve:

A. deutsche marks
B. yen
C. dollars
D. francs

Answer: C
Medium
Page: 287

24. Due to its central role in so many foreign exchange deals, the dollar is a __________ currency.

A. conveyance
B. arbitrage
C. vehicle
D. means

ECONOMIC THEORIES OF EXCHANGE RATE DETERMINATION

Answer: D
Easy
Page: 287

25. At the most basic level, exchange rates are determined by the demand and supply of one currency relative to the:

A. permanent value of another
B. 30-day average of another
C. 90-day average of another
D. demand and supply of another

Answer: A
Hard
Page: 288

26. Most economic theories suggest that three factors have an important impact on future exchange rate movements in a country's currency. These factors are:

A. the country's price inflation, its interest rate, and its market philosophy
B. the country's rate of GNP, its unemployment rate, and its economic policy
C. the country's participation in the World Trade Organization, its monetary policy, and its market philosophy
D. the country's rate of economic growth, its participation in the World Trade Organization, and its economic policy

Answer: A
Medium
Page: 288

27. The three factors that have the most important impact on future exchange rate movements in a country's currency include the country's market philosophy, its price inflation, and its:

A. interest rate
B. unemployment rate
C. growth in GNP
D. participation in regional trade agreements

Answer: C
Medium
Page: 288

28. The three factors that have the most important impact on future exchange rate movements in a country's currency include the country's market philosophy, its interest rate, and its:

A. participation in regional trade agreements
B. unemployment rate
C. price inflation
D. growth in GNP

Answer: A
Medium
Page: 288

29. The __________ states that in competitive markets free of transportation costs and barriers to trade (such as tariffs), identical products sold in different countries must sell for the same price when their price is expressed in terms of the same currency.

A. law of one price
B. principle of equitable pricing
C. model of fair pricing
D. International Fisher Effect

Answer: C
Easy
Page: 288

30. PPP theory stands for:

A. Productivity Power Premium theory
B. Process Productivity Predictor theory
C. Purchasing Power Parity theory
D. Personal Power Predictor theory

Answer: D
Easy
Page: 288

31. A(n) __________ market has no impediments to the free flow of goods and services, such as trade barriers.

A. inefficient
B. classical
C. tolerant
D. efficient

Answer: A
Medium
Page: 288

32. A __________ market is a market in which few impediments to international trade and investment exist.

A. relatively efficient market
B. consistently efficient market
C. absolutely free market
D. untainted market

Answer: B
Hard
Page: 289

33. The __________ theory predicts that changes in relative prices will result in a change in exchange rates.

A. buying power equality (BPE)
B. purchasing power parity (PPP)
C. stability power similarity (SPS)
D. buying prowess equality (BPE)

Answer: A
Hard
Page: 289

34. According to our textbook, when the growth in a country's money supply is faster than the growth in its output, __________ is fueled.

A. price inflation
B. unemployment
C. economic growth
D. per capita savings

Answer: C
Medium
Page: 289

35. The __________ theory tells us that a country with a high inflation rate will see depreciation in its currency exchange rate.

A. law of one price
B. monetary system
C. PPP
D. price inflation

Answer: B
Hard
Page: 290

36. According to our textbook, __________ determines whether the rate of growth in a country's money supply is greater than the rate of growth in output.

A. the international monetary authority
B. government
C. the private sector
D. market mechanisms

Answer: A
Medium
Page: 291

37. PPP theory predicts that changes in __________ will result in a change in exchange rates.

A. relative prices
B. interest rates
C. unemployment rates
D. statutory prices

Answer: B
Hard
Page: 291

38. According to our textbook, PPP theory does not seem to be a particularly good predictor of exchange rate movement for time spans of:

A. one year or less
B. five years or less
C. ten years or less
D. twenty years or less

Answer: C
Medium
Page: 291

39. Economic theory tells us that __________ rates reflect expectations about likely future inflation rates.

A. unemployment
B. exchange
C. interest
D. tariff

Answer: D
Medium
Page: 291

40. The __________ states that a country's "nominal" interest rate (*i*) is the sum of the required "real" rate of interest (*r*) and the expected rate of inflation over the period for which the funds are to be lent (*I*).

A. Miller effect
B. Phillips effect
C. James effect
D. Fisher effect

Answer: C
Hard
Page: 291

41. According to the Fisher effect, if the real rate of interest in a country is 5 percent and the annual inflation is expected to be 10 percent, the nominal interest rate will be:

A. 5 percent
B. 10 percent
C. 15 percent
D. 20 percent

Answer: A
Hard
Page: 291

42. According to our textbook, when investors are free to transfer capital between countries, real interest rates will be:

A. the same in every country
B. fluctuate widely from country to country
C. be higher in industrialized countries than developing countries
D. be higher in developing countries than industrialized countries

Answer: B
Medium
Page: 292

43. The International Fisher Effect states that for any two countries, the __________ exchange rate should change in an equal amount but in the opposite direction to the difference in the nominal interest rates between the two countries.

A. inward
B. spot
C. forward
D. reciprocal

Answer: A
Medium
Page: 292

44. Empirical evidence suggests that neither PPP theory nor the International Fisher Effect is particularly good at explaining __________ movements in exchange rates.

A. short-term
B. intermediate-term
C. long-term
D. permanent

Answer: C
Medium
Page: 293

45. According to our textbook, relative monetary growth, relative inflation rates, and nominal interest rates differentials are all __________ predictors of long-run exchanges in exchange rates.

A. poor
B. moderately poor
C. moderately good
D. excellent

EXCHANGE RATE FORECASTING

Answer: D
Medium
Page: 293

46. The __________ market school argues that forward exchange rates do the best job of forecasting future spot exchange rates, and, therefore, investing in forecasting services would be a waste of money.

A. robust
B. inefficient
C. forward
D. efficient

Answer: B
Medium
Page: 293

47. The __________ market school argues that companies can improve the foreign exchange market's estimate of future exchange rates by investing in forecasting services.

A. robust
B. inefficient
C. efficient
D. forward

Answer: D
Easy
Page: 293

48. A __________ market is one in which prices reflect all available public information.

A. inefficient
B. closed
C. open
D. efficient

Answer: A
Easy
Page: 294

49. A __________ market is one in which prices do not reflect all available information.

A. inefficient
B. statutory
C. free
D. efficient

Answer: B
Medium
Page: 296

50. __________ analysis draws on economic theory to construct sophisticated econometric models for predicting exchange rate movements.

A. Technical
B. Fundamental
C. Basic
D. Primary

Answer: A
Medium
Page: 296

51. __________ analysis uses prices and volume data to determine past trends.

A. Technical
B. Primary
C. Basic
D. Fundamental

Answer: D
Medium
Page: 296

52. __________ analysis is based on the premise that there are analyzable market trends and waves and that previous trends and waves can be used to predict future trends and waves.

A. Fundamental
B. Basic
C. Primary
D. Technical

CURRENCY CONVERTIBILITY

Answer: B
Easy
Page: 296

53. A country's currency is said to be __________ when the country's government allows both residents and nonresidents to purchase unlimited amounts of foreign currency with it.

A. technically convertible
B. freely convertible
C. externally convertible
D. nonconvertible

Answer: B
Medium
Page: 297

54. A country's currency is said to be freely convertible when the country's government:

A. allows only nonresidents to purchase unlimited amounts of a foreign currency with it
B. allows both residents and nonresidents to purchase unlimited amounts of foreign currency with it
C. allows only residents to purchase currency with it
D. allows both residents, nonresidents, and foreign governments to purchase limited amounts of foreign currency with it

Answer: A
Medium
Page: 297

55. A currency is said to be __________ when only nonresidents may convert it into a foreign currency without any limitations.

A. externally convertible
B. freely convertible
C. nonconvertible
D. technically convertible

Answer: B
Medium
Page: 297

56. A currency is __________ when neither residents nor nonresidents are allowed to convert it into a foreign currency.

A. freely convertible
B. nonconvertible
C. externally convertible
D. technically convertible

Answer: C
Hard
Page: 297

57. Governments limit currency convertibility to protect their:

A. national sovereignty
B. domestic interest rates
C. foreign exchange reserves
D. political stature

Answer: B
Easy
Page: 297

58. _________ refers to a range of baterlike agreements by which goods and services can be traded for other goods and services.

A. Separate trade
B. Countertrade
C. Alternative trade
D. Reciprocal trade

Answer: A
Medium
Page: 297

59. If an American grain company exported corn to Russia, and instead of receiving nonconvertible Russian currency in exchange for the corn received Russian crude oil, that would be an example of:

A. countertrade
B. reciprocal trade
C. separate trade
D. synergistic trade

Answer: D
Medium
Page: 297

60. Countertrade makes the most sense when a country's currency is:

A. externally convertible
B. freely convertible
C. nominally convertible
D. nonconvertible

TRUE-FALSE QUESTIONS

INTRODUCTION

Answer: T
Easy
Page: 278

61. The foreign exchange market is a market for converting the currency of one country into that of another country.

Answer: F
Easy
Page: 278

62. The rate at which one currency is converted into another is typically stable over time.

THE FUNCTIONS OF THE FOREIGN EXCHANGE MARKET

Answer: T
Medium
Page: 279

63. The German currency is called the deutsche mark.

Answer: F
Medium
Page: 279

64. The foreign exchange market serves two main functions. The first is to convert the currency of one country into the currency of another. The second is to set interest rates charged to foreign investors.

Answer: T
Easy
Page: 279

65. The exchange rate allows us to compare the relative prices of goods and services in different countries.

Answer: F
Medium
Page: 279

66. Both tourists and companies engaged in international trade and investment are major participants in the foreign exchange market.

Answer: F
Medium
Page: 280

67. Currency speculation typically involves the long-term movement of funds from one currency to another in the hopes of profiting from shifts in exchange rates.

Answer: T
Easy
Page: 280

68. When two parties agree to exchange currency and execute the deal immediately, the transaction is referred to as a spot exchange rate.

Answer: T
Medium
Page: 281

69. The value of currency is determined by the interaction between the demand and supply of that currency relative to the demand and supply of other currencies.

Answer: F
Medium
Page: 282

70. A forward exchange occurs when two parties agree to exchange currency and execute the deal at some undetermined date in the future.

Answer: T
Medium
Page: 282

71. For most currencies, forward exchange rates are quoted for 30 days, 90 days, and 180 days into the future.

Answer: F
Medium
Page: 284

72. A currency sway is the even exchange of a specific number of units of one currency for another (e.g. 100 French francs for 100 Japanese yen).

THE NATURE OF THE FOREIGN EXCHANGE MARKET

Answer: T
Easy
Page: 285

73. The foreign exchange market has been growing at a rapid pace, reflecting a general growth in the volume of cross-border trade and investment.

Answer: F
Medium
Page: 285

74. Tokyo is the largest trading center in the foreign exchange market.

Answer: F
Medium
Page: 286

75. Arbitrage is buying a currency high and selling it low.

Answer: T
Medium
Page: 286

76. Although a foreign exchange transaction can in theory involve any two currencies, most transactions involve dollars.

ECONOMIC THEORIES OF EXCHANGE RATE DETERMINATION

Answer: T
Easy
Page: 287

77. At the most basic level, exchange rates are determined by the demand and supply of one currency relative to the demand and supply of another.

Answer: T
Medium
Page: 288

78. The three factors that have the most important impact on future exchange rate movements in a country's currency include the country's market philosophy, its interest rate, and its price inflation.

Answer: F
Hard
Page: 288

79. The law of one price states that in competitive markets free of transportation costs and barriers to trade (such as tariffs), identical products sold in different countries must sell for different prices when their price is expressed in terms of the same currency.

Answer: T
Hard
Page: 288

80. If the law of one price were true for all goods and services, the purchasing power parity (PPP) exchange rate could be found from any individual set of prices.

Answer: F
Hard
Page: 289

81. In essence, PPP theory predicts that changes in relative prices will result in stability in exchange rates.

Answer: F
Hard
Page: 289

82. The PPP theory tells us that a country with a high inflation rate will see an appreciation in its currency exchange rate.

Answer: T
Medium
Page: 290

83. The inevitable result of excessive growth in money supply is price inflation.

Answer: T
Medium
Page: 291

84. Economic theory tells us that interest rates reflect expectations about likely future inflation rates.

EXCHANGE RATE FORECASTING

Answer: F
Easy
Page: 293

85. An inefficient market is one in which prices reflect all available public information.

Answer: T
Hard
Page: 293

86. If the foreign exchange market is efficient, forward exchange rates should be unbiased predictors of future spot rates.

CURRENCY CONVERTIBILITY

Answer: T
Medium
Page: 297

87. A country's currency is said to be freely convertible when the country's government allows both residents and nonresidents to purchase unlimited amounts of a foreign currency with it.

Answer: F
Medium
Page: 297

88. Governments limit currency convertibility to preserve their political image.

Answer: T
Hard
Page: 297

89. Governments typically impose convertibility restrictions of the currency when they fear that free convertibility will lead to a run on their foreign exchange reserves.

Answer: T
Easy
Page: 297

90. Countertrade refers to a range of barterlike agreements by which goods and services can be traded for other goods and services.

ESSAY QUESTIONS

Medium
Page: 278

91. What are the functions of the foreign exchange market? Would international commerce be possible without its existence?

Answer: The foreign exchange market is a market for converting the currency of one country into that of another. For example, an American exporter that gets paid by a German importer in deutsche marks can convert the deutsche marks to dollars on the foreign exchange market. The two main functions of the foreign exchange market are currency conversion and insuring against foreign exchange risk. In terms of currency conversion, the market has four primary functions for international businesses: (1) converting payments a company receives in foreign currencies into the currency of its home country; (2) converting the currency of a company's home country into another currency when they must pay a foreign company for its products and services in their currency; (3) international businesses may use foreign exchange markets when they have spare cash that they wish to invest for short terms in money markets (of another country); and (4) currency speculation. The second function of the foreign exchange market is to provide insurance to protect against the possible adverse consequences of unpredictable changes in exchange rates. This can be accomplished through the use of a forward exchange.

It is difficult to image how international commerce would work without the existence of the foreign exchange market. Without it, international trade would have to be completed on the basis of barter, rather than currency exchange. As suggested by the author of the textbook, the foreign exchange markets is the lubricant that enables companies based in countries that use different currencies to trade with each other.

Medium
Page: 279

92. For a firm that deals in international markets, what does "foreign exchange risk" mean? How could foreign exchange risk affect the profitability of an American agricultural equipment firm exporting tractors to a German buyer?

Answer: A foreign exchange risk is a risk that the value of currencies will change in the future. A change in foreign exchange rates could have a dramatic impact on a company engaged in international commerce. For example, if a U.S. agricultural equipment firm had a contract to deliver 100 tractors to a German customer in three months, and the U.S. dollar strengthened against the German deutsche mark (i.e. currency values changed), the U.S. agricultural equipment firm would end up with less dollars (after the deutsche marks it was paid were exchanged for dollars) than originally anticipated.

Difficult
Page: 280

93. Explain the difference between spot exchange rates and forward exchange rates. Briefly explain how the forward exchange market works.

Answer: The spot exchange rate is the rate at which a foreign exchange dealer converts one currency into another currency on a particular day. Thus, when a Japanese tourist in Orlando goes to a bank to convert yen into dollars to spend at Disney World, the exchange rate is the spot rate for that day. Spot exchange rates change daily, based on the relative supply and demand for different currencies.

Forward exchange rates are rates for currencies quoted for 30, 90, or 180 days into the future (in some cases, it is possible to get forward exchange rates for several years into the future). Forward exchange rates are available because of the volatile and problematic nature of the spot exchange market. Suppose a U.S. importer agreed to paid a Japanese exporter $100 a piece for a large quantity of cameras. The day of the agreement, the exchange rate for dollars and yen was 1:1 (1 dollar for 1 yen). The U.S. importer planed to sell the cameras for $125, guaranteeing himself a profit of $25 per camera. Further suppose that the payment is not due to the Japanese exporter for 30 days, and during the 30 day waiting period, the dollar unexpectedly depreciates against the yen, forcing the exchange rate to one dollar for every .75 yen. Per the original agreement, the U.S. importer still has to pay the Japanese importer 100 yen per camera, but now the exchange rate is not 1 dollar per yen, but is 1 dollar per .75 yen. As a result, the U.S. importer has to pay $1.33 to buy the equivalent of 1 yen. Now, instead of making $25 per camera ($125 selling price - $100 purchase price), the U.S. importer will lose $8 per camera ($125 selling price - $133 purchase price influenced by currency fluctuations). To avoid this potential problem, the U.S. importer could have entered into a 30-day forward exchange transaction with a foreign exchange dealer at, say, 1 dollar for every .95 yen (the forward rate will typically be somewhat lower than the spot rate). By doing this, the importer is guaranteed that he or she will not have to pay more than 1.05 dollars for every 1 yen, which would still guarantee the importer a $20 per profit on the cameras.

Medium
Page: 287

94. Why is the U.S. dollar referred to as a vehicle currency?

Answer: Due to its central role in so many transactions, the dollar is sometimes referred to as a vehicle currency. While foreign exchange transactions can in theory involve any two currencies, many transactions involve dollars. This is true even when a dealer wants to sell one non-dollar currency and buy another. This is because the volume of transactions in dollars with other currencies is so high that it may be cheaper and more expedient for a trader to exchange French francs (for example) for dollars and then these dollars for Philippine pesos than it would be to try to execute a transaction directly between these relatively minor currencies. There will be plenty of other traders willing to trade dollars for pesos or francs, but few interested in trading pesos for francs.

Medium
Page: 288

95. Why might the law of one price not hold for a particular brand of French wine that can be bought both in France and the U.S., assuming it is readily available on store shelves in both countries?

Answer: The law of one price assumes no transportation costs and efficient markets. As a result, since it costs something to transport the wine from France to the U.S., the price might be higher in the U.S. Taxes can also affect prices. If the tax rate on wine is higher in France than it is in the U.S., the bottle of wine might cost more in France one mile from where it is made than it does in a store in the U.S.

Medium
Page: 289

96. When does inflation occur?

Answer: Inflation occurs when the quantity of money in circulation rises faster than the stock of goods and services; that is, when the money supply increases faster than output increases.

Difficult
Page: 292

97. What is the International Fisher Effect? (note: you do not need to provide the mathematical formula provided in the book)

Answer: The International Fisher Effect states that for any two countries, the spot exchange rate should change in an equal amount but in the opposite direction to the difference in nominal interest rates between the two countries.

Medium
Page: 292

98. Explain how the psychology of investors and bandwagon effects can have an impact on the movement in exchange rates. Do you believe that bandwagon effects really happen? Explain your answer.

Answer: As noted by the author of the textbook, empirical evidence suggests that empirical explanations are not particular good at explaining short-term movements in exchange rates. One reason for this may be the impact of investor psychology on short-run exchange rate movements. Investors, because they are human beings, do not always make decisions based on a rational analysis of the facts. Sometimes investors imitate the actions of someone that is very influential, even if there is no logical reason to do so. Investors also trade based on "hunches" or speculation, which is more psychological in nature than rational. A bandwagon effect in when investors in increasing numbers start following the lead of someone who may be pushing the value of a currency up or down due to psychological reasons. As a bandwagon effect builds up, the expectations of investors become a self-fulfilling prophecy, and the market moves in the way the investors expected.

Ask your students if they believe bandwagon effects actually happen in practice. Most students will say that they do, and have vivid examples to support their conclusions.

Medium
Page: 296

99. In the context of forecasting exchange rate movements, describe the difference between fundamental analysis and technical analysis. Which approach do economists prefer? Why?

Answer: Fundamental analysis draws on economic theory to construct sophisticated econometric models for predicting exchange rate movements. The variables contained in these models typically include relative money supply growth rates, inflation rates, and interest rates. In addition, they may include variables related to a countries' balance-of-payments positions. In contrast, technical analysis uses price and volume data to determine past trends, which are expected to continue into the future. This approach does not rely on a consideration of economic fundamentals. Technical analysis is based on the premise that there are analyzable market trends and waves and that previous trends and waves can be used to predict future trends and waves.

Since there is no theoretical rationale for the assumption of predictability that underlies technical analysis, most economists compare technical analysis to fortune telling, and prefer fundamental analysis. However, despite this skepticism, technical analysis has gained favor in recent years.

Medium
Page:

100. Explain the concept of countertrade. When does countertrade make sense? How does countertrade help solve the nonconvertability problem? Provide a brief example of how countertrade works.

Answer: Countertrade refers to a range of barterlike agreements by which goods and services can be traded for other goods and services. Countertrade makes sense when a country's currency is nonconvertible. For example, the Russian ruble in nonconvertible. What that means it that if an U.S. exporter sold grain to a Russian importer and was paid in rubles, the U.S. exporter could not take the rubles to a bank and have them converted into dollars. The rubles are only of value in Russia. To get around this limitation, the U.S. exporter and the Russian importer might enter into a countertrade agreement, in which the U.S. exporter accepts some type of goods or services in exchange for the grain rather than Russian rubles. For instance, the Russian importer could use rubles to buy Russian crude oil, and exchange the crude oil for the grain. The U.S. exporter could then sell the crude oil for American dollars, and benefit from the transaction.

CHAPTER 10

THE INTERNATIONAL MONETARY FUND

MULTIPLE-CHOICE QUESTIONS

INTRODUCTION

Answer: C
Hard
Page: 307

1. In 1997, only __________ of the world's viable currencies were freely floating; this includes the currencies of many of the world's larger industrial nations such as the United States, Canada, Japan, and Britain.

   A. 12
   B. 33
   C. 51
   D. 77

Answer: B
Easy
Page: 307

2. The Bretton Woods system called for __________ exchange rates against the U.S. dollar.

   A. variable
   B. fixed
   C. floating
   D. fluctuating

Answer: B
Medium
Page: 307

3. Under the fixed exchange rate system established by the Bretton Woods agreement, the value of most currencies in terms of __________ was fixed for long periods and was allowed to change only under a specific set of circumstances.

   A. German deutsche marks
   B. United States dollars
   C. Japanese yen
   D. British pounds

Answer: D
Medium
Page: 307

4. The Bretton Woods conference created two major international institutions, including:

   A. the Bretton Woods Monetary Fund and the World Trade Organization
   B. the World Currency Exchange and the World Bank
   C. the World Trade Organization and the United Nations
   D. the International Monetary Fund and the World Bank

Answer: C
Medium
Page: 307

5. The World Bank and the __________ were created by the Bretton Woods conference.

A. Bretton Woods Monetary Fund
B. World Currency Exchange
C. International Monetary Fund
D. Global Trade Organization

Answer: D
Medium
Page: 307

6. The International Monetary Fund and the __________ were created by the Bretton Woods Conference.

A. Bretton Woods Monetary Fund
B. World Currency Exchange
C. World Trade Organization
D. World Bank

Answer: C
Hard
Page: 307

7. The Bretton Woods system of fixed exchange rates collapsed in:

A. 1951
B. 1965
C. 1973
D. 1990

THE GOLD STANDARD

Answer: B
Medium
Page: 308

8. The practice of pegging currencies to gold and guaranteeing convertibility was referred to as the:

A. premium standard
B. gold standard
C. metal standard
D. federal reserve standard

Answer: C
Medium
Page: 308

9. By 1880, most of the world's major trading nations, including Great Britain, Germany, Japan, and the United States, had adopted the:

A. platinum standard
B. federal reserve standard
C. gold standard
D. metal standard

Answer: D
Medium
Page: 308

10. Under the gold standard, the amount of currency needed to purchase one ounce of gold was referred to as the gold __________ value.

A. arbitrary
B. statutory
C. legal
D. par

Answer: A
Medium
Page: 308

11. The great strength claimed for the gold standard was that it contained a powerful mechanism for achieving __________ by all countries.

A. balance-of-trade equilibrium
A. economic stability
C. interest rate parity
D. equal tariff levels

Answer: B
Medium
Page: 308

12. A country is said to be in balance-of-trade equilibrium when:

A. the income that its residents earn from the export of manufactured goods equals the income that its residents earn from the export of services
B. the income that its residents earn from exports is equal to the money that its residents pay for imports
C. the income that its residents earn from exports in the current fiscal year is equal to the income that its residents earned from exports in the previous fiscal year
D. the income that its residents earn from the export of raw materials is equal to the income that its residents earn from the export of manufactured goods

Answer: C
Hard
Page: 309

13. The gold standard was abandoned in:

A. 1870
B. 1889
C. 1914
D. 1924

THE BRETTON WOODS SYSTEM

Answer: D
Easy
Page: 309

14. In 1944, at the height of World War II, representatives from 44 countries met at __________ to design a new international monetary system.

A. Morris Plains, New Jersey
B. Dayton, Ohio
C. Richmond, Virginia
D. Bretton Woods, New Hampshire

Answer: B
Medium
Page: 309

15. The Bretton Woods agreement called for:

A. variable exchange rates
B. fixed exchange rates
C. freely floating exchange rates
D. a set of "managed" floating exchange rates

Answer: A
Medium
Page: 309

16. The agreement reached at Bretton Woods established two multinational institutions, including:

A. the International Monetary Fund and the World Bank
B. the American-European National Bank and the Import-Export Bank
C. the Global Bank for Sustained Economic Stability and the International Monetary Fund
D. the World Bank and the International Export-Import Institute

Answer: B
Medium
Page: 309

17. The agreement reached at Bretton Woods established two multinational institutions, include the International Monetary Fund and the:

A. Global Bank for Sustained Economic Stability
B. World Bank
C. International Import-Export Institute
D. Import-Export Bank

Answer: D
Medium
Page: 309

18. The task of the World Bank, as established by the Bretton Woods agreement, is to:

A. maintain order in the international monetary system
B. set currency exchange rates
C. arbitrate trade disputes
D. promote general economic development

Answer: B
Medium
Page: 309

19. The task of the International Monetary Fund, as established by the Bretton Woods agreement, is to:

A. promote general economic development
B. maintain order in the international monetary system
C. provide letters of credit on behalf of first-time exporters
D. facilitate the establishment of regional trade agreements

Answer: D
Medium
Page: 310

20. Under the Bretton Woods system, which currency served as the base currency?

A. Japanese yen
B. French franc
C. British pound
D. U.S. dollar

Answer: A
Hard
Page: 310

21. The IMF Articles of Agreement were heavily influenced by all of the following except:

A. the worldwide financial boom
B. competitive devaluations
C. trade wars
D. high unemployment

Answer: D
Medium
Page: 311

22. The official name of the World Bank is the:

A. Global Bank for the Financing of Trade and Development
B. International Bank for Sustained Economic Stability
C. Global Bank for the Promotion of Trade
D. International Bank for Reconstruction and Development

Answer: B
Hard
Page: 311

23. The World Bank lends money under two schemes. Under the IBRD scheme, money is raised:

A. through contributions from participating countries
B. through bond sales in the international capital market
C. through low-interest rate loans from major private sector banks
D. through loans from the International Monetary Fund

THE COLLAPSE OF THE FIXED EXCHANGE RATE SYSTEM

Answer: C
Hard
Page: 311

24. The system of fixed exchange rates established at Bretton Woods collapsed in:

    A. 1959
    B. 1965
    C. 1973
    D. 1981

Answer: C
Hard
Page: 311

25. Which of the following statements accurately depicts what happened to the Bretton Woods system of fixed exchange rates?

    A. the system never got off the ground, and collapsed in the late 1940s
    B. the system worked well for about a decade, then collapsed in the mid-1950s
    C. the system began to show signs of strain in the 1960s, and finally collapsed in 1973
    D. the system remained in place until the early 1990s when an international conference was convened in Finland to develop a managed float system

Answer: A
Medium
Page: 312

26. In the context of the global monetary system, in August 1971 President Nixon made the following two announcements: (1) a new 10 percent tax on imports would remain in effect until the trading partners of the U.S. agreed to revalue their currency against the dollar and (2):

    A. the dollar was no longer convertible into gold
    B. the U.S. would no longer support the World Bank
    C. the U.S. planned to devalue its currency by 20 percent
    D. the U.S. planned to call for a second Bretton Woods conference

Answer: C
Hard
Page: 312

27. The Bretton Woods system had an Achilles' heel: The system could not work if its key currency, the US dollar, was:

    A. overvalued
    B. undervalued
    C. under speculative attack
    D. subject to a low U.S. inflation rate

THE FLOATING EXCHANGE RATE REGIME

Answer: C
Medium
Page: 313

28. The __________ exchange rate regime that followed the collapse of the fixed exchange rate system was formalized in January 1976 when IMF members met in Jamaica and agreed to the rules of the international monetary system that are in place today.

A. closed
B. open
C. floating
D. quasi-fixed

Answer: D
Medium
Page: 313

29. The floating exchange rate regime that followed the collapse of the fixed exchange rate system was formalized in January 1976 when IMF members met in __________ and agreed to the rules of the international monetary system that are in place today.

A. Toronto
B. Spain
A. Brussels
D. Jamaica

Answer: B
Hard
Page: 313

30. The three main elements of the Jamaica Agreement were:

A. the IMF was established, gold was abandoned as a reserve asset, and floating rates were declared unacceptable
B. floating rates were declared acceptable, gold was abandoned as a reserve asset, and total annual IMF quotas were increased to $41 billion
C. floating rates were declared unacceptable, the IMF was abolished, and the World Bank was established
D. fixed rates were declared acceptable, gold was accepted as a reserve asset, and the total annual IMP quotas were increased to $41 billion

Answer: A
Medium
Page: 313

31. Which of the following was not one of the main three elements of the Jamaica agreement?

A. the establishment of the World Bank
B. floating rates were declared acceptable
C. total annual IMF quotas were increased to $41 billion
D. gold was abandoned as a reserve asset

Answer: C
Hard
Page: 314

32. The __________ represents the exchange rate of the U.S. dollar against a weighted basket of the currencies of 19 other industrialized countries.

A. Stanley Assurance Index
B. Phillips Security Index
C. Morgan Guaranty Index
D. Nelson's Assurance Index

Answer: B
Hard
Page: 314

33. The so called "Group of Five" major industrialized nations include:

A. Germany, China, Japan, Great Britain, and the U.S.
B. Great Britain, France, Japan, Germany, and the U.S.
C. U.S., Japan, China, Brazil, and Germany
D. France, Germany, Japan, South Korea, and the U.S.

FIXED VERSUS FLOATING EXCHANGE RATES

Answer: A
Medium
Page: 317

34. The case for floating exchange rates has two main elements. These are:

A. monetary policy autonomy and automatic trade balance adjustments
B. the impracticality of the gold standard and sporadic trade balance adjustments
C. monetary policy control and sporadic trade balance adjustments
D. automatic trade balance adjustments and the impracticality of the gold standard

Answer: C
Medium
Page: 317

35. The case for floating exchange rates has two main elements: monetary policy autonomy and:

A. the impracticality of the gold standard
B. sporadic trade balance adjustments
C. automatic trade balance adjustments
D. money supply adjustments

Answer: C
Medium
Page: 317

36. Advocates of a __________ rate regime argue that removal of the obligation to maintain exchange rate parity would restore monetary control to the government.

A. variable
B. fixed
C. floating
D. quasi-fixed

Answer: A
Easy
Page: 317

37. Floating exchange rates are determined by:

A. market forces
B. the IMF
C. the World Bank
D. an international commission on exchange rate stability

Answer: D
Medium
Page: 318

38. Under the Bretton Woods system, if a country developed a permanent deficit in its balance of trade (importing more than it exported) that could not be corrected by domestic policy, this would require the __________ to agree to a currency devaluation.

A. World Bank
B. United Nations
C. International Economic Council
D. International Monetary Fund

Answer: C
Medium
Page: 319

39. According to our textbook, those in favor of floating exchange rates argue that floating rates:

A. encourage speculation
B. help confuse trade imbalances
C. help adjust trade imbalances
D. have no effect on trade imbalances

EXCHANGE RATE REGIMES IN PRACTICE

Answer: C
Medium
Page: 319

40. "Free float" exchange rates are determined by:

A. governments
B. the IMF
C. market forces
D. the World Bank

Answer: C
Hard
Page: 319

41. Pegged exchange rates are popular among many of the world's:

A. industrialized nations
B. largest nations
C. smaller nations
D. communist nations

Answer: B
Medium
Page: 320

42. There is some evidence that adopting a pegged exchange rate regime:

A. reduces unemployment in a country
B. moderates inflationary pressure in a country
C. increase global GNP
D. decreases global GNP

Answer: B
Hard
Page: 320

43. A recent IMF study concluded that countries with pegged exchange rates regimes had an average annual inflation rate of __________, compared with 14 percent for intermediate regimes and 16 percent for floating regimes.

A. 4 percent
B. 8 percent
C. 14 percent
D. 18 percent

Answer: A
Hard
Page: 320

44. A country that introduces a __________ commits itself to converting its domestic currency on demand into another currency at a fixed exchange rate.

A. currency board
B. monetary review committee
C. certificate board
D. exchange rate review committee

Answer: A
Medium
Page: 321

45. In the context of international monetary systems, the initials EMS stands for:

A. European Monetary System
B. Eastern-European Monetary System
C. Eastern-Asia Monetary System
D. Electronic Monetary Standard

Answer: D
Hard
Page: 321

46. An exchange rate system based on __________ involves a group of countries trying to keep their currencies within a predetermined range, or zone, or other currencies in the group.

A. objective criteria
B. point zones
C. subjective criteria
D. target zones

Answer: C
Hard
Page: 321

47. When the European Monetary System was created in March 1979, it was entrusted with three main objectives: (1) to create a zone of monetary stability in Europe by reducing exchange rate volatility and converging national interest rates; (2) to coordinate exchange rate policies versus non-EU currencies such as the US dollar and the yen; and (3):

A. to control currency rate fluctuations through close monitoring
B. to control currency rate stability through strict controls
C. to control inflation through the imposition of monetary discipline
D. to control unemployment through the imposition of monetary policy

Answer: D
Medium
Page: 321

48. The ECU was a basket of the EU currencies that served as the unit of account for the:

A. International Monetary Fund
B. World Bank
C. Import-Export Bank
D. European Monetary System

RECENT ACTIVITIES AND THE FUTURE OF THE IMF

Answer: B
Medium
Page: 323

49. Many observers initially believed that the collapse of the Bretton Woods system in 1973 would __________ the role of the IMF within the international monetary system.

A. embellish
B. diminish
C. eliminate
D. increase

Answer: D
Medium
Page: 324

50. A __________ crisis occurs when a speculative attack on the exchange value of a currency results in a sharp depreciation in the value of the currency or forces authorities to expend large volumes of international currency reserves and sharply increase interest rates to defend the prevailing exchange rate.

A. foreign debt
B. banking
C. fiduciary
D. currency

Answer: C
Easy
Page: 324

51. A __________ crisis refers to a loss of confidence in the banking system that leads to a run on banks, as individuals and companies withdraw their deposits.

A. currency
B. institutional
C. banking
D. fiduciary

Answer: B
Hard
Page: 325

52. IMF's willingness to help Mexico deal with its recent fiscal crises involved all of the following elements except:

A. rescheduling of Mexico's old debt
B. assumption of the control of Mexico's central bank
C. new loans to Mexico from the IMF, the World Bank, and commercial banks
D. the Mexican government's agreement to abide by a set of IMF-dictated macroeconomic prescriptions for its economy, including tight control over the growth of the money supply and major cuts in governmental spending

Answer: D
Medium
Page: 325

53. The Brady Plan, named after U.S. Treasury secretary Nicholas Brady, was associated with IMF debt relief for:

A. Thailand
B. Brazil
C. South Korea
D. Mexico

Answer: B
Easy
Page: 324

54. A __________ crisis is a situation in which a country cannot service its foreign debt obligations, whether private sector or government debt.

A. international affairs
B. foreign debt
C. currency
D. banking

Answer: A
Medium
Page: 324

55. The __________ crisis had its roots in the OPEC oil price hikes of 1973 and 1979.

A. Third World debt
B. Mexican Currency
C. Russian Ruble
D. Asian

Answer: D
Hard
Page: 326

56. Why was the Mexican peso pegged to the U.S. dollar from the early 1980s to the mid 1990s?

A. to prevent speculative pressures for the devaluation of the peso
B. in was required under NAFTA rules
C. after the U.S. provided Mexico economic assistance in the early 1980s, Mexico voluntarily agreed to peg the peso to the U.S. dollar
D. IMF conditions on its loans that were intended to force Mexico to adopt tight financial policies

Answer: A
Medium
Page: 327

57. The IMF's involvement in Russia came about as the result of:

A. a persistent decline in the value of the Russian ruble
B. high unemployment in Russia and the other republics of the former Soviet Union
C. the easing of international political tensions between Russia and the west
D. negotiations sponsored by the United Nations

Answer: D
Medium
Page: 329

58. According to our textbook, the financial crisis that erupted across __________ during the fall of 1997 has emerged as the biggest challenge yet to the IMF.

A. Russia
B. Mexico
C. Eastern Europe
D. Southeast Asia

Answer: D
Medium
Page: 334

59. __________ arises when people behave recklessly because they know they will be saved if things go wrong.

A. Unethical impropriety
B. Scrupulous hazard
C. Critical impropriety
D. Moral hazard

IMPLICATIONS FOR BUSINESS

Answer: C
Easy
Page: 335

60. The current system of foreign exchange is a _________ system in which a combination of government intervention and speculative activity can drive the foreign exchange market.

A. static
B. fluid
C. mixed
D. statutory

TRUE-FALSE QUESTIONS

INTRODUCTION

Answer: T
Easy
Page: 307

61. The Bretton Woods system called for fixed exchange rates against the U.S. dollar.

Answer: F
Easy
Page: 307

62. The Bretton Woods conference created two major international institutions: the International Monetary Fund and the World Court.

Answer: T
Medium
Page: 307

63. The Bretton Woods system of fixed exchange rates collapsed in 1973.

THE GOLD STANDARD

Answer: T
Easy
Page: 308

64. Pegging currencies to gold and guaranteeing convertibility is know as the gold standard.

Answer: T
Medium
Page: 308

65. The great strength claimed for the gold standard was that it contained a powerful mechanism for achieving balance-of-trade equilibrium by all countries.

Answer: F
Medium
Page: 309

66. The gold standard worked reasonably well from the 1870 until the end of World War II, in 1945.

THE BRETTON WOODS SYSTEM

Answer: F
Easy
Page: 309

67. At the Bretton Woods conference, there was a general consensus that floating exchange rates were preferable to fixed exchange rates.

Answer: F
Medium
Page: 309

68. The task of the World Bank is to maintain order in the international monetary system.

Answer: F
Medium
Page: 309

69. Bretton Woods is a small community is the Yorkshire area of Great Britain.

THE COLLAPSE OF THE FIXED EXCHANGE RATE SYSTEM

Answer: T
Medium
Page: 311

70. The system of fixed exchange rates established at Bretton Woods worked well until the late 1960s, when it began to show signs of strain.

Answer: F
Medium
Page: 312

71. Most economists trace the breakup of the fixed exchange rate system to the European macroeconomic policy package of 1965-68.

Answer: T
Hard
Page: 312

72. In August of 1971, President Nixon announced that the dollar was no longer convertible into gold.

Answer: T
Medium
Page: 312

73. The Bretton Woods system had an Achilles' heel: The system could not work if its key currency, the US dollar, was under speculative attack.

THE FLOATING EXCHANGE RATE REGIME

Answer: F
Medium
Page: 313

74. The floating exchange rate regime that followed the collapse of the fixed exchange rate system was formalized in 1976 when World Bank members met in Brussels and agreed to the rules for the international monetary system that are in place today.

Answer: T
Hard
Page: 313

75. According to our textbook, since March 1973, exchange rates have become much more volatile and less predictable than they were between 1945 and 1973.

Answer: T
Medium
Page: 316

76. The so-called Group of Five major industrial countries includes Great Britain, France, Japan, Germany, and the United States

FIXED VERSUS FLOATING EXCHANGE RATES

Answer: F
Medium
Page: 317

77. Monetary expansion can lead to inflation, which puts upward pressure on a fixed exchange rate.

Answer: T
Medium
Page: 317

78. Advocates of a floating exchange rate regime argue that removal of the obligation to maintain exchange rate parity would restore monetary control to the government.

Answer: T
Medium
Page: 318

79. Critics of a floating exchange rate regime argue that speculation can cause fluctuations in exchange rates.

EXCHANGE RATE REGIMES IN PRACTICE

Answer: F
Medium
Page: 319

80. Pegged exchange rates are popular among many of the world's largest nations.

Answer: T
Medium
Page: 320

81. There is some evidence that adopting a pegged exchange rate regime does moderate inflationary pressures in a country.

Answer: T
Medium
Page: 320

82. A country that introduces a currency board commits itself to converting its domestic currency on demand into another currency at a fixed exchange rate.

Answer: F
Medium
Page: 321

83. In the context of international monetary systems, EMS stands for Electronic Monetary Standard.

RECENT ACTIVITIES AND THE FUTURE OF THE IMF

Answer: F
Easy
Page: 323

84. The activities of the IMF have waned over the past 30 years.

Answer: T
Medium
Page: 324

85. A currency crises occurs when a speculative attack on the exchange value of a currency results in a sharp depreciation in the value of a currency or forces authorities to expend large volumes of international currency reserves and sharply increase interest rates to defend the prevailing exchange rates.

Answer: F
Medium
Page: 324

86. A banking crisis is a situation in which a country cannot service its foreign debt obligations, whether private sector of governmental debt.

Answer: T
Medium
Page: 324

87. The Third World debt crisis had its roots in the OPEC oil price hikes of 1973 and 1979.

Answer: T
Hard
Page: 326

88. The Mexican peso had been pegged to the dollar since the early 1980s when the IMF had made it a condition for lending money to the Mexican government to help bail the country out of 1982 a financial crisis.

Answer: F
Medium
Page: 327

89. The IMF's involvement in Russia came about as the result of a persistent increase in the value of the Russian ruble.

Answer: T
Medium
Page: 329

90. The financial crisis that erupted across Southeast Asia during the fall of 1997 has emerged as the biggest challenge ever for the IMF.

ESSAY QUESTIONS

Hard
Page: 308

91. Explain how the automatic adjustment mechanism for balancing trade disequilibrium works under the gold standard.

Answer: The mechanism for trade balance disequilibrium adjustment can be most easily described with an example. Suppose that there are only two countries in the world - Japan and the U.S. Imagine that Japan's trade balance is in surplus because it exports more to the U.S. than it imports from the U.S. Japanese exporters are paid in U.S. dollars, which they exchange for Japanese yen at a Japanese bank. The Japanese bank submits the dollars to the U.S. government and demands payment of gold in return. Under the gold standard, when Japan has a trade surplus, there will be a net flow of gold from the U.S. to Japan. These gold flows automatically reduce the U.S. money supply and swell Japan's money supply. An increase in money supply will raise prices in Japan, while a decrease in the U.S. money supply will push U.S. prices downward. The rise in the price of Japanese goods will decrease demand for these goods, while the fall in the prices of U.S. goods will increase demand for these goods. Thus, Japan will start to buy more from the U.S., and the U.S. will buy less from Japan, until a balance-of-trade equilibrium is achieved. This same logic can be extended to any number of countries.

Medium
Page: 309

92. Describe what happened at the 1944 Bretton Woods conference. Are the monetary principles established by the Bretton Woods conference still in effect today?

Answer: In 1944, at the height of World War II, representatives from 44 countries met at Bretton Woods, New Hampshire, to design a new international monetary system. The purpose of the conference was to build an economic order that would facilitate postwar economic growth and cooperation. Three primary initiatives resulted from the conference:

a) The establishment of the International Monetary Fund (IMF).
b) The establishment of the World Bank.
c) A call for the establishment of a set of fixed currency exchange rates that would be policed by the IMF.
d) A commitment not to use devaluation as a weapon of competitive trade policy.

The task of the IMF would be to maintain order in the international monetary system, and the World Bank was designed to promote general economic development. In regard to currency exchange rates, all countries were to fix the value of their currency in terms of gold but were not required to exchange their currencies for gold. Only the U.S. dollar remained convertible into gold - at a price of $35 per ounce. Each other country decided what it wanted its exchange rate to be vis-a-vis the dollar and then calculated the gold par value of its currency based on that selected dollar exchange rate. All participating countries agreed to try to maintain the value of their currency within 1 percent of the par value.

Today, the IMF and the World Bank still play a role in the international monetary system. The system of fixed exchange rates established at Bretton Woods worked well until the late 1960s, when it began to show signs of strain. The system finally collapsed in 1973, and since then we have had a managed float system.

Medium
Page: 311

93. Describe the role of the World Bank in the international community. How does the World Bank contribute to the overall stability of the global monetary system?

Answer: The World Bank was established by the 1944 Bretton Woods agreement. The official name for the World Bank is the International Bank for Reconstruction and Development (IBRD). The bank's initial mission was to help finance the building of Europe's war torn economy by providing low-interest loans. As it turned out, the role of the World Bank in Europe was overshadowed by the Marshall Plan, under which the U.S. lent money directly to European nations to help them rebuild in the aftermath of World War II. As a result, the bank turned its attention to lending money for development in Third World nations.

Although the World Bank does not play a direct role in monetary policy, it contributes to the global money system by providing low interest loans to developing countries. These loans, which are used for such things as public-sector projects (i.e. power stations, roads, bridges, etc.), agricultural development, education, population control, and urban development, are intended to promote economic development and increase the standard of living in developing countries.

As the result of some disappointment in regard to loaning money to countries that do not practice sound economy policy, the World Bank has recently devised a new type of loan. In addition to providing funds to support specific projects, the bank will now also provide loans for the government of a nation to use as it sees fit in return for promises on macroeconomic policy.

Medium
Page: 315

94. What explains the rise in the value of the U.S. dollar between 1980 and 1985? Why was the demand for dollars greater than the supply, even though the U.S. was running a large trade deficit?

Answer: The U.S. dollar rose in the early 1980s in spite of the trade deficit. Strong economic growth in the U.S. attracted heavy inflows of capital from foreign investors seeking high returns on capital assets. Moreover, high real interest rates attracted foreign investors seeking high returns on financial assets. At the same time, political turmoil in other parts of the world, along with relatively slow economic growth in the developed countries of Europe, helped create the view that the U.S. was a good place for investment. These inflows of capital increased the demand for dollars in the foreign exchange market, which pushed the value of the dollar upwards against other currencies.

Medium
Page: 317

95. What is the difference between a free floating exchange rate and a managed or dirty float system?

Answer: In a free floating system there is no governmental invention in the market, while in a managed or dirty float system governments intervene to influence the value of their currency.

Hard
Page: 317

96. Describe the difference between fixed and floating exchange rates. Which is better? Explain your answer.

Answer: Under a fixed rate system the value of a currency is fixed (usually in terms of U.S. dollars) and is only allowed to change under a specific set of circumstances. The value of a fixed rate system is that it introduces monetary discipline (on a country level), discourages currency speculation, reduces uncertainty (in regard to future currency movements), and, according to the proponents of fixed rates, has little or no effect on trade balance adjustments. In contrast, under a floating rate system, currencies are allowed to float freely (in practice, the majority of floating rate systems are either managed in some way by government intervention or are pegged to another currency). The benefits of a floating rate system is that it gives countries monetary policy autonomy and, according to the proponents, provides a way for countries to correct trade deficits (i.e. an exchange rate depreciation should correct a trade balance by making a country's exports cheaper and its imports more expensive).

There is no right or wrong answer to this question - we simply don't know which system is better. We do know that a fixed rate system modeled along the lines of the Bretton Woods system will not work. Conversely, advocates of a fixed rate system argue that speculation is a major disadvantage of floating rates. Perhaps a modified fixed rate system will produce the type of economic stability that will contribute to greater growth in international trade and investments.

Medium:
Page: 318

97. Under a system of freely floating exchange rates, how would trade balance disequilibria be adjusted?

Answer: Under a freely floating system if a country is running a trade deficit, the imbalance between the supply and demand of that country's currency in the foreign exchange markets will lead to a depreciation of its exchange rate. In turn, by making its exports cheaper, and its imports more expensive, an exchange rate depreciation should ultimately correct the trade deficit.

Medium
Page: 318

98. How do exchange rates affect individual international businesses? Do international businesses like stable rates or volatile rates? Explain your answer.

Answer: The volatility of the present system of floating exchange rates is a problem for international businesses. Exchange rates are difficult to predict, and introduce a major source of "uncertainty" in international trade that is unnerving for many businesses. For example, a company like Case Tractor may build a high quality product in the U.S. and make a profit by exporting it to Japan. But if the Japanese yen depreciates against the U.S. dollar, the relative cost of the tractor in Japan will go up. This will either lower the demand for the tractor in Japan or force Case to lower its price (and accept a lower profit).

The majority of international businesses would probably prefer stability in exchange rates. As depicted above, exchange rate fluctuations introduce uncertainty into the international business process, which is uncertain enough to begin with. Imagine how frustrating it must be for the mangers of firms like Case Tractor, who may lose sales in an international market or suffer declines in profitability that has nothing to do with the quality of their products, but hinge solely on currency rate volatility. This uncertainty, according to the critics, dampens the growth of international trade and investment across all industries.

Medium
Page: 335

99. What can international business organizations do to help shape global monetary policy and encourage growth in international trade and investment?

Answer: This question is designed to encourage classroom discussion and/or to encourage students to "think" about how international businesses can play a constructive role in shaping monetary policy and increase international trade and investment. Obviously, businesses can lobby their respective governments to encourage steps that minimize currency volatility and maximize international business opportunities. In addition, businesses can act prudently in terms of their individual trade practices, and by doing so, lessen the chance that nations will use their currencies (through devaluation) to protect their local industries. Finally, businesses can help sponsor international forums (like the World Bank) that facilitate the growth in international trade and investment.

Medium
Page: 336

100. Given the current volatility in exchange rates, what actions can firms take to develop strategic flexibility?

Answer: Strategic flexibility can be gained by having production facilities in different locations world wide, and shifting production volumes to take advantage of favorable exchange rates. By contracting out low value added manufacturing, firms can also switch suppliers in order to adjust to changing exchange rates.

CHAPTER 11

THE GLOBAL CAPITAL MARKET

MULTIPLE-CHOICE QUESTIONS

BENEFITS OF THE GLOBAL CAPITAL MARKET

Answer: A
Easy
Page: 344

1. A __________ market brings together those who want to invest money and those who want to borrow money.

A. capital
B. fiduciary
C. sanctioned
D. statutory

Answer: C
Easy
Page: 344

2. A capital market brings together those who want to __________ money and those who want to __________ money.

A. solicit, spend
B. disperse, deposit
C. invest, borrow
D. spend, solicit

Answer: A
Easy
Page: 344

3. __________ are the financial service companies that connect investors and borrowers, either directly or indirectly.

A. Market makers
B. Commerce brokers
C. Economic facilitators
D. Trade brokers

Answer: D
Medium
Page: 344

4. Which statement best describes the role of market makers?

A. market makers arrange for the sale of new issues of stock
B. the liquidity of equities in the equity markets is insured by market makers
C. the electronic network of buyers and sellers is maintained by market makers
D. they are financial service companies that connect investors to borrowers

Answer: B
Medium
Page: 344

5. Commercial banks perform a(n) __________ connection function.

A. direct
B. indirect
C. continuous
D. straight

Answer: C
Medium
Page: 344

6. Investment banks perform a __________ connection function.

A. continuous
B. indirect
C. direct
D. straight

Answer: A
Medium
Page: 345

7. Capital market loans to corporations are either __________ loans or __________ loans.

A. equity, debt
B. debit, credit
C. equity, credit
D. debit, debt

Answer: D
Medium
Page: 345

8. A(n) __________ loan is made when a corporation sells stock to investors.

A. duty
B. credit
C. debt
D. equity

Answer: C
Medium
Page: 345

9. Under which type of financial instrument do firms pay funds to investors in an amount determined by the board of directions, dependent upon the firm's profitability?

A. foreign bond
B. eurobonds
C. equity
D. eurocurrency

Answer: A
Medium
Page: 345

10. A(n) __________ loan requires a corporation to repay a predetermined portion of the loan amount (the sum of the principal plus the specified interest) at regular intervals regardless of how much profit it is making.

A. debt
B. credit
C. equity
D. arrears

Answer: D
Easy
Page: 345

11. In a purely domestic capital market, the pool of investors is limited to:

A. people who are self-employed
B. 401K plans and other qualified investment programs
C. international investment brokers
D. residents of the country

Answer: B
Medium
Page: 345

12. Perhaps the most important drawback of the limited liquidity of a purely domestic capital market is that the cost of capital tends to be:

A. lower than it is in an international market
B. higher than it is in an international market
C. exactly double the cost of capital in a global capital market
D. set by the government

Answer: A
Medium
Page: 345

13. The cost of capital is the:

A. rate of return that borrowers must pay investors
B. the maintenance fees that investors pay on their accounts
C. the "load" or sales fee that investors pay when they buy securities
D. the fixed interest rate set by the government

Answer: C
Easy
Page: 345

14. The cost of capital is frequently referred to as the:

A. dividend rate
B. load
C. price of borrowed money
D. domestic tariff rate

Answer: C
Medium
Page: 346

15. By using the __________ capital market, investors have a much wider range of investment opportunities than in a purely __________ capital market.

A. indigenous, exogenous
B. domestic, global
C. global, domestic
D. local, exogenous

Answer: A
Medium
Page: 348

16. __________ refers to movements in a stock portfolio's value that are attributable to macroeconomic forces affecting all firms in an economy, rather than factors specific to an individual stock.

A. Systematic risk
B. Rational risk
C. Speculative risk
D. Capital risk

Answer: D
Medium
Page: 348

17. The systematic risk is the level of __________ risk in an economy.

A. contractible
B. diversifiable
C. expandable
D. nondiversifiable

Answer: B
Hard
Page: 348

18. The correlation between the movement of stock markets in different countries is:

A. extremely low
B. relatively low
C. almost 100%
D. relatively high

Answer: B
Medium
Page: 348

19. The relatively low correlation between the movement of stock markets in different countries reflects two basic factors. First, countries pursue different macroeconomic policies and face different economic conditions, and second:

A. regulatory controls vary across countries
B. different stock markets are still somewhat segmented from each other by capital controls
C. countries have different currency exchange rates
D. countries trade stock in different time zones

Answer: A
Medium
Page: 348

20. According to our textbook, restrictions on cross-boarder capital flows are:

A. declining rapidly
B. declining slowly
C. increasingly slowly
D. increasing rapidly

Answer: C
Medium
Page: 348

21. Limits on the amount of a firm's stock that a foreigner can own and limits on the ability of a country's citizens to invest their money outside of their respective country are called:

A. monetary controls
B. fiduciary controls
C. capital controls
D. economic controls

Answer: C
Hard
Page: 348

22. According to a classic study cited in our textbook, a fully diversified portfolio that contains stocks from many countries is ________ as a fully diversified portfolio that contains only U.S. stocks.

A. more than twice as risky
B. more than three times as risky
C. less than twice as risky
D. less than three times as risky

GROWTH OF THE GLOBAL CAPITAL MARKET

Answer: D
Hard
Page: 350

23. International bank lending from 1983 to the end of 1997 has:

A. decreased rapidly
B. decreased slightly
C. increased slightly
D. increased rapidly

Answer: D
Medium
Page: 350

24. The __________ has been the favored currency for issuing international bonds.

A. Japanese yen
B. British pound
C. German mark
D. U.S. dollar

Answer: A
Medium
Page: 350

25. During the period between 1985 and 1987, international equity offerings:

A. increased rapidly
B. increased slightly
C. decreased slightly
D. decreased rapidly

Answer: D
Hard
Page: 351

26. According to one study cited in our textbook, the cost of recording, transmitting, and processing information has fallen by __________ since 1964.

A. 10 percent
B. 25 percent
C. 60 percent
D. 95 percent

Answer: C
Medium
Page: 352

27. In country after country, __________ have been the most tightly regulated of all industries.

A. medical services
B. legal services
C. financial services
D. transportation services

Answer: B
Hard
Page: 352

28. In Great Britain, the so-called __________ of October 1986 removed barriers that had existed between banks and stockbrokers and allowed foreign financial service companies to enter the British stock market.

A. market collapse
B. Big Bang
C. Little Bang
D. market explosion

Answer: C
Hard
Page: 352

29. In France, the __________ of 1987 is gradually opening the French stock market to outsiders and to foreign and domestic banks.

A. market collapse
B. market explosion
C. Little Bang
D. Big Bang

Answer: C
Medium
Page: 352

30. In addition to the deregulation of the financial services industry, many countries beginning in the 1970s started to dismantle __________ controls, loosening both restrictions on inward investment by foreigners and outward investment by their own citizens and corporations.

A. economic
B. fiduciary
C. capital
D. monetary

Answer: D
Hard
Page: 353

31. According to the World Bank, capital flows into the emerging economies of the world went from less than $50 billion in 1990 to over __________ in 1997.

A. $77 billion
B. $145 billion
C. $288 billion
D. $336 billion

Answer: D
Hard
Page: 353

32. When Harvard economist Martin Feldstein uses the term "hot money," he is referring to:

A. long-term capital
B. extremely high interest rates
C. extremely low interest rates
D. short-term capital

Answer: B
Hard
Page: 353

33. When Harvard economist Martin Feldstein uses the term "patient money," he is referring to:

A. short-term capital
B. long-term capital
C. extremely low interest rates
D. extremely high interest rates

Answer: C
Hard
Page: 353

34. Harvard economist Martin Feldstein claims that Mexico's economic problems in the mid-1990s were the result of too much __________ money flowing in and out of the country and too little __________ money.

A. patient, hot
B. fluid, diligent
C. hot, patient
D. diligent, fluid

Answer: C
Medium
Page: 354

35. IMF research suggests that the volatility in financial markets over the past 25 years has:

A. increased
B. decreased
C. remained the same
D. disappeared

THE EUROCURRENCY MARKET

Answer: C
Medium
Page: 355

36. A Eurocurrency:

A. cannot be exchanged for a non-Eurocurrency
B. is typically denominated in ECUs
C. is any currency banked outside the country that issued it
D. is planned for 2006

Answer: B
Medium
Page: 355

37. Eurodollars, which account for about two-thirds of all eurocurrencies, are dollars backed outside of:

A. Europe
B. the United States
C. Asia
D. countries with hard currencies

Answer: C
Medium
Page: 355

38. The euro-yen, euro-deutsche mark, and euor-pound are all examples of:

A. European currency markets
B. dual currencies
C. eurocurrencies
D. trade areas

Answer: B
Hard
Page: 355

39. The eurocurrency market was born in the __________ when Eastern European holders of dollars, including the former Soviet Union, were afraid to deposit their holdings of dollars in the U.S. least they be seized by the U.S. government to settle U.S. residents' claims against business losses resulting from the Communist takeover of Eastern Europe.

A. mid-1940s
B. mid-1950s
C. late-1960s
D. early-1080s

Answer: D
Medium
Page: 355

40 What makes eurocurrency deposits so attractive to savers?

A. the spread is more on eurocurrencies than on domestic currencies
B. borrower's reserve requirements are lower
C. all transactions are required to be processed through a European bank
D. banks typically pay higher interest rates on eurocurrency deposits than domestic deposits

Answer: C
Hard
Page: 356

41. The eurocurrency market received a major push in _________ when the British government prohibited British banks from lending British pounds to finance non-British trade, a business that had been very profitable for British banks.

A. 1941
B. 1949
C. 1957
D. 1966

Answer: C
Medium
Page: 356

42. The main factor that makes the eurocurrency market so attractive to both depositors and borrowers is:

A. its favorable exchange rates against other currencies
B. the convertibility of eurocurrency to gold
C. its lack of government regulation
D. its low commission rate for currency trades

Answer: B
Medium
Page: 356

43. What makes eurocurrency loans attractive to borrowers?

A. borrower's reserve requirements are lower
B. banks typically charge lower interest rate for eurocurrency loans than for loans denominated in the domestic currency
C. they can earn higher interest rates on deposits
D. all transactions are required to take place in European country

Answer: A
Medium
Page: 356

44. The eurocurrency market has two drawbacks. First, when depositors use a regulated banking system, they know that the probability of a bank failure that would cause them to lose their deposits is very low. Second,:

A. borrowing funds internationally can expose a company to foreign exchange risk
B. depositors typically receive a higher interest rate on deposits
C. borrowers typically pay a lower interest rate on loans
D. eurocurrencies are subject to high government regulation

Answer: D
Medium
Page: 357

45. The eurocurrency market has two drawbacks. First, borrowing funds internationally can expose a company to foreign exchange risk. Second,:

A. the spread between the eurocurrency deposit rate and the eurocurrency lending rate is less than the spread between the domestic deposit and lending rates
B. eurocurrencies are subject to high government regulation
C. depositors typically receive a higher interest rate on deposits
D. when borrowers use a regulated banking system, they know that the probability of a bank that would cause them to lose their deposits is low

THE GLOBAL BOND MARKET

Answer: D
Hard
Page: 358

46. The global bond market grew rapidly during the:

A. 1920s and 1930s
B. 1940s and 1950s
C. 1970s and 1980s
D. 1980s and 1990s

Answer: C
Easy
Page: 358

47. The most common kind of bond is a __________ rate bond.

A. alterable
B. accelerating
C. fixed
D. variable

Answer: A
Easy
Page: 358

48. International bonds are of two types. These are:

A. foreign bonds and eurobonds
B. world bonds and industrial bonds
C. IMF bonds and eurobonds
D. global bonds and industrial bonds

Answer: B
Easy
Page: 358

49. International bonds are of two types. These are eurobonds and:

A. global bonds
B. foreign bonds
C. IMF bonds
D. industrial bonds

Answer: B
Easy
Page: 358

50. International bonds are of two types. These are foreign bonds and:

A. asia-pacific bonds
B. eurobonds
C. IMF bonds
D. World Bank bonds

Answer: D
Medium
Page: 358

51. __________ are sold outside of the borrower's country and are denominated in the currency of the country in which they are issued.

A. IMF bonds
B. Asia-pacific bonds
C. World Bank bonds
D. Foreign bonds

Answer: A
Medium
Page: 358

52. __________ are normally underwritten by an international syndicate of banks and placed in countries other than the one in whose currency the bond is denominated.

A. Eurobonds
B. World Bank bonds
C. Asiabonds
D. Foreign bonds

Answer: C
Hard
Page: 358

53. A bond issued by a German corporation, denominated in U.S. dollars, and sold to investors outside of the U.S. by an international syndicate of banks is referred to as a:

A. foreign bond
B. asiabond
C. eurobond
D. World Bank bond

Answer: B
Medium
Page: 358

54. __________ account for the lion's share of international bond issues.

A. Foreign bonds
B. Eurobonds
C. IMF bonds
D. World Bank bonds

Answer: D
Hard
Page: 358

55. The following are attractive characteristics of the __________ market: An absence of regulatory inference; less stringent disclosure requirements than in most domestic markets; a favorable tax status.

A. foreign bond
B. World Bank bond
C. IMF bond
D. eurobond

THE GLOBAL EQUITY MARKET

Answer: C
Medium
Page: 359

56. The largest of the domestic equity markets are found in:

A. China, Japan, Germany, and the United States
B. Japan, South Korea, India, and the United States
C. Germany, Japan, Britain, and the United States
D. Canada, Japan, Britain, and the United States

Answer: C
Hard
Page: 359

57. By 1994, individuals and institutions had invested more than __________ in stocks outside their home markets.

A. $500 billion
B. $920 billion
C. $1.3 trillion
D. $2.6 trillion

Answer: A
Hard
Page:359

58. Which of the following was not mentioned in our textbook as a reason that companies list their stocks in the equity markets of foreign countries?

A. for political reasons
B. it is a prelude to issuing stock in that market to raise capital
C. to facilitate future acquisitions of foreign companies
D. the company's stock and stock options can be used to compensate local management and employees

FOREIGN EXCHANGE RISK AND THE COST OF CAPITAL

Answer: A
Medium
Page: 360

59. Our textbook has emphasized repeatedly that a firm:

A. can borrow funds at a lower cost on the global capital market than on the domestic capital market
B. can borrow funds at a lower costs on the domestic capital market than the global capital market
C. can borrows funds on the global capital market and the domestic capital market at the same rate
D. cannot borrow money outside its home country

Answer: D
Easy
Page: 360

60. When a firm borrows funds from the _________ capital market, it must weigh the benefits of a lower interest rate against the risks of an increase in the real cost of capital due to adverse exchange rate movements.

A. local
B. state
C. domestic
D. global

IMPLICATIONS FOR BUSINESS

Answer: A
Medium
Page: 361

61. Government regulation tends to:

A. raise the cost of capital in most domestic capital markets
B. lower the cost of capital in most domestic capital markets
C. have no impact on the cost of capital in most domestic capital markets
D. smooth out the cost of capital in domestic capital markets

Answer: B
Medium
Page: 361

62. According to our textbook, the global capital market will _________ over the next decade.

A. decrease in both importance and degree of integration over the next decade
B. increase in both importance and degree of integration over the next decade
C. increase in importance but decrease in degree of integration over the next decade
D. decrease in importance but increase in degree of integration over the next decade

TRUE-FALSE QUESTIONS

BENEFITS OF THE GLOBAL CAPITAL MARKET

Answer: T
Easy
Page: 344

63. A capital market brings together those who want to invest money and those who want to borrow money.

Answer: F
Medium
Page: 344

64. Commercial banks perform a direct connection function.

Answer: T
Easy
Page: 345

65. Capital market loans to corporations are either equity loans or debt loans.

Answer: F
Medium
Page: 345

66. A debt loan is made when a corporation sells stock to an investor.

Answer: F
Medium
Page: 345

67. A global capital market benefits borrowers and hurts investors.

Answer: T
Medium
Page: 345

68. Perhaps the most important drawback of the limited liquidity of a purely domestic capital market is that the cost of capital tends to be higher than it is in an international market.

Answer: T
Easy
Page: 345

69. The cost of capital is the rate of return that borrowers must pay investors.

Answer: F
Medium
Page: 346

70. By using the global capital market, investors have a much narrower range of investment opportunities than in a purely domestic capital market.

Answer: T
Medium
Page: 348

71. Systematic risk refers to movements in a stock portfolio's value that are attributable to macroeconomic forces affecting all firms in an economy, rather than factors specific to an individual firm.

Answer: F
Medium
Page: 348

72. The Standard & Poor's 500 summarizes stock movements in less developed "emerging economies."

Answer: F
Medium
Page: 348

73. There is a relatively high correlation between the movement of stock markets in different countries.

Answer: T
Medium
Page: 349

74. Floating exchange rates introduce an element of risk into investing in foreign assets.

GROWTH OF THE GLOBAL CAPITAL MARKET

Answer: F
Medium
Page: 350

75. The Japanese yen has been the favored currency for issuing international bonds.

Answer: T
Medium
Page: 352

76. In country after country, financial services have been the most tightly regulated of all industries.

Answer: T
Medium
Page: 353

77. A lack of information about the fundamental quality of foreign investments may encourage speculative flows in the global capital market.

Answer: F
Hard
Page: 354

78. IMF research suggests that there has been a significant increase in the volatility of financial markets over the past 25 years.

THE EUROCURRENCY MARKET

Answer: T
Easy
Page: 355

79. A eurocurrency is any currency banked outside of its country of origin.

Answer: F
Hard
Page: 355

80. Eurodollars, which account for about 25 percent of all eurocurrencies, are dollars banked outside of the United States.

Answer: T
Medium
Page: 356

81. The main factor that makes the eurocurrency market so attractive to both depositors and borrowers is its lack of government regulation.

Answer: F
Hard
Page: 356

82. The spread between the eurocurrency deposit rate and the eurocurrency lending rate is more than the spread between the domestic deposit and lending rates.

Answer: T
Medium
Page: 356

83. Domestic currency deposits are regulated in all industrialized countries.

Answer: T
Medium
Page: 357

84. Clearly, there are very strong financial motivations for companies to use the eurocurrency market. By doing so, they receive a higher interest rate on deposits and pay less for loans.

THE GLOBAL BOND MARKET

Answer: F
Medium
Page: 358

85. International bonds are of two types: foreign bonds and IMF bonds.

Answer: T
Medium
Page: 358

86. Foreign bonds are sold outside of the borrower's country and are denominated in the currency of the country in which they are issued.

Answer: T
Medium
Page: 358

87. Eurobonds are normally underwritten by an international syndicate of banks and placed in countries other than the one in whose currency the bond is denominated.

THE GLOBAL EQUITY MARKET

Answer: T
Medium
Page: 359

88. A consequence of the trend towards international equity investment is the internationalization of corporate ownership.

Answer: F
Medium
Page: 359

89. It is illegal for a company to list its stock on the equity market of foreign country.

FOREIGN EXCHANGE RISK AND THE COST OF CAPITAL

Answer: F
Medium
Page: 360

90. Our textbook has emphasized repeatedly that a firm can borrow funds at a lower cost on the domestic capital market than the global capital market.

Answer: T
Medium
Page: 360

91. Adverse movements in foreign exchange rates can substantially increase the cost of foreign currency loans.

Answer: T
Medium
Page: 360

92. Unpredictable movements in exchange rages can inject risk into foreign currency borrowing.

ESSAY QUESTIONS

Easy
Page: 344

93. Why do we have capital markets? What is their function? Who are the "market makers" in capital markets?

Answer: A capital market brings together those who want to invest money and those who want to borrow money. Market makers are the financial service companies that connect investors and borrowers, either directly or directly. Commercial banks perform an indirect connection function. They take cash deposits from corporations and individuals and pay them a rate of interest in return. They then lend that money to borrowers at a higher rate of interest, making a profit from the difference in interest rates. Investment banks perform a direct connection function. They bring investors and borrowers together and charge commissions for doing do.

Medium
Page: 345

94. What is the difference between an equity loan and a debt loan?

Answer: An equity loan is made when a corporation sells stock to investors. The money the corporation receives in return for its stock can be used to purchase plants and equipment, fund R&D projects, pay wages, and so on. A share of stock gives its holder a claim to a firm's profit stream. The corporation honors this claim by paying dividends to stockholders. The amount of the dividends is not fixed in advance. Rather, it is determined by management based on how much profit the corporation is making. A debt loan is made when a corporation borrows money from a financial institution. A debt loan requires the corporation to repay a predetermined portion of the loan amount at regular intervals regardless of how much profit it is making.

Medium
Page: 345

95. Why are international capital markets needed? What functions do they provide beyond that available in most domestic markets - and especially domestic markets as big as the U.S. and Japan?

Answer: There are two reasons why an international capital market offers an improvement over a purely domestic capital market. First, from a borrower's perspective, it increases the supply of funds available for borrowing and lowers the cost of capital. Second, from an investor's perspective it provides a wider range of investment opportunities, thereby allowing investors to build a portfolio of international investments that diversifies risk.

Hard
Page: 348

96. What explains the relatively low correlation between the movement of stock markets in different countries?

Answer: The relatively low correlation between the movement of stock markets in different countries reflects two basic factors. First, countries pursue different macroeconomic policies and face different economic conditions, so their stock markets respond to different forces and can move in different ways. Second, different stock markets are still somewhat segmented from each other by capital controls - that is, by restrictions on cross-border capital flows (although such restrictions are declining rapidly). The most common restrictions include limits on the amount of a firm's stock that a foreigner can own and limits on the ability of a country's citizens to invest their money outside that country.

Medium
Page: 355

97. What is a eurocurrency? What are eurodollars?

Answer: A eurocurrency is any currency banked outside of its country of origin. Eurodollars, which account for about two-thirds of all eurocurrencies, are dollars banked outside of the United States.

Medium
Page: 358

98. What are the drawbacks or disadvantages of the eurocurrency market?

Answer: The eurocurrency market has two drawbacks. First, when depositors use a regulated banking system, they know that the probability of a bank failure that would cause them to lose their deposits is very low. Regulation maintains the liquidity of the banking system. In an unregulated system such as the eurocurrency market, the probability of a bank failure that would cause depositors to lose their money is greater. Second, borrowing funds internationally can expose a company to foreign exchange risk.

Medium
Page: 358

99. What is the difference between foreign bonds and eurobonds? Which are more common?

Answer: Foreign bonds are bonds sold outside the borrower's country and denominated in the currency of the country in which they are issued. Eurobonds are typically underwritten by an international syndicate of banks and are placed in countries other than the one in whose currency they bond is denominated. Because of their wider coverage and lesser regulation, eurobonds are much more common than foreign bonds.

Medium
Page: 359

100. Critically evaluate the following statement: "Given the international capital markets firms use, it is senseless to any longer refer to firms as "American firms" or "British firms" or "Japanese firms." Firms are now truly stateless organizations with nationality."

Answer: This statement perhaps overstates the current situation, but clearly identifies a trend. Firms are increasingly attracting shareholders from around the world, selling their stock on multiple international exchanges, and floating debt in a number of countries. But this is only true for a small percentage of companies worldwide, and even than a majority of the shareholders and the management team are still typically from a single country.

Hard
Page: 359

101. What motivates firms to list their stock on a foreign equity market?

Answer: There are several reasons that motivate firms to list their stock on a foreign exchange market. First, listing stock on a foreign market is often a prelude to issuing stock in that market to raise capital. The idea is to tap into the liquidity of foreign markets, thereby increasing the funds available for investment and lowering a firm's cost of capital. Second, firms list their stock on foreign equity markets to facilitate future acquisitions of foreign companies. Third, firms list their stock on foreign exchange markets so that they can use their stock and stock options to compensate local management and employees. Finally, companies list their stock of foreign equity markets because it satisfies the desire for local ownership, and it increases their visibility with local employees, customers, suppliers, and bankers.

Medium
Page: 361

102. What has the growth in global capital markets meant to investors and borrowers?

Answer: On the investment side, the growth of the global capital market is providing opportunities for firms, institutions, and individuals to diversify their investments to limit risk. By holding a diverse portfolio of stocks and bonds in different nations, an investor can reduce total risk to a lower level than can be achieved in a purely domestic setting.

On the borrowing side, by using a global capital market, firms can often borrow funds at a lower cost than is possible in a purely domestic capital market. This conclusion holds no matter what form of borrowing a firm uses - equity, bonds, or cash loans. The lower cost of capital on the global market reflects their greater liquidity and the general absence of government regulation.

CHAPTER 12

THE STRATEGY OF INTERNATIONAL BUSINESS

MULTIPLE-CHOICE QUESTIONS

STRATEGY AND THE FIRM

Answer: B
Easy
Page: 379

1. According to our textbook, it is useful to think of the firm as a __________, composed of a series of distinct activities, including production, marketing, materials management, R&D, human resources, information systems, and the firm infrastructure.

A. functional stream
B. value chain
C. inertia chain
D. momentum machine

Answer: D
Medium
Page: 379

2. Value chain activities can be categorized as:

A. primary activities and secondary activities
B. input activities and throughput activities
C. profitable activities and unprofitable activities
D. primary activities and support activities

Answer: A
Easy
Page: 379

3. The __________ activities of a firm have to do with creating the product, marketing and delivering the product to buyers, and providing support and after-sale service to the buyers of the product.

A. primary
B. subordinate
C. ancillary
D. support

Answer: A
Medium
Page: 379

4. In the context of value chain analysis, the primary activities of a firm include:

A. manufacturing, marketing, and sales & service
B. manufacturing, human resources, and materials management
C. infrastructure (structure and leadership, R&D, and human resources
D. human resources, sales & service, and R&D

Answer: D
Medium
Page: 379

5. In the context of value chain analysis, the support activities of a firm include:

A. sales & service, human resources, materials management, R&D
B. marketing, sales & service, infrastructure (structure and leadership, and materials management
C. infrastructure (structure and leadership), human resources, R&D, and materials management
D. manufacturing, sales & service, human resources, and R&D

Answer: B
Medium
Page: 379

6. In the context of value chain analysis, __________ controls the transmission of physical materials through the value chain - from procurement through production and into distribution.

A. manufacturing management
B. materials management
C. marketing management
D. assets management

Answer: C
Easy
Page: 380

7. A firm's __________ can be defined as the actions that managers take to attain the goals of the firm.

A. systems
B. value chain
C. strategy
D. operations

Answer: D
Medium
Page: 381

8. Which of the following statements is not an accurate reflection of the impact of global expansion on firm profitability?

A. a firm can earn a greater return from its core competencies
B. a firm realizes greater experience curve economies, which reduces the cost of value creation
C. a firm realizes location economies by dispersing particular value creation activities to those locations where they can be performed most efficiently
D. a firm typically earns less from its distinctive skills

Answer: D
Easy
Page: 381

9. The term __________ refers to skills within a firm that competitors cannot easily match.

A. discriminate attributes
B. indigenous properties
C. value chain
D. core competencies

Answer: A
Medium
Page: 382

10. According to our textbook, a firm's __________ allow it to reduce the costs of value creation and/or to create value in such a way that premium pricing is possible.

A. core competencies
B. indigenous properties
C. discriminate attributes
D. special attributes

Answer: D
Easy
Page: 383

11. Economies that arise from performing a value creation activity in the optimal location for that activity are called:

A. site expediencies
B. location synergies
C. site commerce
D. location economies

Answer: C
Medium
Page: 383

12. Suppose Ford Motor decided to manufacturer transmissions in Belgium, because a detailed analysis of the country specific advantages indicated that Belgium is the optimal place in the world to produce transmissions. In this example, Ford is capturing __________ by manufacturing transmissions in Belgium.

A. location synergies
B. site expediencies
C. location economies
D. site commerce

Answer: A
Medium
Page: 383

13. Locating a value creation activity in the optimal location for that activity can have one or two effects. First, it can lower the costs of value creation and help the firm to achieve a low-cost position, and/or:

A. it can enable a firm to differentiate its product offering from that of competitors
B. it can lower the cost of marketing and service
C. it can expedite the research and development process
D. it can create political good well

Answer: C
Medium
Page: 383

14. According to our textbook, a firm creates a __________ by dispersing the stages of its value chain to those locations around the globe where the value added is maximized or where the costs of value creation are minimized.

A. international mesh
B. disperse chain
C. global web
D. integrate circle

Answer: A
Medium
Page: 383

15. In theory, a firm that realizes __________ by dispersing each of its value creation activities to its optimal location should have a competitive advantage vis-à-vis a firm that bases all its value creation activities at a single location.

A. location economies
B. site synergies
C. site commerce
D. geographical distinctiveness

Answer: B
Easy
Page: 384

16. The __________ refers to the systematic reductions in production costs that have been observed to occur over the life of a product.

A. forward advantage
B. experience curve
C. positive-sum result
D. managed advantage

Answer: C
Medium
Page: 385

17. If Intel Corporation experienced systematic reductions in the production costs of a particular product over the life of the product, they would be realizing __________ effects.

A. managed production
B. forward advantage
C. experience curve
D. value chain

Answer: C
Medium
Page: 384

18. A number of studies have observed that a product's __________ decline by some characteristic each time accumulated output doubles.

A. financing costs
B. marketing costs
C. production costs
D. R&D costs

Answer: A
Easy
Page: 384

19. __________ refer to cost savings that come from learning by doing.

A. Learning effects
B. Exponential effects
C. Ancillary effects
D. Indirect effects

Answer: B
Medium
Page: 384

20. Learning effects tend to be more significant when a __________ task is repeated because there is more than can be learned about the task.

A. repetitive manufacturing
B. technologically complex
C. standardized service
D. standardized manufacturing

Answer: B
Easy
Page: 385

21. The term __________ refers to the reduction in unit costs achieved by producing a large volume of a product.

A. rent effects
B. economies of scale
C. volume synergies
D. captured savings

Answer: C
Medium
Page: 385

22. Economies of scale have a number of sources, one of the most important of which seems to be the ability to spread:

A. fixed costs over a small volume
B. variable costs over a large volume
C. fixed costs over a large volume
D. variable costs over a small volume

Answer: D
Medium
Page: 385

23. If Honda noticed that the unit costs of Honda Accords went down as the number of Accord's produced went up, Honda would be realizing the benefits of:

A. captured savings
B. volume synergies
C. rent effects
D. economies of scale

Answer: A
Hard
Page: 385

24. The strategic significance of the experience curve is clear. Moving __________ the experience curve allows a firm to __________ the cost of creating value.

A. down, reduce
B. down, increase
C. up, reduce
D. up, increase

Answer: D
Hard
Page: 386

25. The key to progressing downward on the experience curve as rapidly as possible is to increase the __________ produced by a single plant as __________ as possible.

A. quality, slowly
B. variety of products, slowly
C. variety of products, rapidly
D. volume, rapidly

Answer: B
Easy
Page: 386

26. Firms that compete in the global marketplace typically face two types of competitive pressures. They face pressures for cost reductions and:

A. pressures for volume increases
B. pressures to be locally responsive
C. pressures to be politically savvy
D. pressures for price reductions

Answer: C
Medium
Page: 387

27. Pressures for cost reductions can be particularly intense in industries producing commodity products where meaningful differentiation on nonprice factors is difficult and __________ is the main competitive weapon.

A. quality
B. distribution efficiency
C. price
D. sales & service

Answer: A
Medium
Page: 388

28. Which of the following is not a factor that is driving pressures for local responsiveness among global firms?

A. similarities in distribution channels
B. host government demands
C. differences in infrastructure and tradition practices
D. differences in consumer tastes and preferences

Answer: C
Medium
Page: 388

29. Differences in consumer tastes and preferences, differences in infrastructure and traditional practices, differences in distribution channels, and host government demands are factors pressuring firms to be sensitive to __________ in their international strategies.

A. cost containment
B. global standardization
C. local responsiveness
D. integrating more "commodity" like features

Answer: A
Hard
Page: 388

30. Harvard Business School Professor Theodore Levitt has argued that consumer demands for local customization are __________ worldwide.

A. declining
B. leveling out
C. increasing
D. a myth

Answer: D
Medium
Page: 389

31. Pressures for __________ imply that it may not be possible for a firm to realize the full benefits from experience curve and location economies.

A. global responsiveness
B. cost containment
C. international differentiation
D. local responsiveness

STRATEGIC CHOICE

Answer: A
Medium
Page: 390

32. Firms use four basic strategies to compete in the international environment. These are:

A. international, multidomestic, global, and transnational
B. cross-cultural, trade block, regional, and world
C. domestic-based, internationally-focused, local/regional based, and cultural-based
D. international, regional, global, and world

Answer: B
Medium
Page: 390

33. In the international environment, firms use four basic strategies. Theses are an international strategy, a multidomestic strategy, a global strategy, and a __________ strategy.

A. local/regional
B. transnational
C. cross-cultural
D. trade block

Answer: D
Medium
Page: 390

34. In the international environment, firms use four basic strategies. These are an international strategy, a multidomestic strategy, a transnational strategy, and a __________ strategy.

A. trade block
B. cultural-based
C. regional
D. global

Answer: B
Medium
Page: 390

35. In the international environment, firms use four basic strategies. These are an international strategy, a transnational strategy, a global strategy, and a:

A. regional strategy
B. multidomestic strategy
C. global strategy
D. transnational strategy

Answer: D
Medium
Page: 390

36. The appropriateness of the strategy that a firm uses in an international market varies with the extent of pressures for:

A. cost reductions and availability of financing
B. price concessions and quality improvements
C. availability of financing and product standardization
D. cost reductions and local responsiveness

Answer: A
Medium
Page: 390

37. The appropriateness of the strategy that a firm uses in an international market varies the extent of pressures for cost reductions and:

A. local responsiveness
B. availability of financing
C. trade block membership
D. price concessions

Answer: A
Medium
Page: 391

38. Firms that pursue a(n) __________ strategy try to create value by transferring valuable skills and products to foreign markets where indigenous competitors lack those skills and products.

A. international
B. multidomestic
C. global
D. transnational

Answer: C
Medium
Page: 392

39. A(n) __________ strategy makes sense if a firm has a valuable core competence that indigenous competitors in foreign markets lack.

A. transnational
B. multidomestic
C. international
D. global

Answer: B
Hard
Page: 392

40. When cost pressures are high and pressures for local responsiveness are high, a(n) __________ strategy is the most appropriate.

A. multidomestic
B. transnational
C. international
D. global

Answer: C
Hard
Page: 392

41. When cost pressures are low and pressures for local responsiveness are low, a(n) __________ strategy is the most appropriate.

A. global
B. transnational
C. international
D. multidomestic

Answer: C
Hard
Page: 390

42. When cost pressures are high and pressures for local responsiveness are low, a(n) __________ strategy is the most appropriate.

A. multidomestic
B. transnational
C. global
D. international

Answer: D
Hard
Page: 390

43. When cost pressures are low and pressures for local responsiveness are high, a(n) __________ strategy is the most appropriate.

A. international
B. transnational
C. global
D. multidomestic

Answer: B
Medium
Page: 390

44. Firms pursuing a __________ strategy orient themselves toward achieving maximum local responsiveness.

A. transnational
B. multidomestic
C. global
D. international

Answer: C
Hard
Page: 392

45. Which of the following is not a typical characteristic of a multidomestic firm?

A. extensively customize both their product offerings and their marketing strategy to match different national conditions
B. try to establish a complete set of value creation activities in each major national market in which they do business
C. have a low cost structure
D. do a poor job of leveraging core competencies within the firm

Answer: D
Hard
Page: 393

46. A weakness of the __________ strategy is that many of the firms that pursue this strategy have developed into decentralized federations in which each national subsidiary functions in a largely autonomous manner.

A. global
B. international
C. transnational
D. multidomestic

Answer: B
Medium
Page: 393

47. Firms that pursue a __________ strategy focus on increasing profitability by reaping the cost reductions that come from experience curve effects and location economies.

A. multidomestic
B. global
C. transational
D. international

Answer: A
Medium
Page: 393

48. Firms that pursue a __________ strategy are trying to simultaneously achieve low-cost and differentiation advantages.

A. transnational
B. multidomestic
C. international
D. global

Answer: C
Medium
Page: 393

49. Pursuing a __________ strategy involves a simultaneous focus on reducing costs, transferring skills and products, and being locally responsive.

A. global
B. multidomestic
C. transnational
D. international

Answer: A
Medium
Page: 393

50. According to Christopher Bartlett and Sumantra Ghoshal, the flow of skills and product offerings should not be all one way, from home firm to foreign subsidiary. Rather, they argue that the flow should also be from foreign subsidiary to home country, and from foreign subsidiary to foreign subsidiary - a process they call:

A. global learning
B. international education
C. international lore
C. worldwide edification

Answer: C
Medium
Page: 393

51. The work of Christopher Bartlett and Sumantra Ghoshal is associated with:

A. global strategy
B. multidomestic strategy
C. transnational strategy
D. international strategy

Answer: D
Medium
Page: 393

52. According to Bartlett and Ghoshal, the __________ strategy is the only viable international strategy.

A. international
B. multidomestic
C. global
D. transnational

Answer: D
Medium
Page: 396

53. __________ is the flow of skills and product offerings from home firm to foreign subsidiary and from foreign subsidiary to home firm and from foreign subsidiary to foreign subsidiary.

A. Skills and product offerings transfer
B. Technical transfer
C. Knowledge assimilation
D. Global learning

Answer: D
Hard
Page: 396

54. A disadvantage of both the global strategy and the international strategy is:

A. inability to realize location economies
B. failure to exploit experience curve effects
C. failure to transfer distinctive competencies to foreign markets
D. lack of local responsiveness

Answer: B
Hard
Page: 396

55. The distinct disadvantage of the transnational strategy is:

A. lack of local responsiveness
B. it is difficult to implement due to organizational problems
C. failure to exploit experience curve effects
D. inability to realize location economies

Answer: A
Hard
Page: 396

56. A disadvantage of both the international strategy and the multidomestic strategy is:

A. inability to realize location economies
B. both are difficult to implement due to organizational problems
C. lack of local responsiveness
D. failure to transfer distinctive competencies to foreign markets

Answer: C
Hard
Page: 396

57. Two distinct advantages of the global strategy are:

A. reap benefits of global learning and customize product offerings and marketing in accordance with local responsiveness
B. exploit location economies and transfer distinctive competencies to foreign markets
C. exploit experience curve effects and exploit location economies
D. reap benefits of global learning and exploit location economies

Answer: A
Hard
Page: 396

58. A distinct advantage of an international strategy is:

A. transfer distinctive competencies to foreign markets
B. reap benefits of global learning
C. customize product offerings in accordance with local responsiveness
D. exploit local economies

Answer: D
Medium
Page: 396

59. Which of the following represents the list of advantages of a transnational strategy?

A. exploit experience curve effects, exploit location economies
B. transfer distinctive competencies to foreign markets
C. customize product offerings and marketing in accordance with local responsiveness
D. exploit experience curve effects, exploit location economies, customize product offerings and marketing in accordance with local responsiveness, reap benefits of global learning

Answer: A
Hard
Page: 396

60. A lack of local responsiveness, an inability to realize location economies, and a failure to exploit experience curve effects are disadvantages of a __________ strategy.

A. international
B. global
C. transnational
D. multidomestic

TRUE-FALSE QUESTIONS

STRATEGY AND THE FIRM

Answer: T
Medium
Page: 379

61. It is useful to think of the firm as a value chain composed of a series of distinct value creation activities including production, marketing, materials management, R&D, human resources, information systems, and the firm infrastructure.

Answer: F
Easy
Page: 379

62. There are two basic strategies for improving a firm's profitability - a segmentation strategy and a low-cost strategy.

Answer: F
Medium
Page: 379

63. In the context of value chain analysis, the primary activities of a firm include manufacturing, materials management, marketing, and sales & service.

Answer: T
Easy
Page: 380

64. In the context of value chain analysis, support activities provide the inputs that allow the primary activities of production and marketing to occur.

Answer: T
Easy
Page: 380

65. A firm's strategy can be defined as the actions managers take to attain the goals of the firm.

PROFITING FROM GLOBAL EXPANSION

Answer: F
Easy
Page: 381

66. The term principle competence refers to skills within the firm that competitors cannot easily match or imitate.

Answer: T
Medium
Page: 383

67. The economies that arise from performing a value creation activity in the optimal location for that activity are referred to as location economies.

Answer: F
Medium
Page: 383

68. According to our textbook, a firm creates an "integrated circle" by dispersing the stages of its value chain to those locations around the globe where the value added is maximized or where the costs of value creation are minimized.

Answer: T
Medium
Page: 383

69. In theory, a firm that realizes location economies by dispersing each of its value creation activities to its optimal location should have a competitive advantage vis-à-vis a firm that bases all its value creation activities at a single location.

Answer: F
Easy
Page: 384

70. The experience curve refers to the systematic increases in production costs that have been observed to occur over the life of a product.

Answer: T
Easy
Page: 384

71. Learning effects refer to cost savings that come from learning by doing.

Answer: T
Medium
Page: 384

72. Learning effects tend to be more significant when a technologically complex task is repeated because there is more than can be learned about the task.

Answer: F
Medium
Page: 385

73. The term economies of scale refers to the reduction in marketing and administrative costs that take place as a firm exports to an increasingly larger number of countries.

Answer: F
Medium
Page: 385

74. Moving up the experience curve allows a firm to reduce its cost of creating value.

PRESSURES FOR COST REDUCTIONS AND LOCAL RESPONSIVENESS

Answer: T
Medium
Page: 386

75. Firms that compete in the global marketplace typically face two types of competitive pressure. They face pressures for cost reductions and pressures to be locally responsive.

Answer: T
Medium
Page: 387

76. Pressures for cost reductions can be particularly intense in industries producing commodity products where meaningful differentiation on nonprice factors is difficult and price is the main competitive weapon.

Answer: F
Medium
Page: 387

77. Commodity products such as bulk chemicals, petroleum, steel, and sugar are typically not subject to pressures for cost reductions.

Answer: T
Medium
Page: 388

78. Strong pressures for local responsiveness emerge when consumer tastes and preferences differ significantly between countries.

Answer: F
Medium
Page: 389

79. Pressures for local responsiveness increase the probability that firms will realize the full benefits from experience curve and location economies.

STRATEGIC CHOICE

Answer: T
Medium
Page: 391

80. Firms that pursue an international strategy try to create value by transferring valuable skills and products to foreign markets where indigenous competitors lack those skills and products.

Answer: T
Hard
Page: 392

81. When cost pressures are high and the pressures for local responsiveness are low, a global strategy is the most appropriate.

Answer: F
Hard
Page: 392

82. When cost pressures are high and the pressures for local responsiveness are high, a multidomestic strategy is the most appropriate.

Answer: T
Hard
Page: 392

83. When cost pressures are low and pressures for local responsiveness are low, an international strategy is the most appropriate.

Answer: F
Medium
Page: 392

84. Firms pursuing a global strategy orient themselves toward achieving maximum local responsiveness.

Answer: T
Medium
Page: 393

85. Firms that pursue a global strategy focus on increasing profitability by reaping the cost reductions that come from experience curve effects and location economics.

Answer: F
Medium
Page: 393

86. The work of Christopher Barlett and Sumantra Ghoshal is most closely associated with the multidomestic strategy.

Answer: F
Hard
Page: 393

87. A transnational strategy makes sense when there are high pressures for cost reductions and low pressures for local responsiveness.

Answer: T
Medium
Page: 396

88. A distinct disadvantage of a transnational strategy is that it is difficult to implement due to organizational problems.

Answer: T
Medium
Page: 396

89. An advantage of a multidomestic strategy is that it customizes product offerings and marketing in accordance with local responsiveness.

Answer: F
Medium
Page: 396

90. A disadvantage of the global strategy and the transnational strategy is the lack of local responsiveness.

ESSAY QUESTIONS

Easy
Page: 380

91. What is a firm's strategy?

Answer: A firm's strategy can be defined as the actions managers take to attain the goals of the firm.

Medium
Page: 381

92. Can firms that expand globally increase their profitability in ways that are not available to them in domestic markets? What are the constraints on taking full advantage of the potential for increasing profits in international markets?

Answer: Expanding globally allows firms to increase their profitability in ways not available to purely domestic enterprises. Firms that operate internationally are able to (1) earn a greater return from their distinctive skills or core competencies; (2) realize location economies by dispersing particular value creation activities to those locations where they can be performed most efficiently; and (3) realize greater experience curve economies, which reduces the cost of value creation.

Unfortunately, a firm's ability to increase its profitability by pursuing these strategies is constrained by the need to customize its product offerings, marketing strategy, and business strategy to differing national conditions/

Easy
Page: 381

93. Describe the concept of "core competence." What types of core competencies are the most valuable for penetrating foreign markets?

Answer: The term core competence refers to the skills within the firms that competitors cannot easily match or imitate. These skills may exist in any of the firm's value creation activities (i.e. manufacturing, marketing, sales, materials management, etc.). These skills typically enable a firm to produce a product or service that competitors find difficult to duplicate. For instance, Home Depot has a core competence in managing home improvement superstores. Home Depot's competitors have found this core competence difficult to imitate.

Core competencies are the most valuable as a tool for helping firms enter foreign markets when they are unique, when the value placed on them by consumers is great, and when there are very few capable competitors with similar skills and/or products in foreign markets.

According to the textbook, firms with unique and valuable skills can often realize enormous returns by applying those skills, and the products they produce, to foreign markets where indigenous competitors lack similar skills and products.

Medium
Page: 384

94. What is the experience curve? How can an involvement in overseas markets help a firm capture experience curve advantages more rapidly?

Answer: The experience curve refers to the systematic reductions in production costs that have been observed to occur over the life of a product. In general, the experience curve suggests that as a firm produces more of a particular product, the unit price of the product drops. This phenomenon occurs because of learning effects and economies of scale. Learning effects refer to the cost savings that come from learning by doing. Economies of scale refers to the reduction in unit costs achieved by producing a large volume of a product as a result of the ability to spread fixed costs over a larger volume.

Firms can typically move down the experience curve (i.e. realize a reduction in production costs by selling more of a product) faster through involvement in overseas markets. The simple logic is that by going global, a firm expands its customer base and is able to sell a higher volume of its product. By selling a higher volume of its product, a firm can experience learning effects and economies of scale benefits more rapidly.

Medium
Page: 384

95. What is the difference between learning effects and economies of scale?

Answer: Learning effects refer to cost savings that come from learning by doing. Labor, for example, learns by repetition how to carry out a task, such as assembling airframes, most efficiently. The term economies of scale refers to the reduction in unit cost achieved by producing a large volume of a product. Economies of scale have a number of sources, one of the most important of which seem to be the ability to spread fixed costs over a large volume.

Medium
Page: 387

96. In what types of industries are the pressures for cost reductions the greatest?

Answer: Pressures for cost reductions are greatest in industries producing commodity type products where price is the main competitive weapon. This tends to be the case for products that serve universal needs. Universal needs exist when the tastes and preferences of consumers in different nations are similar. This is the case for conventional commodity products such as bulk chemicals, petroleum, steel, sugar, and the like. Pressures for cost reductions are also intense in industries where major competitors are based in low-cost locations, where there is persistent excess capacity, and where consumers are powerful and face low switching costs.

Medium
Page: 388

97. Firms that compete in global markets often face pressures for local responsiveness. Describe what is meant by local responsiveness, and identify the underlying reasons that local responsiveness pressures exist.

Answer: Many firms enter global markets with the idea of selling essentially the same product in each market that they enter. This approach becomes problematic when the citizens of a particular country ask that the product be customized to fit their particular needs. When the consumer in a country ask that a product be modified to suite their particular tastes, they are in effect asking the international company to be "locally responsive" to their needs. This is where the term local responsiveness comes from.

Pressures for local responsiveness arise from a number of sources. These sources include: (1) Differences in consumer tastes and preferences across markets; (2) Differences in infrastructure and traditional practices across markets; (3) Differences in distribution channels across markets; and (4) Host government demands.

Hard
Page: 388

98. Harvard Business Professor Theodore Levitt has argued that consumer demands for local customization are declining worldwide. What is the gist of Levitt's argument? Do you agree or disagree with Levitt's conclusions.

Answer: According to Levitt, modern communications and transportation technologies have created the conditions for a convergence of the tastes of consumers from different nations. The result is the emergence of enormous global markets for standardized consumer products. Levitt cites worldwide acceptance of McDonalds hamburgers, Coca-Cola, Levis Strauss jeans, and Sony television sets, all of which are sold as standardized products, as evidence of the increasing homogeneity of the global marketplace.

The second half of the question is designed to stimulate classroom discussion. Some critics see Levitt's arguments are extreme, and argue that he goes "too far" in his characterization of the globalization of markets.

Hard
Page: 390

99. Describe the four basic strategies that firms use to compete in international markets. Which strategy is the best?

Answer: The four basic strategies that firms use to compete in international markets are: an international strategy, a multidomestic strategy, a global strategy, and a transnational strategy. Each of the strategies is briefly described below.

International Strategy - Firms that pursue an international strategy try to create value by transferring valuable skills and products to foreign markets where indigenous competitors lack those skills and products. These firms tend to centralize product development functions at home, and establish manufacturing and marketing functions in each major country in which they do business. An international strategy makes sense if a firm has a valuable core competence that indigenous competitors in foreign markets lack and if the firm faces relatively weak pressures for local responsiveness and cost reductions. Typically, local responsiveness is fairly modest.

Multidomestic Strategy - Firms pursuing a multidomestic strategy orient themselves toward achieving maximum local responsiveness. These firms tend to transfer skills and products developed at home to foreign markets. Consistent with their strategy of local responsiveness, however, they tend to establish a complete set of value creation activities - including production, marketing, and R&D - in each major market in which they do business. A multidomestic strategy makes sense when there are high pressures for local responsiveness and low pressures for cost reductions. The high cost structure associated with the duplication of production facilities makes this strategy inappropriate in industries where cost pressures are intense.

Global Strategy - Firms that pursue a global strategy focus upon increasing profitability by reaping the cost reductions that come from experience curve effects and location economies. That is, they are pursuing a low cost strategy. The majority of the value chain activities for a global firm are concentrated in a few favorable locations. Global firms are not very locally responsive. Instead, they prefer to market a standardized product worldwide. This strategy makes most sense in those cases where there are strong pressures for cost reductions, and where demands for local responsiveness are minimal.

Transnational Strategy - A transnational strategy is an ambitious strategy in which a firm tries to simultaneously exploit experience-base cost economies and location economies, transfer distinctive competencies within the firm, and pay attention to pressures for local responsiveness. This type of strategy makes sense when a firm faces high pressures for cost reductions and high pressures for local responsiveness. Barlett and Ghoshal admit that building an organization that is capable of supporting a transnational strategic posture is complex and difficult. In essence, a transnational strategy requires a firm to simultaneously achieve cost efficiencies, global learning, and local responsiveness. These are contradictory demands which are difficult to achieve at the same time in practice.

Which strategy is the best? There is no compelling answer to this question. The most advantageous strategy is the one that best complements a firm's distinctive competencies and its ultimate goals and objectives.

Medium
Page: 393

100. Describe Christopher Bartlett and Sumantra Ghoshal's concept of global learning.

Answer: Christopher Bartlett and Sumantra Ghoshal have argued that in today's environment, competitive conditions are so intense that to survive in the global marketplace, firms must exploit experience-based cost economies and location economies, they must transfer core competencies within the firm, and they must do all this while paying attention to pressures for local responsiveness. They note that in the modern multinational enterprise, core competencies do not reside just in the home country. They can develop in any of the firm's worldwide operations. Thus, they maintain that the flow of skills and product offerings should not be all one way, from home firm to foreign subsidiary, as in the case of firms pursuing an international strategy. Rather, the flow should also be from foreign subsidiary to home country, and from foreign subsidiary to foreign subsidiary - a process they refer to as global learning.

CHAPTER 13

THE ORGANIZATION OF INTERNATIONAL BUSINESS

MULTIPLE-CHOICE QUESTIONS

VERTICAL DIFFERENTIATION

Answer: B
Easy
Page: 403

1. A firm's __________ determines where in its hierarchy the decision-making power is concentrated.

   A. diagonal differentiation
   B. vertical differentiation
   C. horizontal differentiation
   D. parallel differentiation

Answer: A
Hard
Page: 404

2. There are four main arguments for centralization. These are:

   A. facilitates coordination, helps ensure that decisions are consistent with organizational objectives, gives top-level managers the means to bring about needed major organizational changes, avoids the duplication of activities that occurs when similar activities are carried on by various subunits within the organization
   B. decision-making authority is equally dispersed throughout the organization, top management is not overburdened, greater flexibility, emphasizes employee empowerment
   C. helps ensure that decisions are consistent with organizational objectives, avoids the duplication of activities that occurs when similar activities are carried on by various subunits within the organization, greater flexibility, decision-making authority is equally dispersed throughout the organization
   D. can facilitate coordination, emphasizes employee empowerment, greater flexibility, top management is not overburdened

Answer: B
Medium
Page: 402

3. There are four main arguments for centralization. These are: facilitates coordination, gives top level managers the means to bring about needed major organizational changes, avoids the duplication of activities that occurs when similar activities are carried on by various subunits within the organization, and:

A. emphasizes employee empowerment
B. helps ensure that decisions are consistent with organizational objectives
C. decision-making authority is equally dispersed throughout the organization
D. greater flexibility

Answer: B
Hard
Page: 404

4. There are five main arguments for decentralization. These are:

A. facilitates coordination, avoids the duplication of activities that occurs when similar activities are carried on by various subunits within the organization, can result in better decisions because decisions are made closer to the spot, greater flexibility, decreases control
B. frees top managers to focus on critical issues by delegating more routine issues to lower-level managers, provides employees a greater degree of individual freedom and control over their work, greater flexibility, can result in better decisions because decisions are made closer to the spot, increases control
C. gives top managers the means to bring about needed organizational changes, greater flexibility, facilitates coordination, emphasizes total quality management, increases control
D. facilitates coordination, can result in better decisions because decisions are made closer to the spot, greater flexibility, gives top managers the means to bring about needed organizational changes, increases supervision

Answer: D
Medium
Page: 404

5. Which of the following decisions is typically centralized at a firm's headquarters?

A. production decisions
B. human resource management
C. marketing decisions
D. financial objectives

Answer: C
Medium
Page: 404

6. All of the following decisions are typically centralized at a firm's headquarters except:

A. overall firm strategy
B. major financial expenditures
C. marketing decisions
D. financial objectives

Answer: A
Medium
Page: 404

7. The emphasis on local responsiveness in multidomestic firms creates strong pressures for __________ operating decisions to foreign subsidiaries.

A. decentralizing
B. centralizing
C. consolidating
D. integrating

Answer: C
Medium
Page: 404

8. International firms tend to maintain __________ control over their core competency and to __________ other decisions to foreign subsidiaries.

A. decentralized, centralize
B. integrated, centralize
C. centralized, decentralize
D. parallel, decentralize

Answer: D
Hard
Page: 405

9. In transnational firms, the need to realize location and experience curve economies requires some degree of __________ control over global production centers. However, the need for local responsiveness dictates the __________ of many operating decisions, particularly for marketing, to foreign subsidiaries.

A. integrated, parallel decentralization
B. decentralized, centralization
C. integrated, parallel centralization
D. centralized, decentralization

Answer: B
Medium
Page: 405

10. The pursuit of a transnational strategy requires a high degree of:

A. centralization
B. decentralization
C. quasi-centralization
D. quasi-decentralization

HORIZONTAL DIFFERENTIATION

Answer: A
Easy
Page: 405

11. __________ is basically concerned with how the firm decides to divide itself into subunits.

A. Horizontal differentiation
B. Parallel differentiation
C. Vertical Differentiation
D. Network Differentiation

Answer: B
Medium
Page: 405

12. Decision making in a functional structure tends to be:

A. decentralized
B. centralized
C. horizontal
D. characterized by a high degree of employee empowerment

Answer: A
Medium
Page: 406

13. With a __________ structure, each division is responsible for a distinct product line.

A. product division
B. consumer division
C. domestic division
D. output division

Answer: C
Easy
Page: 406

14. Historically, when firms have expanded abroad, they have typically grouped all their international activities in a(n) __________ division.

A. product
B. geographic
C. international
D. functional

Answer: C
Medium
Page: 408

15. A __________ tends to be favored by firms with a low degree of diversification and a domestic structure based on function.

A. worldwide product division structure
B. global matrix structure
C. worldwide area structure
D. global network structure

Answer: A
Medium
Page: 408

16. A worldwide area structure tends to be favored by firms with a __________ degree of diversification and a domestic structure based on __________.

A. low, function
B. high, matrix
C. high, function
D. high, division

Answer: B
Medium
Page: 408

17. Which of the following structures facilitates local responsiveness?

A. global network structure
B. worldwide area structure
C. global matrix structure
D. worldwide product division structure

Answer: D
Medium
Page: 408

18. The weakness of the worldwide area structure is that it:

A. is often clumsy and bureucratic
B. creates a dual-hierarchy which is difficult to administrate
C. gives a limited voice to area or country managers, since they are seen as subservient to product division managers
D. encourages fragmentation of the organization into highly autonomous entities

Answer: C
Medium
Page: 409

19. Which of the following structures is consistent with a multidomestic strategy but little else?

A. worldwide product division structure
B. global matrix structure
C. worldwide area structure
D. global geographic division structure

Answer: B
Medium
Page: 410

20. A __________ tends to be adopted by firms that are reasonably diversified and, accordingly, originally had domestic structures based on product divisions.

A. global geographic division structure
B. worldwide product division structure
C. global matrix structure
D. worldwide area structure

Answer: A
Hard
Page: 410

21. The __________ structure is designed to help overcome the coordination problems that arise with the international division and worldwide area structures.

A. worldwide product division
B. global matrix
C. global network
D. global geographic division

Answer: B
Medium
Page: 410

22. A worldwide product division structure is appropriate for firms pursuing __________ strategies

A. multidomestic or international
B. global or international
C. multidomestic or global
D. cross-cultural of multidomestic

Answer: C
Hard
Page: 411

23. In the classic global matrix structure, horizontal differentiation proceeds along two dimensions. These are:

A. geographic area and functional area
B. markets served and functional area
C. product division and geographic area
D. markets served and geographic area

Answer: A
Medium
Page: 411

24. Which of the following structures has a dual-hierarchy?

A. global matrix structure
B. worldwide product division structure
C. global product division structure
D. worldwide area structure

INTEGRATING MECHANISMS

Answer: C
Easy
Page: 412

25. According to our textbook, the need for coordination between the subunits of a firm varies with the __________ of the firm.

A. nationality
B. industry
C. strategy
E. culture

Answer: D
Medium
Page: 412

26. In terms of the organization of a firm, the need for coordination is lowest in __________ companies.

A. international
B. transnational
C. global
D. multidomestic

Answer: B
Medium
Page: 412

27. In terms of the organization of a firm, the need for coordination is highest in __________ companies

A. multidomestic
B. transnational
C. global
D. international

Answer: A
Medium
Page: 412

28. Which of the following types of firms is likely to operate with a worldwide area structure in which each area has considerable autonomy and its own set of value creation functions?

A. multidomestic
B. international
C. transnational
D. global

Answer: D
Hard
Page: 412

29. Which of the following types of firms requires coordination between foreign subunits and the firm's globally dispersed value creation activities to ensure that any product offering and marketing strategy is sufficiently customized to local conditions.

A. international
B. global
C. multidomestic
D. transnational

Answer: D
Hard
Page: 412

30. Which of the following selections correctly lists the international strategies in terms of the lowest level of coordination needed to the highest?

A. multidomestic, transnational, international, global
B. transnational, multidomestic, global, international
C. global, international, transnational, global
D. multidomestic, international, global, transnational

Answer: A
Hard
Page: 412

31. Which of the following selections correctly lists the international strategies in terms of the highest level of coordination needed to the lowest?

A. transnational, global, international, multidomestic
B. global, international, transnational, multidomestic
C. international, multidomestic, transnational, global
D. multidomestic, global, transnational, international

Answer: D
Medium
Page: 412

32. __________ managers are typically concerned with issues such as capacity utilization, cost control, and quality control.

A. General
B. Marketing
C. Service
D. Production

Answer: B
Medium
Page: 414

33. __________ managers are concerned with issues such as pricing, promotions, distribution, and market value.

A. Production
B. Marketing
C. General
D. Matrix

Answer: C
Medium
Page: 414

34. __________ contact between subunit managers is the simplest integrating mechanism.

A. Indirect
B. Circular
C. Direct
D. Unplanned

Answer: B
Medium
Page: 414

35. The person in a subunit that is responsible for coordination with another subunit is referred to as a:

A. manager
B. liaison
C. coordinator
D. facilitator

Answer: D
Hard
Page: 415

36. __________ structures tend to be bureaucratic, inflexible, and characterized by conflict rather than cooperation.

A. Functional
B. Divisional
C. Network
D. Matrix

Answer: C
Hard
Page: 415

37. Which of the following selections correctly lists the formal integrating mechanisms from the lowest level of complexity to the highest?

A. teams, liaison roles, direct contact, matrix structure
B. liaison roles, direct contact, matrix structure, teams
C. direct contact, liaison roles, teams, matrix structure
D. matrix structure, teams, direct contact, and liaison roles

Answer: C
Medium
Page: 415

38. In attempting to alleviate or avoid the problems associated with formal integrating mechanisms in general, and matrix structures in particular, firms with a high need for integration have been experimenting with two informal integrating mechanisms. These are:

A. management cadres and organizational citizenship behavior
B. organizational culture and management cadres
C. management networks and organizational culture
D. organizational citizenship behavior and management networks

Answer: C
Medium
Page: 415

39. In attempting to alleviate or avoid the problems associated with formal integrating mechanisms in general, and matrix structures in particular, firms with a high need for integration have been experimenting with two informal integrating mechanisms. These are organizational culture and:

A. management cadres
B. management cohorts
C. management networks
D. organizational citizenship behavior

Answer: C
Medium
Page: 415

40. A __________ is a system of informal contacts between managers within an enterprise.

A. management cadre
B. management web
C. management network
D. management cohort

Answer: B
Medium
Page: 415

41. A system of informal contracts between managers within an organization is referred to as a:

A. management cohort
B. management network
C. management web
D. management cadre

Answer: A
Medium
Page: 417

42. Traditionally, firms have tried to achieve coordination by adopting:

A. formal integrating mechanisms
B. informal integrating mechanisms
C. formal facilitation mechanisms
D. informal facilitation mechanisms

CONTROL SYSTEMS

Answer: C
Medium
Page: 417

43. Four types of control systems are used in multinational firms. These are:

A. feedforward controls, output controls, input controls, and bureaucratic controls
B. feedback controls, hierarchical controls, input controls, and cultural controls
C. personal controls, bureaucratic controls, output controls, and cultural controls
D. input controls, concurrent controls, hierarchical controls, and personal controls

Answer: D
Medium
Page: 417

44. Four types of control systems are used in multinational firms. These are personal controls, bureaucratic controls, output controls, and:

A. concurrent controls
B. feedforward controls
C. hierarchical controls
D. cultural controls

Answer: C
Medium
Page: 417

45. Four types of control systems are used in multinational firms. These are personal controls, bureaucratic controls, cultural controls, and:

A. input controls
B. feedback controls
C. output controls
D. cultural controls

Answer: B
Medium
Page: 417

46. Which type of control tends to be most widely used in small firms, where it is seen in the direct supervision of subordinates' actions?

A. bureaucratic control
B. personal control
C. output control
D. cultural control

Answer: A
Medium
Page: 418

47. __________ control is control through a system of rules and procedures that direct the actions of subunits.

A. Bureaucratic
B. Output
C. Cultural
D. Personal

Answer: C
Medium
Page: 418

48. __________ controls involve setting goals for subunits to achieve.

A. Personal
B. Cultural
C. Output
D. Bureaucratic

Answer: A
Hard
Page: 418

49. The linking of management reward systems and incentive schemes is typically reinforced through the use of:

A. output controls
B. bureaucratic controls
C. cultural controls
D. personal controls

Answer: C
Medium
Page: 418

50. __________ controls exist when employees "buy into" the norms and value systems of the firm.

A. Personal
B. Output
C. Cultural
D. Bureaucratic

Answer: C
Hard
Page: 419

51. To reduce the high costs of controls, firms with a high degree of interdependence between subunits (e.g., transnationals) must develop:

A. bureaucratic controls
B. output controls
C. cultural controls
D. personal controls

Answer: D
Hard
Page: 419

52. The degree of subunit interdependence - and, hence, performance ambiguity and the costs of control - is a function of the firm's strategy. It is:

A. lowest in international firms, higher in transnational firms, higher still in global firms, and highest in multidomestic firms
B. lowest in global firms, higher in multidomestic firms, higher still in transnational firms, and highest in international firms
C. lowest in transnational firms, higher in international firms, higher still in multidomestic firms, and highest in global firms
D. lowest in multidomestic firms, higher in international firms, higher still in global firms, and highest in transnational firms

Answer: A
Easy
Page: 419

53. __________ exists when the causes of a subunit's poor performance are ambiguous.

A. Performance ambiguity
B. Output skepticism
C. Performance haziness
D. Output uncertainty

Answer: B
Hard
Page: 420

54. The key to understanding the relationship between international strategy and control system is the concept of:

A. output skepticism
B. performance ambiguity
C. performance haziness
D. output uncertainty

Answer: C
Hard
Page: 420

55. Which of the following correctly matches an international strategy with its level of interdependence?

A. multidomestic, high
B. global, very high
C. international, moderate
D. transnational, low

Answer: A
Hard
Page: 420

56. Which of the following correctly matches an international strategy with its level of performance ambiguity?

A. multidomestic, low
B. international, very high
C. global, moderate
D. transnational, high

Answer: D
Hard
Page: 420

57. Which of the following correctly matches an international strategy with its cost of control?

A. multidomestic, high
B. international, low
C. global, moderate
D. transnational, very high

SYNTHESIS: STRATEGY AND STRUCTURE

Answer: C
Hard
Page: 421

58. Which of the following international strategies requires no specific integrating mechanisms, has low performance ambiguity, and has a low need for cultural controls?

A. global
B. transnational
C. multidomestic
D. international

Answer: B
Hard
Page: 421

59. Which of the following international strategies requires very many integrating mechanisms, has a very high performance ambiguity, and has a very high need for cultural controls?

A. international
B. transnational
C. global
D. multidomestic

Answer: B
Medium
Page: 422

60. The need for coordination is particularly high in __________ firms.

A. global
B. transnational
C. multidomestic
D. international

TRUE-FALSE QUESTIONS

VERTICAL DIFFERENTIATION

Answer: T
Medium
Page: 403

61. A firm's vertical differentiation determines where in its hierarchy the decision-making power is concentrated.

Answer: F
Medium
Page: 404

62. One drawback of centralization is that it interferes with the ability of top-management to establish the means to bring about needed major organizational changes.

Answer: T
Medium
Page: 404

63. One argument against centralization is that top management can become overburdened with decision-making responsibilities.

Answer: F
Medium
Page: 404

64. Centralization permits greater flexibility than decentralization.

Answer: T
Easy
Page: 404

65. The emphasis on local responsiveness in multidomestic firms creates strong pressures for decentralizing operating decisions to foreign subsidiaries.

HORIZONTAL DIFFERENTIAITON

Answer: F
Medium
Page: 408

66. A worldwide area structure tends to be favored by firms with a high degree of diversification and a domestic structure based on division.

Answer: T
Medium
Page: 408

67. A worldwide area structure facilitates local responsiveness.

Answer: T
Medium
Page: 410

68. A worldwide product division structure tends to be adopted by firms that are reasonably diversified and, accordingly, originally had domestic structures based on product divisions.

Answer: F
Medium
Page: 410

69. The main problem with a worldwide area structure is the limited voice it gives to area or country managers, since they are seen as subservient to product division managers.

Answer: F
Medium
Page: 411

70. In the classic global matrix structure, horizontal differentiation proceeds along two dimensions: product division and functional area.

Answer: T
Medium
Page: 411

71. A dual-hierarchy structure is associated with a global matrix structure.

INTEGRATING MECHANISMS

Answer: F
Medium
Page: 412

72. The need for coordination between the subunits of a firm varies with the strategy of the firm. The need is highest in multidomestic firms and lowest in transnational firms.

Answer: T
Medium
Page: 412

73. The need for coordination is greatest in transnational firms.

Answer: T
Easy
Page: 414

74. Direct contact between subunit managers is the simplest integrating mechanism.

Answer: F
Medium
Page: 415

75. The formal integrating mechanism with the highest complexity of integrating mechanism is teams.

Answer: F
Medium
Page: 415

76. The formal integrating mechanism with the lowest complexity of integrating mechanisms is liaison roles.

Answer: T
Medium
Page: 415

77. A management network is a system of informal contracts between managers within an enterprise.

Answer: T
Easy
Page: 417

78. Traditionally, firms have tried to achieve coordination by adopting formal integrating mechanisms.

CONTROL SYSTEMS

Answer: F
Hard
Page: 417

79. The four main types of control systems used in multinational firms are output controls, feedforward controls, feedback controls, and input controls.

Answer: T
Easy
Page: 417

80. Personal control is control by personal contact with subordinates.

Answer: F
Medium
Page: 418

81. Output control is control through a system of rules and procedures that direct the actions of subunits.

Answer: F
Medium
Page: 418

82. Bureaucratic controls involve setting goals for subunits to achieve; expressing those goals in terms of relatively objective criteria such as profitability; and then judging the performance of subunit management by their ability to achieve those goals.

Answer: T
Medium
Page: 418

83. Cultural controls exist when employees "buy into" the norms and value systems of the firm.

Answer: T
Easy
Page: 419

84. Performance ambiguity exists when the causes of a subunit's poor performance are ambiguous.

Answer: F
Medium
Page: 420

85. Performance ambiguity tends to be highest in multidomestic firms.

Answer: F
Hard
Page: 420

86. Global firms have a high level of interdependence, a high level of performance ambiguity, and a low cost of controls.

Answer: F
Hard
Page: 420

87. International firms have a low level of interdependence, a high level of performance ambiguity, and a high cost of controls.

Answer: T
Medium
Page: 420

88. Transnational firms have the highest cost of controls.

SYNTHESIS: STRATEGY AND STRUCTURE

Answer: F
Medium
Page: 421

89. Firms pursuing a global strategy focus on local responsiveness.

Answer: T
Medium
Page: 421

90. Firms pursuing an international strategy attempt to create value by transferring core competencies from home to foreign markets.

ESSAY QUESTIONS

Easy
Page: 413

91. What is determined by a firm's vertical differentiation? (provide several examples of organizational issues that are determined by a firm's vertical differentiation).

Answer: A firm's vertical differentiation determines where in its hierarchy the decision-making power is concentrated. For example, are production and marketing decisions centralized in the offices of upper-level managers, or are they decentralized to lower-level managers? Where does the responsibility for R&D decisions lie? Are strategic and financial control responsibilities pushed down to operating units, or are they concentrated in the hands of top management. These are the types of issues that are determined by a firm's vertical differentiation.

Medium
Page: 403

92. What are the arguments for the centralization of decision making?

Answer: There are four main arguments for centralization (1) centralization can facilitate coordination, (2) centralization can help ensure that decisions are consistent with organizational objectives, (3) by concentrating power and authority in one individual or a top-management team, centralization can give top-level managers the means to bring about needed major organizational changes, and (4) centralization can avoid the duplication of activities that occurs when similar activities are carried on by various subunits within the organization.

Easy
Page: 404

93. What are the arguments for decentralization?

Answer: There are five main arguments for decentralization: (1) top management can become overburdened when decision-making authority is centralized, and this can result in poor decisions, (2) motivational research favors decentralization - behavioral scientists have long argued that people are willing to give more to their jobs when they have a greater degree of individual freedom and control over their work, (3) decentralization permits greater flexibility - more rapid response to environmental changes - because decisions do not have to be "referred up the hierarchy" unless they are exceptional, (4) decentralization can result in better decisions because decisions are made closer to the spot by individuals who have better information than managers several levels up in a hierarchy, and (5) decentralization can increase control.

Medium
Page: 405

94. What is determined by a firm's horizontal differentiation?

Answer: Horizontal differentiation is basically concerned with how the firm decides to divide itself into subunits. The decision is typically made on the basis of function, type of business, or geographic area. In many firms, just one of these criteria predominates, but more complex solutions are adopted in others. This is particularly likely in the case of international firms, where the conflicting demands to organize the company around different products and different markets must be reconciled.

Medium
Page: 410

95. Briefly describe the worldwide product division structure. What are the advantages and disadvantages of this structure?

Answer: A worldwide product division structure tends to be adopted by firms that are reasonably diversified and, accordingly, originally had domestic structures based on product divisions. As with the domestic product division structure, each division is a self-contained, largely autonomous entity with full responsibility for its own value creation activities. The headquarters retains the responsibility for the overall strategic development and financial controls of the firm.

The primary strength of the worldwide product division structure is that it provides an organizational context in which it is easier to pursue the consolidation of value creation activities at key locations necessary for realizing location and experience curve economies. It also facilitates the transfer of core competencies within a division's worldwide operations and the simultaneous worldwide introduction of new products. The main problem with the structure is the limited voice it gives to area or country managers, since they are seen as subservient to the product division managers. This can lead to a lack of local responsiveness.

Hard
Page: 410

96. Under what conditions are worldwide area structures and worldwide product division structures appropriate? Briefly describe the strengths and weaknesses of each structure.

Answer: Both the worldwide area structure and the worldwide product division structure have strengths and weaknesses. The worldwide area structure facilitates local responsiveness, but it can inhibit the realization of location and experience curve economies and the transfer of core competencies between areas. The worldwide product division structure provides a better framework for pursuing location and experience curve economies and for transferring core competencies, but it is weak in local responsiveness. Other things being equal, this suggests that a worldwide area structure is more appropriate if the firm's strategy is multidomestic, whereas a worldwide product division structure is more appropriate for firms pursuing global or international strategies.

Medium
Page: 411

97. What have been the major problems experienced with the global matrix structure?

Answer: In practice, the global matrix structure has turned out to be clumsy and bureaucratic. It can require so many meeting that it is difficult to get anything done. Often, the need to get an area and a product division to reach a decision slows decision making and produces an inflexible organization unable to respond quickly to market shifts or to innovate. The dual-hierarchy structure can also lead to conflict and perpetual power struggles between the area and the product divisions, catching many managers in the middle. To make matters worse, it can prove difficult to ascertain accountability in this structure.

Medium
Page: 412

98. How does the need for coordination between the subunits of a firm vary across the four primary international strategies? Which strategies have the lowest and highest needs for coordination.

Answer: The need for coordination between subunits varies with the strategy of the firm. The need for coordination is lowest in multidomestic companies, is higher in international companies, higher still in global companies, and highest of all in the transnational.

Medium
Page: 417

99. What are the four main types of control systems utilized by multinational firms? Why do different firms emphasize different systems?

Answer: There are four main types of control systems that we find in international firms - personal controls, bureaucratic controls, output controls, and cultural controls. In most firms, all four are used, their relative emphasis tends to vary with the strategy of the firm.

Medium
Page: 419

100. What causes performance ambiguity?

Answer: Performance ambiguity arises when the causes of poor performance by a sub-unit are ambiguous. This performance ambiguity is most likely to be the case when the performance of a sub-unit is in part dependent upon its relationship with other sub-units of the firm. The level of performance ambiguity is a function of the extent of interdependence between sub-units within an organization.

CHAPTER 14

ENTRY STRATEGY AND STRATEGIC ALLIANCES

MULTIPLE-CHOICE QUESTIONS

INTRODUCTION

Answer: A
Easy
Page: 429

1. __________ are cooperative agreements between actual or potential competitors.

   A. Strategic alliances
   B. Cooperative interrelationships
   C. Competitive synergies
   D. Tactical partnerships

Answer: C
Easy
Page: 429

2. The term __________ is often used loosely to embrace a variety of arrangements between actual or potential competitors including cross-shareholding deals, licensing arrangements, formal joint ventures, and informal cooperative arrangements.

   A. tactical partnerships
   B. competitive associations
   C. strategic alliances
   D. cooperative interrelationships

BASIC ENTRY DECISIONS

Answer: B
Easy
Page: 431

3. The advantages frequently associated with entering a market early are commonly known as:

   A. inaugural advantages
   B. first-mover advantages
   C. initial-entrant premiums
   D. proactive-mover benefits

Answer: D
Medium
Page: 431

4. Which of the following is not a first-mover advantage?

A. the ability to preempt rivals and capture demand by establishing a strong brand name
B. the ability to build sales volume in a country and ride down the experience curve ahead of rivals
C. the ability to create switching costs that tie customers to a company's products or services
D. the ability to increase a firm's changes of survival by entering a foreign market before industry rivals

Answer: A
Easy
Page: 431

5. The disadvantages associated with entering a market early are commonly known as:

A. first-mover disadvantages
B. inaugural disadvantages
C. initial-entrant disadvantages
D. proactive-mover losses

Answer: C
Medium
Page: 431

6. __________ are costs that an early entrant has to bear that a later entrant can avoid.

A. Untried costs
B. Introductory costs
C. Pioneering costs
D. Experimental costs

Answer: A
Medium
Page: 431

7. __________ arise when the business system in a foreign country is so different from that in a firm's home market that the enterprise has to devote considerable effort, time, and expense to learning the rules of the game.

A. Pioneering costs
B. Introductory costs
C. Inaugural costs
D. Experimental costs

Answer: D
Easy
Page: 432

8. A __________ is a decision that has a long-term impact and is difficult to reverse.

A. operational pledge
B. functional assurance
C. tactical covenant
D. strategic commitment

Answer: B
Medium
Page: 432

9. __________ entry allows a firm to learn about a foreign market while limiting the firm's exposure to that market.

A. Minimal-commitment
B. Small-scale
C. Reduced-commitment
D. Minimal-scale

ENTRY MODES

Answer: A
Medium
Page: 434

10. Exporting has two distinct advantages. These are:

A. it avoids the cost of establishing manufacturing operations in the host country and it may help a firm achieve experience curve and location economies
B. it is politically acceptable and it provides a firm access to the knowledge of its local partners
C. it is politically acceptable and the licensee puts up most of the capital necessary to get the overseas operation going
D. a firm is relieved of many of the costs and risks of opening a foreign market on its own and it provides a firm access to the knowledge of its local partners

Answer: C
Hard
Page: 434

11. All of the following are disadvantages of exporting except?

A. exporting from a firm's home base may not be appropriate if there are lower-cost locations for manufacturing the product abroad
B. tariff barriers can make exporting uneconomical
C. it may help a firm achieve experience curve economies
D. high transportation costs can make exporting uneconomical

Answer: C
Medium
Page: 434

12. High transportation costs, trade barriers, and problems with local marketing agents are all disadvantages of:

A. licensing
B. turnkey projects
C. exporting
D. franchising

Answer: D
Medium
Page: 434

13. Consider the following scenario: Sunshine Manufacturing wants to sell its products overseas, but only if it can act on its own and manufacturer its product in a central location. Based on these objectives, the appropriate foreign entry mode for Sunshine is:

A. wholly owned subsidiary
B. franchising
C. licensing
D. exporting

Answer: C
Easy
Page: 435

14. In a _________ project, the contractor agrees to handle every detail of the project for a foreign client, including the training of operating personnel.

A. beginning to end
B. A to Z
C. turnkey
D. front-to-back

Answer: B
Medium
Page: 435

15. Which of the following industries are turnkey projects the most common in?

A. fresh fruit, grain, and meat products
B. chemical, pharmaceutical, and metal refining
C. electronics, computer chips, and automotive parts
D. apparel, shoes, and leather products

Answer: D
Medium
Page: 435

16. Turnkey projects are a means of exporting __________ to another country.

A. commodities
B. manufactured goods
C. services
D. process technology

Answer: D
Medium
Page: 436

17. Which foreign market entry strategy has the following disadvantages: lack of long-term market presence, may inadvertently create a competitor, risk selling a firm's competitive advantage

A. wholly owned subsidiary
B. exporting
C. franchising
D. turnkey project

Answer: A
Medium
Page: 436

18. Suppose Texaco, a U.S. company, was contracted by a Saudi Arabian company to build an oil refinery in Saudi Arabia, and the contract specified that Texaco would handle every aspect of the construction of the refinery, including the training of the operating personnel. This type of project is referred to as a:

A. turnkey project
B. A to Z endeavor
C. throughput endeavor
D. front to back project

Answer: B
Medium
Page: 436

19. Which of the following foreign market entry modes takes advantage of a firm's competency in the area of assembling and running technologically complex projects?

A. exporting
B. turnkey project
C. wholly owned subsidiary
D. joint venture

Answer: D
Medium
Page: 436

20. An ability to earn returns from process technology skills in countries where foreign direct investment is realized is a distinct advantage of:

A. joint ventures
B. wholly owned subsidiaries
C. franchising
D. turnkey projects

Answer: B
Easy
Page: 436

21. A __________ agreement is an arrangement whereby a licensor grants the rights to intangible property to another entity (the licensee) for a specified period, an in turn, the licensor receives a royalty payment from the licensee.

A. franchising
B. licensing
C. turnkey
D. joint venture

Answer: C
Medium
Page: 436

22. Which of the following is not an argument in favor of licensing as a means of foreign market entry?

A. is attractive when a firm in unwilling to commit substantial financial resources to an unfamiliar market
B. a firm wants to participate in a foreign market but is prohibited from doing so by barriers to investment
C. a firm wants to maintain tight control over the manufacturing and marketing of its product or service
D. a firm does not have to bear the development costs and risks associated with opening a foreign market

Answer: A
Medium
Page: 436

23. Lack of control over technology, an inability to realize location and experience curve economies, and an inability to engage in global strategic coordination are disadvantages of:

A. licensing
B. wholly owned subsidiary
C. exporting
D. franchising

Answer: D
Medium
Page: 436

24. Suppose 3M Corporation granted a Belgium firm the rights to manufacture "Post-it-Notes" in Belgium in exchange for a royalty fee. This type of arrangement is referred to as a:

A. turnkey project
B. joint venture
C. franchise agreement
D. licensing agreement

Answer: A
Medium
Page: 436

25. Patents, inventions, formulas, processes, designs, copyrights, and trademarks are examples of __________ property.

A. intangible
B. nondescript
C. tangible
D. discernible

Answer: B
Medium
Page: 437

26. Under a __________ agreement, a firm might license some valuable intangible property to a foreign partner, but in addition to a royalty payment, the firm might also request that the foreign partner license some of its valuable know-how to the firm.

A. reciprocal-licensing
B. cross-licensing
C. parity-licensing
D. fair-licensing

Answer: C
Easy
Page: 437

27. __________ is basically a specialized form of licensing in which the franchisor not only sells intangible property to the franchisee, but also insists that the franchisee agree to abide by strict rules as to how it does business.

A. Leasing
B. Chartering
C. Franchising
D. Exporting

Answer: C
Medium
Page: 437

28. The two forms of foreign market entry that results in a firm in the host country paying a royalty to the firm that has the rights to a product, service, or business process are:

A. joint venture and licensing
B. wholly owned subsidiary and exporting
C. franchising and licensing
D. exporting and turnkey project

Answer: A
Medium
Page: 438

29. Whereas licensing is pursued primarily by __________ firms, franchising is employed primarily by __________ firms.

A. manufacturing, service
B. agricultural, manufacturing
C. service, mining
D. mining, service

Answer: B
Medium
Page: 439

30. One of the most significant potential disadvantages of franchising is:

A. the need for coordination of manufacturing to achieve experience curve and location economies
B. quality control
C. high development costs
D. high financial risks

Answer: A
Medium
Page: 440

31. If Mobil and a Russian firm established a jointly owned entity for the purpose of exploring for oil in Northern Siberia, that would be an example of a:

A. joint venture
B. licensing agreement
C. wholly owned subsidiary
D. turnkey project

Answer: D
Easy
Page: 440

32. A __________ entails establishment of a firm that is jointly owned by two or more otherwise independent firms.

A. franchise
B. wholly owned subsidiary
C. turnkey project
D. joint venture

Answer: D
Medium
Page: 441

33. Which of the following modes of foreign market entry has the following advantages: firms benefit from a local partner's knowledge of the host country's competitive conditions; a firm shares development costs with a local partner; and in many countries political considerations necessitate this form of entry

A. wholly owned subsidiary
B. franchising
C. exporting
D. joint venture

Answer: B
Medium
Page: 440

34. The most typical joint venture is:

A. 80/20, in which there are two partners and one partners hold a substantial majority share
B. 50/50, in which there are two partners and each partner holds an equal share
C. 25/25/25/25, in which there are four partners and each partner holds an equal share
D. 51/49, in which there are two partners and one partner holds a slight majority share

Answer: A
Easy
Page: 441

35. In a wholly owned subsidiary, the firm owns __________ of the stock.

A. 100 %
B. at least 51 %
C. none
D. at least 33.3 %

Answer: D
Medium
Page: 442

36. Protection of technology, the ability to engage in global strategic coordination, and the ability to realize location and experience curve economies are distinct advantages of a __________ entry mode.

A. franchising
B. licensing
C. exporting
D. wholly owned subsidiary

Answer: D
Medium
Page: 442

37. The most costly form of foreign market entry is:

A. exporting
B. licensing
C. franchising
D. wholly owned subsidiary

Answer: C
Hard
Page: 443

38. If a firm's competitive advantage is based on control over proprietary technological know how, which of the following foreign market entry modes should be avoided?

A. exporting and wholly owned subsidiary
B. turnkey project and exporting
C. licensing and joint venture
D. wholly owned subsidiary and exporting

Answer: D
Medium
Page: 443

39. If a high-tech firms sets up operations in a foreign country to profit from a core competency in technological know-how, it will probably do so through a:

A. licensing agreement
B. franchise agreement
C. joint venture
D. wholly owned subsidiary

Answer: A
Medium
Page: 444

40. Many service firms favor a combination of franchising and __________ to control the franchises within particular countries or regions.

A. subsidiaries
B. turnkey project partners
C. licensing agreements
D. strategic alliances

Answer: C
Hard
Page: 444

41. The greater the pressures for cost reductions are, the more likely a firm will want to pursue some combination of:

A. licensing and joint venture
B. franchising and exporting
C. exporting and wholly owned subsidiaries
D. joint ventures and wholly owned subsidiaries

Answer: B
Hard
Page: 444

42. The greater the pressures for __________ are, the more likely a firm will want to pursue some combination of exporting and wholly owned subsidiaries.

A. quality improvements
B. cost reductions
C. sales increases
D. service contracts

STRATEGIC ALLIANCES

Answer: D
Easy
Page: 444

43. Cooperative agreements between potential or actual competitors are referred to as:

A. tactical partnerships
B. cooperative interrelationships
C. competitive synergies
D. strategic alliances

Answer: B
Easy
Page: 444

44. __________ run the range from formal joint ventures to short-term contractual agreements.

A. Cooperative synergies
B. Strategic alliances
C. Tactical partnerships
D. Franchise organizations

Answer: B
Medium
Page: 444

45. The 1980s and 1990s have seen __________ in the number of strategic alliances.

A. a collapse
B. an explosion
C. a slight increase
D. a slight decrease

Answer: D
Medium
Page: 445

46. Which of the following is a disadvantage of strategic alliances?

A. may facilitate entry into a foreign market
B. allow firms to share fixed costs
C. is a way for firms to bring together complementary skills and assets
D. give competitors a low-cost route to new technology and markets

Answer: B
Medium
Page: 445

47. One of the primary disadvantages of strategic alliances is that they:

A. give competitors a low-cost route to new technology and markets
B. entail high costs and risks
C. can involve problems with local marketing agents
D. are typically only practiced by large companies

Answer: C
Hard
Page: 445

48. Robert Reich and Eric Mankin have argued that __________ between U.S. and Japanese firms are part of an implicit Japanese strategy to keep higher-paying, higher-value-added jobs in Japan while gaining the project engineering and production process skills that underlie the competitive success of many U.S. companies.

A. licensing agreements
B. franchise agreements
C. strategic alliances
D. turnkey projects

Answer: A
Medium
Page: 445

49. One of the principle risks with strategic alliances is:

A. a firm can give away more than it receives
B. that they bring together the complementary skills of alliance partners
C. alliances may facilitate entry into foreign markets
D. that they allow firms to share fixed costs

MAKING ALLIANCES WORK

Answer: A
Medium
Page: 446

50. The failure rate for strategic alliances is:

A. quite high
B. moderately high
C. moderately low
D. quite low

Answer: C
Hard
Page: 446

51. One study of 49 international strategic alliances found that two-thirds run into serious managerial and financial troubles within two years of their formation, and that although many of these problems are solved, __________ are ultimately rated as failures by the parties involved.

A. 15 percent
B. 25 percent
C. 33 percent
D. 50 percent

Answer: C
Hard
Page: 446

52. Which of the following is not an attribute of a good strategic alliance partner?

A. is unlikely to opportunistically exploit the alliance for its own ends
B. shares the firm's vision for the purpose of the alliance
C. must have capabilities identical to its partner
D. helps the firm achieve its strategic goals

Answer: B
Hard
Page: 446

53. Which of the following is not one of the four safeguards against opportunism by alliance partners mentioned in our textbook?

A. walling off critical technology
B. avoiding the practice of swapping valuable skills and technologies
C. establishing contractual safeguards
D. seeking credible commitments

Answer: C
Medium
Page: 446

54. There are four main safeguards against opportunism in alliance relationships. These are walling off critical technology, establishing contractual safeguards, seeking credible commitments, and:

A. only entering into alliances with firms that have a track record of successful alliances relationships
B. only entering into alliances with large (i.e., Fortune 500) firms
C. agreeing to swap valuable skills and technologies
D. avoiding cross-licensing agreements

Answer: D
Medium
Page: 446

55. There are four main safeguards against opportunism in alliance relationships. These are walling off critical technology, agreeing to swap valuable skills and technologies, seeking credible commitments, and:

A. only entering into alliances with firms that are smaller than your own
B. avoiding cross-licensing agreements
C. avoid partnering with multinational firms
D. establishing contractual safeguards

Answer: B
Medium
Page: 446

56. There are four main safeguards against opportunism in alliance relationships. These are walling establishing contractual safeguards, agreeing to swap valuable skills and technologies, seeking credible commitments, and:

A. avoiding cross-licensing agreements
B. walling off critical technology
C. establishing a legally binding escape clause
D. avoid partnering with strictly domestic firms

Answer: C
Medium
Page: 446

57. Walling off critical technology, establishing contractual safeguards, agreeing to swap valuable skills and technologies, and seeking credible commitments are safeguards against __________ by an alliance partner.

A. expediency
B. theft
C. opportunism
D. self-interest

Answer: C
Medium
Page: 447

58. Which of the following safeguards against opportunism by alliance partners can be achieved through the use of cross-licensing agreements?

A. walling off critical technology
B. establishing contractual safeguards
C. agreeing to swap valuable skills and technologies
D. seeking credible commitments

Answer: B
Hard
Page: 446

59. After a five-year study of 15 strategic alliances between major multinationals, Gary Hamel, Yves Doz, and C.K. Prahalad concluded that a major determinant of how much a company gains from an alliance is:

A. the amount of cost sharing that has been achieved
B. its ability to learn from its alliance partners
C. the number of new foreign markets that have been penetrated
D. the product and service quality improvement that have been realized

Answer: A
Medium
Page: 448

60. To maximize the learning benefits of an alliance, a firm must:

A. try to learn from its partner and then apply the knowledge within its own organization
B. set clear objectives in regard to what it wants to learn
C. stay in the alliance for a minimum of three years
D. establish a "learning" organizational culture

TRUE-FALSE QUESTIONS

BASIC ENTRY DECISIONS

Answer: T
Easy
Page: 429

61. Strategic alliances are cooperative agreements between actual and potential competitors.

Answer: T
Easy
Page: 430

62. We say that entry is early when an international business enters a foreign market before other foreign firms and late when it enters after other international businesses have already established themselves.

Answer: F
Easy
Page: 431

63. The advantages frequently associated with entering a market early are commonly known as proactive-mover advantages.

Answer: T
Medium
Page: 431

64. Pioneering costs are costs that an early entrant has to bear that a later entrant can avoid.

Answer: F
Medium
Page: 432

65. A tactical commitment is a decision that has a long-term impact and is difficult to reverse.

ENTRY MODES

Answer: T
Medium
Page: 434

66. Exporting may help a firm achieve experience curve and location economies.

Answer: F
Medium
Page: 434

67. Most manufacturing firms begin their global expansion through licensing.

Answer: T
Medium
Page: 434

68. Exporting has two distinct advantages. First, it avoids the often-substantial costs of establishing manufacturing operations in the host country. Second, exporting may help a firm achieve experience curve and location economies.

Answer: F
Medium
Page: 434

69. Exporting from the firm's home base is particularly appropriate if there are lower-cost locations for manufacturing the product abroad.

Answer: F
Medium
Page: 435

70. In a turnkey project, the contractor agrees to handle every detail of the project for a foreign client, with the exception of training the operating personnel.

Answer: F
Medium
Page: 435

71. Wholly owned subsidiary is particularly useful where FDI is limited by host-government regulations.

Answer: T
Medium
Page: 435

72. Turnkey projects are most common in the chemical, pharmaceutical, petroleum refining, and metal refining industries.

Answer: T
Medium
Page: 436

73. A licensing agreement is an arrangement whereby a licensor grants the rights to intangible property to another entity for a specified period, and in return, the licensor receives a royalty fee from the licensee.

Answer: F
Medium
Page: 436

74. Licensing gives a firm tight control over the manufacturing, marketing, and strategy that is required for realizing experience curve and location economies.

Answer: F
Medium
Page: 436

75. A primary advantage of licensing is total control over technology.

Answer: T
Medium
Page: 437

76. In the typical international licensing deal, the licensee puts up most of the capital necessary to get the overseas operation going.

Answer: T
Medium
Page: 437

77. Whereas licensing is pursued primarily by manufacturing firms, franchising is employed primarily by service firms.

Answer: T
Easy
Page: 438

78. Franchising is basically a specialized form of licensing in which the franchisor not only sells intangible property to the franchisee, but also insists that the franchisee agree to abide by strict rules as to how it does business.

Answer: T
Medium
Page: 438

79. A primary advantage of franchising is low development costs and risks.

Answer: T
Medium
Page: 440

80. A significant disadvantage of franchising is quality control.

Answer: F
Easy
Page: 440

81. A joint venture entails establishing a new firm from two separate divisions of an existing firm.

Answer: T
Medium
Page: 440

82. A primary advantage of joint ventures is the sharing of development costs and risks.

Answer: T
Easy
Page: 441

83. In a wholly owned subsidiary, the firm owns 100% of the stock.

Answer: F
Medium
Page: 442

84. One of the primary disadvantages of a wholly owned subsidiary is that it gives the firm little control over operations in different countries that is necessary for engaging in global strategic coordination.

Answer: T
Medium
Page: 443

85. A disadvantage of wholly owned subsidiaries is high costs and risks.

Answer: T
Hard
Page: 444

86. Many service firms favor a combination of licensing and subsidiaries to control the franchises within particular countries or regions.

STRATEGIC ALLIANCES

Answer: T
Easy
Page: 444

87. Strategic alliances refer to cooperative agreements between potential or actual competitors.

Answer: F
Medium
Page: 444

88. Strategic alliances are rarely used as an entry strategy into foreign markets.

MAKING ALLIANCES WORK

Answer: F
Medium
Page: 446

89. The failure rate for international strategic alliances is quite low.

Answer: T
Medium
Page: 447

90. The four safeguards against opportunism in alliance relationships are walling off critical technology, establishing contractual safeguards, agreeing to swap valuable skills and technologies, and seeking credible commitments.

ESSAY QUESTIONS

Medium
Page: 431

91. What are pioneering costs? When do these costs arise?

Answer: Pioneering costs are costs that an early entrant has to bear that a later entrant can avoid. Pioneering costs arise when the business system in a foreign country is too different from that in a firm's home market that the enterprise has to devote considerable effort, time, and expanse to learning the rules of the game.

Easy
Page: 432

92. What is a strategic commitment? Does entering a foreign market qualify as a strategic commitment?

Answer: A strategic commitment is a decision that has a long-term impact and is difficult to reverse. Deciding whether entering a foreign market qualifies as a strategic commitment depends on the scale of a domestic firm's commitment. Deciding to enter a foreign market on a significant scale is a major strategic commitment. Occasionally exporting a product to a foreign country, with little investment involved, may be only a minor commitment on the part of a firm.

Hard
Page: 434

93. What are the six different ways for a firm to enter a foreign market? Provide a brief description of each of these foreign market entry strategies.

Answer: The six different ways for a firm to enter a foreign market include:

A. Exporting – involves manufacturing a product in a central location and shipping it to foreign markets for sale.
B. Turnkey projects – in a turnkey project, a contractor from one country handles every detail of the design, construction, and start-up of a facility in a foreign country, and then hands the foreign client the key to a facility that is ready for operation.
C. Licensing – in a licensing agreement, a company from one country grants the rights to intangible property (such as patents, processes, and trademarks) to a company in another country in exchange for a royalty fee.
D. Franchising – is a specialized form of licensing in which the franchiser sells intangible property (normally processes and trademarks) to a franchisee, but also insists that the franchisee agree

to abide by strict rules as to how it does business. The McDonalds Corporation, for example, has been very successful in selling franchises to both domestic and foreign franchisees.

E. Joint Ventures – entails establishing a firm that is jointly owned by two or more otherwise independent firms.

F. Wholly Owned Subsidiary – this form of foreign market entry entails setting up a new operation (or acquiring an existing company) in a foreign country.

Medium
Page: 435

94. What is a turnkey project? What are the advantages of a turnkey project compared to foreign direct investment (FDI)?

Answer: In a turnkey project, the contractor agrees to handle every detail of the project for a foreign client, including the training of operating personnel. At the completion of the contract, the foreign client is handed the "key" to a plant that is ready for full operation.

The know-how required to assemble and run a technologically complex process (like a chemical plant) is a valuable asset. Turnkey projects are a way of earning great economic returns from that asset. The strategy is particularly useful where FDI is limited by host-government regulations. A turnkey strategy can also be less risky than conventional FDI. In a country with unstable political and economic environments, a longer-term investment might expose a firm to unacceptable political and/or economic risks.

Medium
Page: 436

95. From the perspective of a domestic firm, what are the advantages and disadvantages of licensing the rights to the company's production process and trademark to a firm in a foreign country?

Answer: The primary advantage of licensing is that the firm does not have to bear the development costs and risks associated with opening a foreign market. As a result, licensing is a very attractive option for firms that lack the capital or risk bearing ability to open overseas markets. Licensing is also an attractive option when a firm is interested in pursuing a foreign market but does not want to commit substantial resources to an unfamiliar or potentially volatile foreign market. Licensing is also used when a firm wishes to participate in a foreign market, but is prohibited from doing so by barriers to investment. Finally, licensing is used when a firm possesses some intangible property (like its trademark) but does not want to pursue a potential application itself. For example, Coca-Cola has licensed its familiar trademark to clothing manufacturers, which have incorporated the design into their clothing.

There are three main drawbacks to licensing. First, if a firm licenses any of its proprietary know-how (such as its production processes) to another company, it risks losing control over this knowledge by permitting access to it by another firm. According to the textbook, many firms have made the mistake of thinking they could maintain control over their know-how within the framework of a licensing agreement. Second, licensing is not an effective way of realizing experience curve and location economies by manufacturing a product in a centralized location. If these attributes are important to a firm, licensing may be a poor choice. Finally, competing in a global market may require a firm to coordinate strategic moves across countries by using profits from one country to support competitive attacks in another. Licensing severely limits a firm's ability to do this. A licensee is unlikely to allow a multinational firm to use its profits (beyond the royalty payments) to support a different licensee operating in another country.

Medium
Page: 436

96. What is the difference between licensing and franchising in an international context?

Answer: Conceptually there is really little difference between licensing and franchising. In both cases the firm gives up something it has to allow a foreign firm to be more successful in a foreign market (in exchange for a royalty payment). In the case of licensing, this usually involves the right to use some technological product or know how. In the case of franchising, the franchisee usually gets access to a brand name and a business process that it can use to establish a business. Franchising agreement tend to be for longer terms than licensing agreements.

Medium
Page: 437

97. What are some of the ways that a firm can reduce the risk of losing its proprietary know-how to foreign companies through licensing agreements?

Answer: A licensor can reduce the risk of losing proprietary know-how to a foreign partner by entering into a cross-licensing agreement. Under a cross-license agreement, a firm licenses some valuable intangible property (such as a production process) to a foreign partner, but in addition to royalty payments, the firm also requires the foreign partner to license some of its valuable know-how to the firm. Cross-licensing agreements enable forms to hold each other "hostage," there by reducing the risk they will behave in an opportunistic manner towards each other.

Medium
Page: 441

98. What is meant by the term "wholly owned subsidiary?" Under what circumstances is the establishment of a wholly owned subsidiary an appropriate foreign entry strategy?

Answer: A wholly owned subsidiary is a company that is completely owned by another company. One choice that a firm has for entering a foreign market is to setup a new operation in that market or purchase an existing firm. In either case, if the original company owns 100% of the new operation, it is "wholly owned subsidiary" of the original firm.

Establishing a wholly owned subsidiary as an entry strategy into a foreign market is appropriate when a firm's competitive advantage is based on technological competence. By establishing a wholly owned subsidiary, a firm reduces the risk of losing control over that competence. This is a particularly important concern for firms that have important proprietary technology. Other forms of foreign market entry, such as licensing and joint venture, do a poorer job of protecting a firm's proprietary technology.

Establishing a wholly owned subsidiary may be appropriate for two additional reasons. First, expanding via the wholly owned subsidiary route gives a firm tight control over its operations in various countries. This strategy maximizes a firm's potential to engage in global strategic coordination (i.e., using profits from one country to support competitive attacks in another). Second, a wholly owned subsidiary strategy may be required if a firm is trying to realize location and experience curve economies.

Easy
Page: 444

99. What are strategic alliances? Are strategic alliances on the rise or decline?

Answer: Strategic alliances are cooperative agreements between potential or actual competitors. Strategic alliances run the range from formal joint ventures, in which two or more firms have equity stakes, to short-term contractual arrangements, in which two companies agree to cooperate on a particular task. Strategic alliances are definitely on the rise. The 1980s and 1990s have seen an explosion in the number of strategic alliances that have been formed worldwide.

Medium
Page: 446

100. What are the four main ways that firms can safeguard themselves against opportunism in alliance relationships?

Answer: (1) walling off critical technology; (2) establishing contractual safeguards, (3) agreeing to swap valuable skills and technologies, and

(4) seeking credible commitments

CHAPTER 15

EXPORTING, IMPORTING, AND COUNTERTRADE

MULTIPLE-CHOICE QUESTIONS

INTRODUCTION

Answer: A
Easy
Page: 484

1. Evidence suggests that the volume of export activity in the world economy, by firms of all sizes, is likely to __________ in the near future.

   A. increase
   B. decrease
   C. remain the same
   D. disappear

THE PROMISE AND PITFALL OF EXPORTING

Answer: B
Medium
Page: 485

2. Despite the obvious opportunities associated with exporting, studies have shown that while many large firm tend to be __________ about seeking opportunities for profitable exporting, many medium sized and small firms are very __________.

   A. reluctant, proactive
   B. proactive, reactive
   C. reserved, optimistic
   D. reactive, proactive

Answer: A
Hard
Page: 485

3. According to the U.S. Small Business Administration, less than __________ of U.S. firms export.

   A. 2 percent
   B. 5 percent
   C. 10 percent
   D. 15 percent

Answer: D
Medium
Page: 485

4. Exporters account for __________ of U.S. firms.

   A. a very large percent
   B. a large percent
   C. a small percent
   D. a very small percent

Answer: B
Medium
Page: 485

5. Common pitfalls to successful export operations include all of the following except:

A. poor market analysis
B. relatively small revenue and profit opportunities are found in foreign markets
C. a poor understanding of competitive conditions in the foreign market
D. lack of an effective distribution program

Answer: D
Hard
Page: 485

6. According to a UN report on trade and development, a typical international trade transaction may involve __________ different parties.

A. 8
B. 15
C. 20
D. 30

Answer: B
Hard
Page: 485

7. The United Nations has calculated that the time involved in preparing export related documents, along with the costs of common errors in paperwork, often amounts to __________ of the final value of the goods exported.

A. 5 percent
B. 10 percent
C. 15 percent
D. 20 percent

IMPROVING EXPORT PERFORMANCE

Answer: A
Easy
Page: 486

8. In the context of exporting, the acronym EMC refers to:

A. export management company
B. experienced multinational corporation
C. export medical clearance
D. European Monetary Commission

Answer: C
Hard
Page: 486

9. There are __________ different countries that represent potential export markets.

A. 95
B. 135
C. 180
D. 215

Answer: C
Medium
Page: 486

10. MITI is the __________ Ministry of International Trade and Industry.

A. South Korean
B. Italian
C. Japanese
D. British

Answer: A
Hard
Page: 486

11. In Japan, the *sogo shosha* are:

A. trading houses
B. export finance companies
C. exporters
D. importers

Answer: D
Medium
Page: 486

12. The most comprehensive source of export related information in the U.S. is the:

A. U.S. Department of Agricultural
B. World Bank
C. International Monetary Fund
D. U.S. Department of Commerce

Answer: A
Medium
Page: 486

13. In the United States, the __________ is the most comprehensive source of information about export advice.

A. U.S. Department of Commerce
B. U.S. Department of State
C. World Trade Organization
D. U.S. Department of Agricultural

Answer: B
medium
Page: 486

14. Within the U.S. Department of Commerce are two organizations dedicated to providing businesses with intelligence and assistance for attacking foreign markets. These organizations are:

A. Agency for Export Promotion and Development and the International Trade Administration
B. International Trade Administration and the United States and Foreign Commercial Service Agency
C. U.S. Export-Import Bank and the Agency for Export Promotion and Development
D. United States and Foreign Commercial Service Agency and the U.S. Export-Import Bank

Answer: A
Medium
Page: 486

15. Within the U.S. Department of Commerce are two organizations dedicated to providing businesses with intelligence and assistance for attacking foreign markets. These organizations are the United States and Foreign Commercial Service Agency and the:

A. International Trade Administration
B. U.S. Export-Import Bank
C. Agency for Export Promotion and Development
D. U.S. Commission for Export Excellence

Answer: D
Medium
Page: 487

16. Which of the following is not a function of the U.S. Department of Commerce?

A. organize trade events that help potential exporters make foreign contacts and explore export opportunities
B. organizes exhibitions at international trade shows
C. maintains a matchmaker program, in which department representatives accompany groups of U.S. businesspeople abroad to meet with qualified agents, distributors, and customers
D. act as an export marketing department or international department for their client firms

Answer: A
Easy
Page: 487

17. One way for first-time exporters to identify the opportunities associated with exporting and to avoid many of the associated pitfalls is to hire an:

A. export management company
B. international intermediaries
C. export accounting agencies
D. overseas marketing companies

Answer: A
Medium
Page: 487

18. Export management companies are export specialists who act as the __________ department for their client firms.

A. marketing or international
B. manufacturing or operations
C. finance or accounting
D. human resource management or personnel

Answer: C
Hard
Page: 487

19. Export management companies normally accept two types of export assignments: they start export operations for a firm with the understanding that the firm will take over operations after they are well established, or:

A. they perform start-up with the understanding that the export management company will remain committed for a period of at least ten years
B. they perform start-up with the understanding that the export management company will remain committed for a period of at least five years
C. they perform start-up with the understanding that they will have continuing responsibility for selling the firm's products
D. they perform start-up with the understanding that the export management company will acquire an equity interest in the exporting firm

Answer: B
Medium
Page: 487

20. In theory, the advantage of EMCs is that:

A. they are required for entering some foreign markets
B. they are experienced specialists who can help the neophyte exporter
C. they are subsidized by the Department of Commerce
D. are required to be not-for-profit organizations

Answer: D
Hard
Page: 487

21. Which of the following was not mentioned in our textbook as a strategy for effective exporting?

A. it is important to hire local personnel to help the firm establish itself in a foreign market
B. particularly for a new exporter, it helps to hire an export management company
C. in many countries it is important to devote a lot of attention to building strong and enduring relationships with local distributors and/or customers
D. it often makes sense to focus on a large number of markets initially

EXPORT AND IMPORT FINANCING

Answer: A
Medium
Page: 490

22. The three mechanisms for financing exports and imports include:

A. the letter of credit, the draft, and the bill of lading
B. the open note, the bill of cargo, and the stamp of credit worthiness
C. the stamp of credit worthiness, the open note, and the bill of cargo
D. the guaranteed note, the letter of credit, and the bill of shipping

Answer: D
Medium
Page: 490

23. The three mechanisms for financing exports and imports include the letter of credit, the draft, and the:

A. open note
B. stamp of credit worthiness
C. guaranteed note
D. bill of lading

Answer: A
Medium
Page: 490

24. The three mechanisms for financing exports and imports include the letter of credit, the bill of lading, and the:

A. draft
B. bill of cargo
C. stamp of credit worthiness
D. certified note

Answer: D
Medium
Page: 490

25. The three mechanisms for financing exports and imports include the bill of lading, the draft, and the:

A. stamp of credit worthiness
B. bill of cargo
C. guaranteed note
D. letter of credit

Answer: C
Easy
Page: 490

26. In the context of international commerce, the abbreviation L/C stands for:

A. letter of certification
B. liability clearance
C. letter of credit
D. liberal commerce

Answer: B
Medium
Page: 490

27. Issued by a bank at the request of an importer, the __________ states that the bank will pay a specified sum of money to a beneficiary, normally the exporter, on presentation of particular, specified documents.

A. stamp of credit worthiness
B. letter of credit
C. draft
D. bill of lading

Answer: B
Hard
Page: 491

28. The service fee for a letter of credit is usually between __________ of the value of the letter of credit, depending on the importer's creditworthiness and the size of the transaction.

A. 0.25 and 1 percent
B. 0.5 and 2 percent
C. 1 and 3 percent
D. 2 and 4 percent

Answer: D
Medium
Page: 490

29. An importer can guarantee to an exporter that it will get paid through a:

A. certificate of trust
B. draft
C. bill of lading
D. letter of credit

Answer: A
Medium
Page: 492

30. The disadvantage of using a letter of credit from the importer's perspective is:

A. that a service fee must be paid
B. only importers with questionable credit use letters of credit
C. a reciprocal letter of credit must be issued to the exporter
D. that it reveals financial information about the importer to the exporter

Answer: D
Easy
Page: 492

31. A __________, sometimes referred to as a bill of exchange, is the instrument normally used in international commerce for payment.

A. bill of lading
B. open note
C. stamp of credit worthiness
D. draft

Answer: A
Easy
Page: 492

32. The instrument normally used in international commerce for payment is referred to as a:

A. draft
B. stamp of credit worthiness
C. bill of lading
D. open note

Answer: C
Easy
Page: 492

33. International practice is to use __________ to settle transactions.

A. open notes
B. letters of credit
C. drafts
D. stamps of credit worthiness

Answer: B
Medium
Page: 492

34. A __________ is simply an order written by an exporter instructing an importer, or an importer's agent, to pay a specified amount of money at a specified time.

A. letter of credit
B. draft
C. stamp of credit worthiness
D. open note

Answer: A
Medium
Page: 492

35. International practice is to use __________ to settle trade transactions. This differs from domestic practice in which a seller usually ships merchandise on a(n) _________, followed by a commercial invoice that specifies the amount due and the terms of payment.

A. drafts, open account
B. letters of credit, restricted account
C. stamps of credit worthiness, probationary account
D. letters of credit, closed account

Answer: C
Easy
Page: 492

36. Drafts fall into two categories. These are:

A. inspection drafts and duration drafts
B. credit drafts and cash drafts
C. sight drafts and time drafts
D. inspection drafts and cash drafts

Answer: B
Easy
Page: 492

37. Drafts fall into two categories: sight drafts and __________ drafts.

A. duration
B. time
C. cash
D. credit

Answer: A
Easy
Page: 492

38. Drafts fall into two categories: time drafts and __________ drafts.

A. sight
B. credit
C. cash
D. duration

Answer: C
Medium
Page: 492

39. A __________ draft is payable on presentation to the drawee.

A. cash
B. credit
C. sight
D. time

Answer: D
Medium
Page: 492

40. A __________ draft allows for a delay in payment - normally 30, 60, 90, or 120 days.

A. sight
B. cash
C. credit
D. time

Answer: A
Medium
Page: 492

41. A __________ draft is presented to the drawee, who signifies acceptance of it by writing or stamping a notice of acceptance on its face.

A. time
B. sight
C. credit
D. cash

Answer: C
Medium
Page: 492

42. When a time draft is drawn on and accepted by a bank, it is called a:

A. trade acceptance
B. creditor's acceptance
C. banker's acceptance
D. drawee's acceptance

Answer: B
Medium
Page: 492

43. When a time draft is drawn on and accepted by a business firm, it is called a:

A. drawee's acceptance
B. trade acceptance
C. banker's acceptance
D. merchant's acceptance

Answer: C
Medium
Page: 492

44. __________ drafts are negotiable instruments; that is, one the draft is stamped with an acceptance, the maker can sell the draft to an investor at a discount from its face value.

A. Merchant
B. Maker
C. Time
D. Commerce

Answer: B
Easy
Page: 493

45. The __________ is issued to the exporter by the common carrier transporting the merchandise.

A. acceptance certificate
B. bill of lading
C. bill of tender
D. stamp of receipt

Answer: C
Medium
Page: 493

46. A bill of laden is issued to an exporter by:

A. a commercial bank
B. an export-import company
C. the common carrier transporting the merchandise
D. a custom's inspector

Answer: A
Medium
Page: 493

47. A bill of laden serves three purposes. These are:

A. it is a receipt, a contract, and a document of title
B. it is a certificate of authenticity, proof of insurance, and a contract
C. it is a certificate of authenticity, a letter of credit, and a document of title
D. it is proof of payment, a certificate of tariff payment, and a contract

Answer: A
Medium
Page: 493

48. A bill of laden serves three purposes - it is a receipt, a contract, and a:

A. document of title
B. letter of credit
C. proof of insurance
D. poof of customs clearance

Answer: B
Medium
Page: 493

49. A bill of laden serves three purposes - it is a contract, a document of title, and a:

A. proof of customs clearance
B. receipt
C. letter of credit
D. proof of environmental safety

Answer: C
Medium
Page: 493

50. A bill of laden serves three purposes - it is a receipt, a document of title, and a:

A. proof of insurance
B. proof of customs clearance
C. contract
D. letter of credit

Answer: C
Medium
Page: 493

51. As a __________, the bill of laden specifies that the carrier is obligated to provide a transportation service in return for a certain charge.

A. receipt
B. letter of understanding
C. contract
D. document of title

EXPORT ASSISTANCE

Answer: D
Easy
Page: 494

52. The mission of the __________ is to provide financing aid that will facilitate exports, imports, and the exchange of commodities between the United States and other countries.

A. International Trade Administration
B. International Monetary Fund
C. United States and Foreign Commercial Service Agency
D. Export-Import Bank

Answer: D
Medium
Page: 494

53. The __________ guarantees repayment of medium and long-term loans U.S. commercial banks made to foreign borrowers for purchasing U.S. exporters.

A. International Trade Administration
B. World Bank
C. United States and Foreign Commercial Service Agency
D. Export-Import Bank

Answer: A
Medium
Page: 495

54. In the United States, export credit insurance is provided by the:

A. Foreign Credit Insurance Association
B. Export-Import Bank
C. International Trade Administration
D. U.S. Department of Commerce

COUNTERTRADE

Answer: B
Medium
Page: 495

55. Countertrade is an alternative means of structuring an international sale when:

A. an importer is unable to raise the cash to make settlement
B. conventional means of payment are difficult, costly, or nonexistent
C. an importer is unable to obtain a letter of credit
D. an importer does not belong to the International Monetary Fund

Answer: C
Easy
Page: 496

56. __________ is the direct exchange of goods and/or services between two parties without a cash transaction.

A. Counterpurchase
B. Offset
C. Barter
D. Counterexchange

Answer: D
Easy
Page: 496

57. __________ is a reciprocal buying agreement.

A. Counterexchange
B. Barter
C. Offset
D. Counterpurchase

Answer: A
Easy
Page: 497

58. _________ is similar to counterpurchase insofar as one party agrees to purchase goods and services with a specified percentage of the proceeds from the original sale.

A. Offset
B. Switch Trading
C. Counterexchange
D. Countertrade

Answer: D
Easy
Page: 497

59. _________ refers to the use of a specialized thirdparty trading house in a countertrade arrangement.

A. Counterexchange
B. Barter
C. Offset
D. Switch Trading

Answer: B
Medium
Page: 498

60. A _________ occurs when a firm builds a plant in a country - or supplies technology, equipment, training, or other services to the country - and agrees to take a certain percentage of the plant's output as partial payment for the contract.

A. turnkey arrangement
B. buyback
C. quid pro quo
D. repurchase

TRUE-FALSE QUESTIONS

THE PROMISE AND PITFALLS OF EXPORTING

Answer: F
Medium
Page: 485

61. Studies have shown that while many small firms tend to be proactive about seeking opportunities for profitable exporting, many large firms are very reactive.

Answer: T
Hard
Page: 485

62. Exporters account for only about two percent of U.S. firms.

IMPROVING EXPORT PERFORMANCE

Answer: F
Medium
Page: 486

63. The most comprehensive source of export related information for American exporters is the U.S. Department of State.

Answer: T
Easy
Page: 487

64. Export management companies are export specialists who act as the export marketing department or international department for their client firms.

EXPORT AND IMPORT FINANCING

Answer: T
Easy
Page: 487

65. The three mechanisms for financing exports and imports include the letter of credit, the draft, and the stamp of credit worthiness.

Answer: T
Medium
Page: 490

66 A letter of credit states that a bank will pay a specified sum of money to a beneficiary, normally the exporter, on presentation of particular, specified documents.

Answer: F
Hard
Page: 491

67 Service fees for letters of credit normally run between 3 and 5 percent of the value of the letter of credit.

Answer: T
Medium
Page: 492

68. Service fees for letters of credit are paid by importers.

Answer: T
Easy
Page: 492

69. A draft, sometimes referred to as a bill of exchange, is the instrument normally used in international commerce for payment.

Answer: F
Easy
Page: 492

70. International practice is to use cash to settle trade transactions.

Answer: F
Medium
Page: 492

71. Drafts fall into two categories, bearer drafts and time drafts.

Answer: T
Medium
Page: 492

72. A sight draft is payable on presentation to the drawee.

Answer: T
Medium
Page: 492

73. Time drafts are negotiable instruments.

Answer: F
Medium
Page: 492

74. A time draft allows for a delay in payment - normally six months, one year, or three years.

Answer: T
Medium
Page: 492

75. When a time draft is drawn on and accepted by a bank, it is called a banker's acceptance.

Answer: F
Medium
Page: 492

76. When a time draft is drawn on and accepted by a business firm, it is called a client's acceptance.

Answer: T
Easy
Page: 493

77. The bill of lading is issued to the exporter by the common carrier transporting the merchandise.

Answer: F
Medium
Page: 493

78. Bill's of lading are issued by banks.

Answer: T
Medium
Page: 493

79. As a receipt, the bill of lading indicates that the carrier has received the merchandise described on the face of the document.

EXPORT ASSISTANCE

Answer: F
Medium
Page: 494

80. The Export-Import Bank is an agency of the World Bank.

Answer: T
Medium
Page: 494

81. The mission of the Export-Import bank is to provide financing aid that will facilitate exports, imports, and the exchange of commodities between the United States and other countries.

Answer: F
Medium
Page: 495

82. In the United States, export credit insurance is provided by U.S. Department of State.

COUNTERTRADE

Answer: T
Medium
Page: 495

83. Countertrade is an alternative means of structuring an international sale when conventional means of payment are difficult, costly, or nonexistent.

Answer: T
Hard
Page: 496

84. According to some estimates, more than 20 percent of world trade by value in 1998 was in the form of countertrade.

Answer: F Medium Page: 496	85. Barter is a reciprocal buying agreement.
Answer: T Hard Page: 496	86. Although barter is the simplest method of trade, it is not common.
Answer: F Medium Page: 496	87. Counterpurchase is the direct exchange of goods and/or services between two parties without a cash transations.
Answer: T Medium Page: 497	88. Offset is similar to counterpurchase insofar as one party agrees to purchase goods and services with a specified percentage of the proceeds from the original sale.
Answer: F Medium Page: 497	89. Switch trading refers to the use of commercial banks in a countertrade arrangement.
Answer: T Medium Page: 498	90. A buyback occurs when a firm builds a plant in a country - or supplies technology, equipment, training, or other services to the country - and agrees to take a certain percentage of the plant's output as partial payment for the contract.

ESSAY QUESTIONS

Easy
Page: 485

91. How have large U.S. firms and medium to small-sized U.S. firms differed in their reaction to export opportunities abroad?

Answer: Despite the obvious opportunities associated with exporting, studies have shown that while many large firms tend to be proactive about seeking opportunities for profitable exporting, many medium sized and small firms are very reactive. Typically, such reactive firms do not even consider exporting under their domestic market is saturated and the emergence of excess productive capacity at home forces them to look for growth opportunities in foreign markets.

Medium
Page: 485

92. What are the common pitfalls to profitable exporting, particularly for neophyte exporters?

Answer: Common pitfalls include poor market analysis, a poor understanding of competitive conditions in foreign markets, a failure to customize the product offering to the needs of foreign customers, lack of an effective distribution program, and a poorly executed promotional campaign in the foreign market.

Medium
Page: 487

93. What is an export management company? What should a company do before it hires an export management company to help with its export operations?

Answer: An export management company (EMC) is a firm that specializes in helping other firms initiate and manage their export operations. EMCs typically accept two types of assignments. First, they can start exporting operations for a firm with the understanding that the firm will take over operations after they are well established. Second, they can perform start-up export operations for a firm with the understanding that they will maintain an ongoing relationship with the company. EMC are valuable because they specialize in export operations, which often involves a lot of export specific paperwork, knowledge, and networking. By using an EMC, a firm can move much quicker than it could if it had to learn all of the export specific regulations itself, and had to start from scratch in terms of making contacts in foreign countries.

Studies have revealed that there is a wide variation in the quality of EMCs. While some perform their functions very well, others appear to add little value to the exporting companies. Therefore, an exporter should carefully review a number of EMCs, and check references from an EMC's past clients, before deciding on a particular EMC.

Hard
Page: 490

94. Describe the mechanisms for financing export and imports. Do you belief that the complexity of export financing deters small firms from becoming involved in exporting? Explain your answer.

Answer: There are three principle mechanisms used to finance exports and imports. These are the letter of credit, the draft (or bill of exchange), and the bill of lading. The following is a description of each one of these items.

Letter of Credit: A letter of credit is issued by a bank at the request of an importer. The letter of credit states the bank will pay a specified sum of money to a beneficiary, normally the exporter, on presentation of particular, specified documents. This process is reflected in the following example. If Goodyear Tire sold 10,000 tires to a company in France, the French company could go to a bank and request a letter of credit to assure Goodyear that it will get paid. If the French company is creditworthy, the bank would issue a letter of credit. The letter of credit would stipulate that upon receipt of the 10,000 tires by the French Company, the bank would pay Goodyear the agreed upon amount. This type of arrangement helps the system of international commerce work. Without some assurance of payment, a company like Goodyear may be reluctant to ship products to a foreign company that it is not very familiar with.

Draft: A draft, sometimes referred to as a bill of exchange, is the instrument normally used in international commerce for payment. A draft is simply an order written by an exporter instructing an importer, or an importer's agency, to pay a specified amount of money at specified time.

Bill of Lading: The third critical document for financing international trade is the bill of lading. The bill of lading is issued to the exporter by the common carrier transporting the merchandise. It serves three purposes: it is a receipt, a contract, and a document of title. As a receipt, the bill of laden indicates the carrier has received the merchandise described on the face of the document. As a contract, it specifies that the carrier is obligated to provide a transportation service in return for a certain charge. As a document of title, it can be used to obtain payment or a written promise of payment before the merchandise is released to the importer. The bill of laden can also function as collateral against which funds may be advanced by the exporter to its local bank before or during shipment and before final payment by the importer.

Does the complexity of this system discourage small businesses from becoming more actively involved in exporting? Probably. This question provides a platform for classroom discussion.

Medium
Page: 492

95. What is the difference between a sight draft and a time draft?

Answer: A sight draft is payable on presentation to the drawee. A time draft allows for a delay in payment - normally 30, 60, 90, or 120 days. It is presented to the drawee, who signifies acceptance of it by writing or stamping a notice of acceptance on its face. Once accepted, the time draft becomes a promise to pay by the accepting party. Time drafts are negotiable instruments; that is, once the draft is stamped with an acceptance, the maker can sell the draft to an investor at the discount from its face value.

Medium
Page: 494

96. What is the Export-Import Bank? What is its mission?

Answer: The Export-Import Bank is an independent agency of the U.S. government. Its mission is to provide financing aid that will facilitate exports, imports, and the exchange of commodities between the United States and other countries. The Export-Import bank pursues this mission with various loan and loan guarantee programs.

Medium
Page: 495

97. What types of risks are covered by foreign credit insurance?

Answer: Foreign credit insurance protects exporters against the risk of nonpayment by foreign importer. In the U.S., export credit insurance is provided by the Foreign Credit Insurance Association (FDIA), an association of private commercial institutions operating und

Medium:
Page: 495

98. What are the advantages of countertrade for American firms interested in selling their products overseas?

Answer: Countertrade is an alternative means of structuring an international sale when conventional means of payment are difficult, costly, or nonexistent. Many foreign countries have currencies that are not freely convertible into other currencies. This is problematic for exporters. Few exporters are interested in accepting payment for their goods or services in a nonconvertible currency. Countertrade is often the solution. Countertrade denotes a whole range of baterlike agreements; its principle is to trade goods and services for other goods and services when they cannot be traded for money.

Medium
Page: 496

99. What is barter? What are the two main problems with barter?

Answer: Barter is the direct exchange of goods and/or services between two parties without a cash transition. There are two main problems with barter. First, if goods are not exchanged simultaneously, one party ends up financing the other for a period. Second, firms engaged in barter run the risk of having to accept goods they do not want, cannot use, or have difficulty reselling at a reasonable price.

Hard
Page: 498

100. In the context of international trade, what is referred to by "buybacks?"

Answer: A buyback occurs when a firm builds a plant in a country - or supplies technology, equipment, training, or other services to the country - and agrees to take a certain percentage of the plant's output as partial payment for the contract. For example, Occidental Petroleum negotiated a deal with the former Soviet Union under which Occidental would build several ammonia plants in the Soviet Union and, as partial payment for their work, would receive ammonia from the plant over a 20 year period.

CHAPTER 16

GLOBAL MANUFACTURING AND MATERIALS MANAGEMENT

MULTIPLE-CHOICE QUESTIONS

STRATGY, MANUFACTURING, AND MATERIALS MANAGEMENT

Answer: D
Easy
Page: 504

1. The process of creating a product is called:

A. materials management
B. bureaucracy
C. administration
D. production

Answer: A
Easy
Page: 504

2. __________ is the activity that controls the transportation of physical materials through the value chain, from procurement through production and into distribution.

A. Materials management
B. Production
C. Operations
D. Bureaucracy

Answer: B
Easy
Page: 504

3. The activity that controls the transportation of physical materials through the value chain, from procurement through production and into distribution, is called:

A. conveyance management
B. materials management
C. transportation management
D. bureaucratic management

Answer: D
Easy
Page: 504

4. Materials management includes __________, which refers to the procurement and physical transmission of material through the supply chain, from suppliers to customers.

A. interchange
B. conveyance
C. reciprocation
D. logistics

Answer: A
Easy
Page: 504

5. The procurement and physical transmission of material through the supply chain, from suppliers to customers, is referred to as:

A. logistics
B. conveyance
C. interchange
D. reciprocation

Answer: C
Medium
Page: 505

6. Two important objectives shared by both manufacturing and materials management are to simultaneously:

A. increase quality and increase revenues
B. increase product awareness and lower costs
C. lower costs and increase quality
D. increase revenues and decrease customer complaints

Answer: A
Medium
Page: 505

7. Two important objectives shared by both manufacturing and materials management are to simultaneously increase quality and:

A. lower costs
B. increase revenues
C. increase product awareness
D. decrease customer complaints

Answer: C
Medium
Page: 505

8. Which of the following is not a result of improved quality control?

A. lower warranty costs
B. lower scrap costs
C. higher rework
D. increased productivity

Answer: D
Easy
Page: 505

9. The main management technique that companies are utilizing to boost their product quality is referred to as:

A. materials management
B. total feature management
C. logistics
D. total quality management

Answer: A
Easy
Page: 505

10. __________ is a management philosophy that takes as its central focus the need to improve the quality of a company's products and services.

A. Total quality management
B. Total enhancement management
C. Complete features management
D. Complete throughput management

Answer: B
Medium
Page: 505

11. The TQM concept was developed by a number of American consultants such as:

A. Martin Wolf, R.B. Weber, and Raymond Vernon
B. W. Edwards Deming, Joseph Juran, and A.V. Feigenbaum
C. J.H. Dunning, M. McQueen, and Michael Porter
D. Paul Krugman, Raymond Vernon, and A.V. Fiegenbaum

Answer: B
Medium
Page: 506

12. In Europe, the European Union requires that the quality of a firm's manufacturing processes and products be certified under a quality standard known as __________ before the firm is allowed access to the European marketplace.

A. total quality management
B. ISO 9000
C. BT 12000
D. reengineering

Answer: D
Medium
Page: 506

13. ISO 9000 is a standard designed to ensure the quality of a firm's manufacturing processes and products before a firm's is permitted access to the:

A. MERCOSUR marketplace
B. Andean Group marketplace
C. European Union marketplace
D. NAFTA marketplace

WHERE TO MANUFACTURER

Answer: B
Medium
Page: 506

14. The key decision factors that pertain to where an international firm locates its manufacturing facilities can be grouped under three broad headings. These are:

A. political factors, economic factors, and legal factors
B. country factors, technological factors, and product factors
C. product factors, service factors, and transportation factors
D. language factors, cultural factors, and transportation factors

Answer: C
Medium
Page: 506

15. The key decision factors that pertain to where an international firm locates it manufacturing facilities can be grouped under three broad headings. These are country factors, technological factors, and:

A. political
B. economic
C. product
D. labor

Answer: A
Medium
Page: 507

16. Three characteristics of a manufacturing technology that are of particular interest to an international firm when making a manufacturing location decision are:

A. fixed costs, minimum efficient scale, and flexible manufacturing
B. variable costs, technological sophistication, and the cost of moving manufacturing executives overseas
C. minimum efficient scale, computer compatibility, and variables costs
D. the cost of moving manufacturing executives overseas, fixed costs, and computer compatibility

Answer: D
Medium
Page: 507

17. Three characteristics of a manufacturing technology that are of particular interest to an international firm when making a manufacturing location decision are fixed costs, flexible manufacturing, and:

A. variable costs
B. computer compatibility
C. technological sophistication
D. minimum efficient scale

Answer: C
Easy
Page: 507

18. In some cases the __________ costs of setting up a manufacturing plant are so high that a firm must serve the world market from a single location of from a very few locations.

A. reoccurring
B. variable
C. fixed
D. transient

Answer: A
Medium
Page: 507

19. The concept of economies of scale tells us that as plant output expands, unit costs:

A. decrease
B. increase
C. increase exponentially
D. remain the same

Answer: B
Hard
Page: 507

20. The __________ declines with output until a certain output level is reached; at which point further increases in output realize little reduction in unit costs.

A. component cost slope
B. unit cost curve
C. unit expense line
D. component expense curve

Answer: C
Medium
Page: 508

21. Which of the following is not one of the objectives of flexible manufacturing technology, or lean production?

A. increase utilization of individual machines through scheduling
B. improve quality control at all stages of the manufacturing process
C. bring a factory into compliance with ISO 9000
D. reduce setup times for complex equipment

Answer: B
Medium
Page: 508

22. The term __________ refers to the ability to produce a wider variety of end products at a unit cost that at one time could be achieved only through the mass production of a standardized output.

A. assembly-line like customization
B. mass customization
C. economies of customization
D. standardized customization

Answer: A
Medium
Page: 508

23. __________ implies that a firm may be able to customize its product range to suit the needs of different customer groups without bearing a cost penalty.

A. Mass customization
B. Standardized customization
C. Economic customization
D. Assembly-like customization

Answer: A
Medium
Page: 508

24. Research suggests that the adoption of __________ manufacturing technologies may increase efficiency and lower unit costs relative to what can be achieved by the mass production of standardized output.

A. flexible
B. elastic
C. malleable
D. rigid

Answer: D
Hard
Page: 509

25. A __________ is a grouping of various types of machinery, a common materials handler, and a centralized cell controller.

A. malleable manufacturing unit
B. rigid machine unit
C. elastic manufacturing station
D. flexible machine cell

Answer: D
Medium
Page: 427

26. All of the following are advantages of flexible manufacturing except:

A. improved efficiency
B. flexible manufacturing technologies allow companies to customize products to suite the unique demands of small consumer groups
C. increased customer responsiveness
D. flexible manufacturing technologies help firms standardize products for different national markets

Answer: B
Medium
Page: 510

27. In terms of making a manufacturing location decision, when fixed costs are substantial, the minimum efficient scale of production is high, and flexible manufacturing technologies are available, it makes sense to:

A. manufacture the product in every country in which it is sold
B. concentrate production at a few choice locations
C. spread production over as many locations as possible
D. outsource production to a third party

Answer: A
Medium
Page: 510

28. In terms of making a manufacturing location decision, when fixed costs are low, the minimum efficient scale of production is low, and flexible manufacturing technologies are not available, it makes sense to:

A. manufacture in each major market in which the firm is active
B. outsource production to a third party
C. concentrate production at a few choice locations
D. manufacture the product in every country in which it is sold

Answer: D
Medium
Page: 510

29. Two product factors impact location decisions. These are:

A. the product's technological sophistication and the product's shape
B. the product's content and the product's point-of-origin
C. the product's shape and the product's weight
D. the product's value-to-weight ratio and whether the product serves universal needs

Answer: A
Medium
Page: 510

30. Two product factors impact location decisions. These are the product's value-to-weight ratio and:

A. whether the product serves universal needs
B. the product's content
C. the product's weight
D. the product's point-of-origin

Answer: B
Easy
Page: 510

31. Needs that are the same all over the world are called:

A. national needs
B. universal needs
C. shared needs
D. individualistic needs

Answer: D
Medium
Page: 511

32. Concentrating manufacturing makes sense for all of the following reasons except:

A. the product serves universal needs
B. the product's value-to-weight ratio is high
C. trade barriers are low
D. volatility in important exchange rates is expected

Answer: A
Medium
Page: 511

33. Decentralization of manufacturing makes sense for all of the following reasons except:

A. the production technology has high fixed costs, a high minimum efficient scale, or a flexible manufacturing technology exists
B. trade barriers are high
C. the product's value-to-weight ratio is low
D. the product does not serve universal needs

THE STRATEGIC ROLE OF FOREIGN FACTORIES

Answer: B
Easy
Page: 513

34. Initially, many foreign factories are established where:

A. labor costs are high
B. labor costs are low
C. labor costs are on par with the manufacturer's typical costs
D. labor intensive manufacturing is the exception rather than the norm

MAKE-OR-BUY DECISIONS

Answer: A
Easy
Page: 515

35. International businesses frequently face __________ decisions, which are decisions about whether they should make or buy the component parts that go into their finished products.

A. sourcing
B. inception
C. originating
D. conception

Answer: C
Easy
Page: 515

36. __________ decisions are decisions about whether firms should make or buy the component parts to go into their finished products.

A. Conception
B. Inception
C. Sourcing
D. Originating

Answer: C
Hard
Page: 515

37. The arguments that support making components parts in-house (i.e. vertical integration) are fourfold. These are:

A. facilitate the scheduling of adjacent processes, ability to support total quality management, higher quality, and strategic flexibility
B. offsets, lower costs, strategic flexibility, and higher quality
C. lower costs, facilitate investments in highly specialized assets, protect proprietary product technology, and facilitate the scheduling of adjacent processes
D. facilitate investments in highly specialized assets, lower costs, offsets, and higher quality

Answer: B
Medium
Page: 515

38. The arguments that support making components parts in-house (i.e. vertical integration) are fourfold. These are lower costs, facilitate investments in highly specialized assets, protect proprietary product technology, and:

A. offsets
B. facilitate the scheduling of adjacent processes
C. ability to support TQM
D. strategic flexibility

Answer: A
Medium
Page: 515

39. The arguments that support making components parts in-house (i.e. vertical integration) are fourfold. These are lower costs, protect proprietary product technology, facilitate the scheduling of adjacent processes, and:

A. facilitate investments in highly specialized assets
B. ability to support TQM
C. strategic flexibility
D. offsets

Answer: C
Easy
Page: 516

40. Proprietary product technology is technology:

A. unique to an industry
B. unique to a trade group
C. unique to a firm
D. unique to a country

Answer: C
Hard
Page: 518

41. The arguments that support buying component parts from independent suppliers are threefold. These are:

A. lower costs, improved scheduling, proprietary product technology protection
B. facilitates investments in highly specialized assets, lower costs, and offsets
C. strategic flexibility, lower costs, and offsets
D. improved scheduling, strategic flexibility, and proprietary product technology protection

Answer: C
Medium
Page: 518

42. The arguments that support buying component parts from independent suppliers are threefold. These are strategic flexibility, lower costs, and:

A. proprietary product technology protection
B. supports TQM
C. offsets
D. improved scheduling

Answer: A
Medium
Page: 518

43. The arguments that support buying component parts from independent suppliers are threefold. These are lower costs, offsets, and:

A. strategic flexibility
B. improved scheduling
C. proprietary product technology protection
D. supports TQM

Answer: D
Medium
Page: 518

44. According to our textbook, the greatest advantage of buying component parts from independent suppliers is:

A. lower costs
B. offsets
C. supports TQM
D. strategic flexibility

Answer: D
Medium
Page: 519

45. The term __________ refers to the practice of outsourcing the production of some component parts to a foreign country in hopes that it may help the firm capture more orders from that country.

A. reciprocal trade tactic
B. neutralize trade
C. countertrade
D. offset

Answer: B
Medium
Page: 519

46. The benefits of __________ seem to be greatest when highly specialized assets are involved, when vertical integration is necessary for protecting proprietary technology, or when the firm is simply more efficient than external suppliers at performing a particular activity.

A. buying component parts from independent suppliers
B. manufacturing components in-house
C. buying components from a merchandise mart
D. buying components at a trade show

Answer: B
Hard
Page: 520

47. Strategic alliances with suppliers was pioneered in:

A. American by large chemical producers like Dow
B. Japan by large auto companies such as Toyota
C. Europe by large electronics firms like Philips
D. Germany by telecommunications companies like Deutsche Telekom

Answer: C
Hard
Page: 520

48. In general, the trends toward just-in-time systems (JIT), computer-aided design (CAD), and computer-aided manufacturing seem to have increased pressures for firms to establish __________ relationships with their suppliers.

A. arms-length
B. short term
C. long term
D. permanent

COORDINATING A GLOBAL MANUFACTURING SYSTEM

Answer: B
Easy
Page: 520

49. __________, which encompasses logistics, embraces the activities necessary to get materials to a manufacturing facility, through the manufacturing process, and out through a distribution system to the end user.

A. Operations management
B. Materials management
C. Conveyance management
D. Scheduling management

Answer: A
Easy
Page: 521

50. The potential for reducing costs through more efficient materials management is:

A. enormous
B. moderate
C. minor
D. insignificant

Answer: D
Hard
Page: 521

51. For the typical manufacturing enterprise, material costs account for between __________ of revenues, depending on the industry.

A. 20 and 40 percent
B. 30 and 50 percent
C. 40 and 60 percent
D. 50 and 70 percent

Answer: C
Medium
Page: 521

52. Pioneered by __________ firms during the 1950s and 1960s, just-in-time inventory systems now play a major role in most manufacturing firms.

A. German
B. American
C. Japanese
D. British

Answer: D
Medium
Page: 521

53. The basic philosophy behind __________ systems is to economize on inventory holding costs by having materials arrive at a manufacturing plant just in time to enter the production process and not before.

A. total quality management
B. reengineering
C. maximum fluency
D. just in time

Answer: B
Hard
Page: 521

54. The major cost savings associated with just in time come from speeding up:

A. product deliveries
B. inventory turnover
C. administrative paperwork
D. production model changeovers

Answer: B
Hard
Page: 521

55. The drawback of a just in time system is that it leaves a firm without:

A. a sufficient number of employees to fill large orders
B. a buffer stock of inventory
C. an adequate cash reserve
D. an adequate staff to fulfill administrative responsibilities

Answer: C
Medium
Page: 521

56. As the number and dispersion of domestic and foreign markets and sources grow, the number and complexity of organizational linkages:

A. decreases correspondingly
B. remains the same
C. increases correspondingly
D. decreases exponentially

Answer: B
Medium
Page: 523

57. Under a __________ materials management structure, most materials management decisions are made at the corporate level.

A. decentralized
B. centralized
C. horizontal
D. parallel

Answer: D
Medium
Page: 524

58. Under a decentralized materials management structure, most management decisions are made at the:

A. corporate level
B. task force level
C. process team level
D. manufacturer plant level

Answer: D
Medium
Page: 524

59. Under a __________ materials management structure, most materials management decisions are delegated to the level of individual manufacturing plants with the firm.

A. vertical
B. corporate
C. centralized
D. decentralized

Answer: B
Easy
Page: 524

60. Under a decentralized materials management structure, most ________ decisions are delegated to the level of individual manufacturing plants within the firm.

A. materials management
B. production
C. marketing
D. human resources

TRUE-FALSE QUESTIONS

STRATEGY, MANUFACTURING, AND MATERIALS MANAGEMENT

Answer: T
Easy
Page: 504

61. Material management is the activity that controls the transmission of physical materials through the value chain, from procurement through production and into distribution.

Answer: T
Medium
Page: 504

62. Two important objectives shared by both manufacturing and materials management are to lower costs and to simultaneously increase product quality.

Answer: F
Medium
Page: 505

63. Improved quality control reduces costs by increasing rework.

Answer: F
Medium
Page: 505

64. The main management technique that companies are utilizing to boost their productivity is just in time inventory control.

Answer: T
Easy
Page: 505

65. TQM is a management philosophy that takes as its central focus the need to improve the quality of a company's products and services.

Answer: F
Medium
Page: 506

66. ISO 9000 is an Asian quality certification process.

WHERE TO MANUFACTURER

Answer: F
Medium
Page: 507

67. The key decision factors that pertain to where an international firm locates its manufacturing facilities can be grouped under the broad headings of country factors, technological factors, and tariff effects.

Answer: T
Easy
Page: 507

68. The concept of economies of scale tells us that as plant size expands, unit costs decrease.

Answer: T
Medium
Page: 508

69. Flexible manufacturing technologies allow a company to produce a wider variety of end products at a unit costs that at one time could be achieved only through the mass production of a standardized output.

Answer: F
Medium
Page: 509

70. A flexible machine cell is a group of manufacturing specialists that work together to troubleshoot manufacturing problems.

Answer: T
Hard
Page: 509

71. Improved capacity utilization and reductions in work in progress and waste are major efficiency benefits of flexible machine cells.

Answer: F
Medium
Page: 510

72. Other things being equal, when fixed costs are substantial it does not make sense to concentrate manufacturing activities in a few choice locations or even a single location.

Answer: T
Medium
Page: 510

73. Other things being equal, when flexible manufacturing technologies are available it makes sense to concentrate manufacturing activities in a few choice locations or even a single location.

Answer: F
Medium
Page: 510

74. When fixed costs are low, the minimum efficient scale of production is low, and flexible manufacturing technologies are not available, it makes sense to concentrate manufacturing activities in a few choice locations or even a single location.

Answer: F
Medium
Page: 510

75. It doesn't make sense to export a product with a very high value-to-weight ratio.

Answer: T
Easy
Page: 510

76. Needs that are the same all over the world are called universal needs.

Answer: T
Medium
Page: 511

77. Concentration of manufacturing makes sense when important exchange rates are expected to remain relatively stable.

Answer: F
Medium
Page: 511

78. Concentration of manufacturing makes sense when trade barriers are high.

Answer: T
Medium
Page: 511

79. Decentralization of manufacturing is appropriate when the product does not serve a universal need.

Answer: F
Medium
Page: 511

80. Decentralization of manufacturing is appropriate when the product's value-to-weight ratio is high.

MAKE-OR-BUY DECISIONS

Answer: T
Easy
Page: 515

81. Sourcing decisions are decisions about whether a firm should make or buy a component part.

Answer: T
Hard
Page: 515

82. The arguments that support making components parts in-house are fourfold: lower costs, facilitates investments in highly specialized assets, protect proprietary product technology, and facilitate the scheduling of adjacent processes.

Answer: T
Medium
Page: 516

83. In general, we can predict that when substantial investments in specialized assets are required to manufacturer a component, the firm will prefer to make the component internally rather than contract it out to a supplier.

Answer: F
Easy
Page: 516

84. Proprietary product technology is technology unique to an industry.

Answer: F
Hard
Page: 516

85. The strongest argument for vertical integration is that production cost savings result from it because it makes planning, coordination, and scheduling of adjacent processes easier.

Answer: T
Medium
Page: 518

86. The greatest advantage of buying component parts from independent suppliers is that the firm can maintain its flexibility, switching orders between suppliers as circumstances dictate.

COORDINATING A GLOBAL MANUFACTURING SYSTEM

Answer: F Hard Page: 521	87. For the typical manufacturing enterprise, material costs account for between 30 and 40 percent of revenues.
Answer: F Medium Page: 521	88. Pioneered by German firms during the 1950s and 1960s, just-in-time inventory systems now play a major role in manufacturing firms.
Answer: T Medium Page: 521	89. The drawback of a JIT system is that it leaves a firm without a buffer stock of inventory.
Answer: T Easy Page: 525	90. Information technology, particularly EDI, plays a major role in materials management.

ESSAY QUESTIONS

Medium
Page: 504

91. Discuss the overall objectives of international firms in terms of manufacturing and materials management.

Answer: International firms have four principle objectives in the area of manufacturing and materials management. The first two objectives are to lower costs and increase quality. In this respect, international firms are no different than their strictly domestic counterparts. Cost reductions can be realized through improved efficiency and through eliminating defective products from both the supply chain and the manufacturing process. Implementing Just-In-Time manufacturing is an important step in achieving these objectives. Quality improvement can be realized through a number of initiatives, including total quality management (TQM) and ISO 9000 certification.

The second two objectives that are shared by the majority of international firms in this area relate directly to their international efforts. First, a firm's manufacturing and materials management functions must be able to accommodate demands for local responsiveness. For instance, an American exporter may have to vary the design of a product that is manufactured and sold in the U.S. to meet European standards. Second, a firm's manufacturing and materials management function must be able to respond quickly to shifts in consumer demand. For instance, if a trend developed in Asia towards a preference for lower-fat foods, the importers of food products to Asia that respond to this trend the most rapidly would have a substantial advantage.

Easy
Page: 505

92. Define the term "total quality management (TQM)." What is the relationship between TQM and manufacturing?

Answer: TQM is a management philosophy that takes as its central focus the need to improve the quality of a company's products and services. TQM is the main management technique that is utilized to improve the quality of the products that emerge from manufacturing processes.

Hard
Page: 506

93. How does an international firm decide where to locate its manufacturing activities? Include in your answer a discussion of country factors, technological factors, and product factors.

Answer: The key factors involved in making location decisions, which entail the dual considerations of minimizing costs and increasing quality, can be grouped under three broad headings: country factors, technological factors, and product factors.

Country Factors: This is a large area of consideration, which encompasses a lot of factors. As described throughout the textbook, the advantage of producing in one country opposed to another varies along a number of dimensions. In earlier chapters in the textbook, for example, we saw that due to differences in factor costs, certain countries have a comparative advantage for producing certain products. Moreover, we saw how differences in political economy and national culture influence the desirability of location decisions. In this regard, all other things being equal, a firm should locate its manufacturing activities in countries that have hospitable political, economy, and factor cost environments.

Other country specific factors play a role in location decisions. These factors include formal and informal trade barriers and rules and regulations regarding foreign direct investment. Another country factor is expected movements in currency exchange rates. Adverse changes in exchange rates can quickly alter a country's attractiveness as a manufacturing site. Firms should consider the potential living conditions of their expatriate managers when making locations decision, and also the quality of the local labor pool.

Technological Factors: The three primary factors that drive location decisions in terms of technology are a manufacturing activity's level of fixed costs, its minimum efficient scale, and its flexibility. In terms of fixed costs, when the fixed costs of setting up a manufacturing operation are high, a firm must serve the world market from a single location or from a few locations. This is the case with aircraft manufacturing, for example. On the other hand, when fixed costs are low, a firm can scatter its manufacturing activities throughout the world to better accommodate local markets. In terms of minimum efficient scale, the larger the minimum efficient scale of a plant, the greater is the argument for centralized production at a single location. This factor motivates companies like Caterpillar Tractor, which makes heavy construction equipment in huge plants, to locate in a single location. Finally, in regard to flexibility, when flexible manufacturing technologies are available, a firm can manufacture products customized to various national markets at a single factory at the optimal location.

Product Factors: Two product features impact location decisions. The first is the product's value-to-weight ratio because of its influence on transportation costs. If a product has a high value-to-weight ratio, like semiconductors, it can be shipped around the world, and the shipping cost would represent only a small portion of the total cost of the product. Conversely, a product with a low value-to-weight ratio, like soft drinks, almost have to be mixed and bottled in the location in which they are sold, because the cost of shipping a 50 cent can of Coke from one country to another would represent a significant part of the value of the product. The second product consideration pertains to whether the product serves universal needs. If so, the need for local responsiveness is reduced, and the product can be produced at its ideal location.

As this discussion indicates, location decisions are complex for international firms. A consideration and weighing of all of the issues involved will result in the best overall decision.

Medium
Page: 508

94. Describe the terms flexible manufacturing and mass customization.

Answer: The term flexible manufacturing - or lean production as it is often called - covers a range of manufacturing that are designed to (a) reduce setup times for complex equipment, (b) increase utilization of individual machines through better scheduling, and (c) improve quality control at all stages of the manufacturing process. Flexible manufacturing technologies allow a company to produce a wider variety of end products at a unit costs that at one time could be achieved only through the mass production of a standardized output. The term mass customization has been coined to describe this ability. Mass customization implies that a firm may be able to customize its product range to suit the needs of different customer groups without bearing a cost penalty. Research suggests that the adoption of flexible manufacturing technologies may increase efficiency and lower unit costs relative to what can be achieved by the mass production of a standardized output.

Hard
Page: 509

95. What is a flexible machine cell?

Answer: Flexible machine cells are a common flexible manufacturing technology. A flexible machine cell is a grouping of various types of machinery, a common materials handler, and a centralized cell controller (computer). Each cell normally contains four to six machines capable of performing various operations. The typical cell is dedicated to the production of a family of parts or products. The settings on machines are computer controlled. This allows each cell to switch quickly between the production of different parts or products.

Medium
Page: 515

96. What are Make-or-Buy Decisions? What are the advantages of make versus buy and visa-versa? Are these decisions harder for international opposed to strictly domestic firms? Explain your answer.

Answer: A make-or-buy decision pertains to whether a business should make or buy the component parts that go into its final product. In other words, should a firm vertically integrate to manufacture its own component parts or should it purchase the parts from outside suppliers? For many firms, the make-or-buy decision is a difficult one, because there are good arguments to support either position.

The Advantages of Make: The arguments that support making component parts in-house (i.e. vertical integration) include: lower costs, facilitating specialized investments, proprietary product technology protection, and improved scheduling. In terms of lower costs, it may pay a firm to manufacture its own component parts, if no cheaper source (assuming quality remains consistent) is available. In terms of facilitating specialized investments, when a firm needs a component part that is highly customized and specialized, it is often best for the firm to manufacturer the part itself. Having a supplier manufacture the part would be awkward, because the supplier would rely strictly on one buyer to purchase the part and the buyer would typically have only the one supplier to furnish the part. In terms of protecting proprietary product technology, the more involvement that a firm has with suppliers, the more likely it is that proprietary information will be lost. As a result, a firm that has highly sensitive proprietary technology may be ahead to produce its own component products. Finally, improved scheduling can result from producing in-house rather than relying upon suppliers. The author of the textbook indicates that this is the weakest argument for vertical integration.

The Advantages of Buy: The advantages of buying component parts from independent suppliers is that it gives the firm greater flexibility, it can help drive down the firm's cost structure, and it may help the firm to capture orders from international customers. In regard to flexibility, by outsourcing the manufacture of its component parts, a firm can switch suppliers as circumstances dictate. This could provide a firm a substantial advantage in a rapidly changing environment. In terms of costs, using suppliers to manufacture component parts allows a firm to narrow its scope, and the resulting administrative overhead costs may be smaller. Finally, an advantage of buying rather than making component parts is that the relationships that are established through buying parts may lead to sales of the firm's final product. For example, if an American firm negotiated the purchase of component parts from several Brazilian firms, that would put the American firm in a position to develop a network of contacts in Brazil that might ultimately result in sales of its finished product.

The make-buy decision is harder for international firms than domestic firms because their decision set is simply more complex. For instance, it may appear desirable to purchase parts from a foreign supplier, but what about political stability in the supplier's country, foreign exchange risk, and the host of other questions that must be answered in international trade?

Medium
Page: 519

97. Discuss the advantages of entering into strategic alliances with suppliers? In general, is alliance formation a good idea for international firms?

Answer: This question is designed to elicit classroom discussion. It is also a good "thought" question for an exam. The number of strategic alliances between firms from different countries is growing and is becoming an increasingly important option for international firms. For example, in recent years we have seen an alliance between Kodak and Canon, under which Canon builds photocopiers to be sold by Kodak.

There are a number of advantages and disadvantages of alliances that may be pointed out by students. The advantages include a sharing of production costs and risks, along with joint marketing and R&D. Also, the long-term relationship that develops between the alliance partners may engender trust and be beneficial for both firms. On the other hand, many of the disadvantages of using suppliers rather than producing products in-house apply to strategic alliances. For instance, proprietary technology may be lost to an alliance partner. This represents a compelling disadvantage of strategic alliances, particularly if the alliance partners are in the same industry.

There is no right or wrong answer to the question of whether alliances are good or bad for international businesses. This topic, however, provides an excellent forum for classroom discussion.

Medium
Page: 521

98. Describe the concept of "just-in-time" systems. What are the advantages and disadvantages of the just-in-time system?

Answer: The basic philosophy behind just-in-time (JIT) systems is to economize on inventory holding costs by having materials arrive at a manufacturing plant "just in time" to enter the product process. This results in potential cost savings and quality improvements. The cost savings come from speeding up inventory turnover, thus reducing inventory holding costs, as well as warehousing and storage costs. In addition, JIT systems can lead to quality improvements. Under a JIT system, parts enter the manufacturing process immediately. This allows defective inputs to be spotted right away. The problem can then be traced to the supply source and fixed before more defective parts are produced. The disadvantage of a JIT system is that it leaves a firm without a buffer stock of inventory. As a result, a labor dispute at a supplier's plant or a disruption in the transportation system could leave a manufacturer without adequate component parts.

Medium
Page: 522

99. Discuss the advantages and disadvantages of decentralization from the materials management perspective of a multinational firm?

Answer: A decentralized organizational decision making structure delegates most materials management decisions to the level of individual manufacturing plants within the firm, although corporate headquarters retains responsibility for overseeing the function. The great advantage of decentralizing is that it allows plant-level materials management groups to develop the knowledge and skills needed for interacting with foreign suppliers that are important to their particular plant. This can lead to better decision making. The disadvantage is that a lack of coordination between plants can result in less than optimal global sourcing. It can also lead to duplication of materials management efforts.

Medium
Page: 525

100. How can electronic data Interchange (EDI) help an international firm coordinate its activities with its suppliers and increase its overall efficiency?

Answer: Firms increasingly use EDI to coordinate the flow of materials into manufacturing, through manufacturing, and out to customers. EDI systems require computer links between a firm, it suppliers, and its shippers. Sometimes customers also are integrated into the system. These electronic links are then used to place orders with suppliers, to register parts leaving a supplier, to track them as they travel toward a manufacturing plant, and to register their arrival. Suppliers typically use an EDI link to send invoices to the purchasing firm. One consequence of an EDI system is that suppliers, shippers, and the purchasing firm can communicate with each other with no time delay, which increases the flexibility and responsiveness of the whole supply system. A second consequence is that much of the paperwork between suppliers, shippers, and the purchasing firm is eliminated. Good EDI systems can help a firm decentralize materials management decisions to the plant level by giving corporate level managers the information they need for coordinating and controlling decentralized materials management groups.

CHAPTER 17

GLOBAL MARKETING AND R&D

MULTIPLE-CHOICE QUESTIONS

INTRODUCTION

Answer: B
Easy
Page: 532

1. A __________ marketing strategy that views the world's consumers as similar in their tastes and preferences is consistent with the mass production of a standardized output.

A. domestic
B. global
C. national
D. indigenous

Answer: A
Medium
Page: 533

2. The following four elements constitute a firm's marketing mix:

A. product attributes, distribution strategy, communication strategy, and pricing strategy
B. transportation strategy, warehousing strategy, availability of financing, and pricing strategy
C. promotions strategy, pricing strategy, availability of financing, and distribution strategy
D. product attributes, promotions strategy, communication strategy, and transportation strategy

Answer: D
Medium
Page: 533

3. The four elements that constitute a firm's marketing mix include product attributes, communication strategy, pricing strategy, and:

A. promotions strategy
B. warehousing strategy
C. availability of financing
D. distribution strategy

Answer: C
Medium
Page: 533

4. A firm's marketing mix includes pricing strategy, product attributes, distribution strategy, and:

A. availability of financing
B. customization strategy
C. communication strategy
D. promotions strategy

Answer: B
Easy
Page: 533

5. The marketing mix is the set of choices the firm offers to:

A. its vendors
B. its targeted markets
C. its employees
D. its external stakeholders

THE GLOBALIZATION OF MARKETS

Answer: A
Easy
Page: 533

6. Levitt has argued that, due to the advent of modern communications and transport technology, consumer tastes and preferences are becoming __________, which is creating global markets for standardized consumer products.

A. global
B. localized
C. cross-regional
D. individualistic

Answer: D
Medium
Page: 533

7. In his 1983 *Harvard Business Review* article, Theodore Levitt argued that due to the advent of modern communications and transport technology, consumer tastes and preferences are becoming global, which is creating global markets for standardized consumer products. In regard to these arguments, the current consensus among academics seems to be that Levitt:

A. was right on
B. understated his case
C. was way off base
D. overstated his case

MARKET SEGMENTATION

Answer: B
Easy
Page: 535

8. __________ refers to identifying distinct groups of consumers whose purchasing behavior differs from others in important ways.

A. Consumer differentiation
B. Market segmentation
C. Demographic profiling
D. Customer analysis

Answer: A
Medium
Page: 536

9. When managers in an international business consider market segmentation in foreign countries, they need to be cognizant of two main issues. These are:

A. the differences between countries in the structure of marketing segments, and the existence of segments that transcend national borders
B. the differences between countries in terms of tariff rates, and the difference between countries in terms of exchange rates
C. the differences between countries in terms of barriers to entry, and the differences between countries in terms of tariff rates
D. the differences between countries in terms of culture, and the differences between countries in terms of exchange rates

PRODUCT ATTRIBUTES

Answer: C
Easy
Page: 536

10. A product can be viewed as a bundle of:

A. qualities
B. needs
C. attributes
D. wants

Answer: A
Medium
Page: 537

11. According to our textbook, the most important aspect of a countries' culture from the perspective of a multinational firm's marketing strategy is:

A. tradition
B. language
C. geographic location
D. the availability of national resources

Answer: D
Medium
Page: 537

12. Across the world, consumer tastes and preferences are becoming more:

A. ethnocentric
B. parochial
C. indigenous
D. cosmopolitan

Answer: C
Hard
Page: 538

13. Contrary to Levitt's suggestions, consumers in the most developed countries are often:

A. willing to sacrifice their preferred attributes for lower prices
B. willing to accept a global product if it is accepted by consumers in underdeveloped countries
C. not willing to sacrifice their preferred attributes for lower prices
D. willing to sacrifice their preferred attributes regardless of the impact on price

DISTRIBUTION STRATEGY

Answer: B
Easy
Page: 538

14. A critical element of a firm's marketing strategy is its __________ strategy, which is the means it chooses for delivering the product to the consumer.

A. materials management
B. distribution
C. logistics
D. communication

Answer: D
Medium
Page: 539

15. In terms of their distribution strategies, countries differ along three main dimensions. These are:

A. end-user identification, channel integration, and transportation strategy
B. customer concentration, channel breadth, and warehousing strategy
C. wholesale concentration, channel depth, and transportation strategy
D. retail concentration, channel length, and channel exclusivity

Answer: B
Medium
Page: 539

16. In terms of their distribution strategies, countries differ along three main dimensions. These are retail concentration, channel length, and:

A. transportation strategy
B. channel exclusivity
C. channel depth
D. warehousing strategy

Answer: A
Medium
Page: 539

17. In terms of their distribution strategies, countries differ along three main dimensions. These are channel length, channel exclusivity, and:

A. retail concentration
B. wholesale concentration
C. preferred mode of transportation
D. channel depth

Answer: D
Easy
Page: 539

18. A __________ retail system is one in which there are many retailers, no one of which has a major share of the market.

A. concentrated
B. focused
C. consolidated
D. fragmented

Answer: A
Medium
Page: 539

19. Most of the differences in the retail concentrations of different countries are rooted in:

A. history and tradition
B. economic stature and religious beliefs
C. current events and trade status
D. geographic location and language

Answer: B
Hard
Page: 539

20. In terms of retail concentration, developed countries tend to have a higher degree of concentration than developing countries for all of the following reasons except:

A. increases in car ownership
B. a tradition of established local neighborhoods in which people walk to stores
C. number of households with refrigerators and freezers
D. number of two-income households that accompany development

Answer: C
Easy
Page: 539

21. Channel __________ refers to the number of intermediaries between the producer (or manufacturer) and the consumer.

A. reach
B. distance
C. length
D. exclusivity

Answer: B
Easy
Page: 539

22. The number of intermediaries between the producer (or manufacturer) and the consumer is referred to as:

A. channel distance
B. channel length
C. channel exclusivity
D. channel reach

Answer: D
Medium
Page: 539

23. If the producer sells directly to the consumer, the channel is __________. If the producer sells through an import agent, a wholesaler, and a retailer, a __________ channel exists.

A. short, intermediate
B. long, very short
C. intermediate in length, long
D. very short, long

Answer: C
Medium
Page: 540

24. Which of the following countries is often cited as the classic example of a fragmented retail system with long channels.

A. United States
B. Germany
C. Japan
D. Great Britain

Answer: A
Easy
Page: 540

25. An __________ distribution channel is one that is difficult for others to access.

A. exclusive
B. open
C. penetrable
D. malleable

Answer: A
Hard
Page: 540

26. According to our textbook, __________ distribution system is often held up as an example of a very exclusive system.

A. Japan's
B. France's
C. Germany's
D. South Korea's

Answer: D
Easy
Page: 540

27. A choice of __________ strategy determines which channel the firm will use to reach potential consumers.

A. transportation
B. communications
C. operations
D. distribution

Answer: B
Medium
Page: 540

28. The optimal distribution strategy for any firm is determined by:

A. product strategy and pricing strategy
B. the relative costs and benefits of each alternative
C. geographic location and tradition
D. industry and country of origin

Answer: A
Hard
Page: 541

29. All other things equal, the longer a channel:

A. the greater is the aggregate markup, and the higher the price that consumers are charged for the final product
B. the lower is the aggregate markup, and the lower the price that consumers are charged for the final product
C. the lower is the aggregate markup, and the higher the price that consumers are charged for the final product
D. the greater is the aggregate markup, and the lower the price that consumers are charged for the final product

COMMUNICATION STRATEGY

Answer: A
Easy
Page: 541

30. Direct selling, sales promotions, direct marketing, and advertising are all part of a firm's __________ strategy.

A. communications
B. distribution
C. product
D. operations

Answer: D
Easy
Page: 541

31. Direct selling, sales promotion, direct marketing, and __________ are all part of a firm's communications strategy.

A. pricing
B. rengineering
C. warehousing
D. advertising

Answer: D
Medium
Page: 541

32. The effectiveness of a firm's international communications can be jeopardized by three potentially critical variables. These are:

A. technological barriers, geographic barriers, and political barriers
B. economic factors, political-legal barriers, and noise levels
C. technological factors, source effects, and political barriers
D. cultural barriers, source effects, and noise levels

Answer: B
Medium
Page: 541

33. The effectiveness of a firm's international communications can be jeopardized by three potentially critical variables. These are cultural barriers, source effects, and:

A. political barriers
B. noise levels
C. technological factors
D. geographic barriers

Answer: A
Medium
Page: 541

34. The effectiveness of a firm's international communications can be jeopardized by three potentially critical variables. These are cultural barriers, noise levels, and:

A. source effects
B. geographic barriers
C. technological factors
D. geographic barriers

Answer: B
Medium
Page: 542

35. The best way for a firm to overcome cultural barriers is to:

A. hire a large number of local managers
B. develop cross-cultural literacy
C. provide training in culture awareness
D. operate in markets culturally similar to its home market

Answer: C
Medium
Page: 542

36. __________ occur when the receiver of the message (i.e. the potential customer) evaluates the message based on the status or image of the sender.

A. Direct effects
B. Temporal effects
C. Source effects
D. Synergistic effects

Answer: A
Medium
Page: 542

37. The types of effects that occur when the receive of a message (i.e. the potential customer) evaluates the message based on the status or image of the sender:

A. source effects
B. concentric effects
C. temporal effects
D. indirect effects

Answer: B
Easy
Page: 542

38. In the context to barriers to communication, __________ refer(s) to the amount of other messages competing for a potential consumer's attention.

A. channels effects
B. noise
C. source effects
D. alternative signals

Answer: A
Medium
Page: 542

39. In highly developed countries such as the United States, noise is:

A. extremely high
B. extremely low
C. moderate
D. not a factor in communications

Answer: D
Medium
Page: 542

40. The main decision with regard to communications strategy is the choice between a:

A. external strategy and an internal strategy
B. aggressive strategy and a conservative strategy
C. loud strategy and a soft strategy
D. push strategy and a pull strategy

Answer: D
Medium
Page: 542

41. In regard to communication strategy, a __________ strategy emphasizes personal selling rather than mass media advertising in the promotional mix.

A. reverse
B. pull
C. forward
D. push

Answer: A
Medium
Page: 542

42. In regard to communication strategy, which of the following strategies emphasizes personal selling rather than mass media advertising in the promotional mix?

A. push
B. pull
C. reverse
D. forward

Answer: C
Medium
Page: 543

43. Which of the following communications strategies relies primarily on mass media advertising rather than personal selling?

A. forward
B. pull
C. push
D. reverse

Answer: C
Hard
Page: 543

44. The three main factors that determine the relative attractiveness of push and pull strategies include:

A. advertising costs, product types relative to consumer sophistication, and channel exclusivity
B. geographic dispersion of buyers, channel length, and channel exclusivity
C. product type relative to consumer sophistication, channel length, and channel exclusivity
D. channel exclusivity, advertising costs, and cultural diversity of buyers

Answer: A
Hard
Page: 544

45. Push strategies tend to be emphasized:

A. for industrial products and/or complex new products
B. for consumer goods
C. when distribution channels are long
D. when sufficient print and electronic media are available to carry the marketing message

Answer: A
Hard
Page: 544

46. Pull strategies tend to be emphasized:

A. when distribution channels are long
B. when few print or electronic media are available
C. when distribution channels are short
D. for industrial products and/or complex new products

Answer: D
Medium
Page: D

47. Which of the following is not a justification for global advertising?

A. it has significant economic advantages
B. because creative talent is scarce, one large effort to develop a campaign will produce better results than 40 or 50 smaller efforts
C. many brand names are global
D. cultural differences among nations are such that a message that works in one national can fail in another

Answer: C
Hard
Page: 544

48. There are two main arguments against global advertising. These are:

A. many brand are global; country differences in advertising regulations may block implementation of global messages
B. language difficulties, cost considerations
C. cultural differences among nations are such that a message that works in one national can fail in another; country difference in advertising regulations may block implementation of global messages
D. many brands are global; it has significant economic advantages

PRICING STRATEGY

Answer: A
Medium
Page: 546

49. In an international context, __________ exists whenever consumers in different countries are charged different prices for the same product.

A. price discrimination
B. global pricing
C. predatory pricing
D. standardized pricing

Answer: B
Medium
Page: 546

50. If a consumer in Italy paid $45,000 for a Lexus and a consumer in Canada paid $60,000 for the identical vehicle, that would be an example of:

A. standardized pricing
B. price discrimination
C. global pricing
D. predatory pricing

Answer: D
Medium
Page: 546

51. Two conditions are necessary for profitable price discrimination: the firm must be able to keep its national markets separate and:

A. the firm must sell a highly standardized product
B. the firm must rely upon substantial economies of scale
C. the firm must sell in multiple countries
D. the existence of different price elasticities of demand in different countries must exist

Answer: C
Hard
Page: 547

52. According to our textbook, the elasticity of demand for a product in a given country is determined at least in part by the following two important factors:

A. geographic location and economic stability
B. currency exchange rates and interest rates
C. income level and competitive conditions
D. tax rates and standard of living

Answer: D
Medium
Page: 549

53. The use of price as a competitive weapon to drive weaker competitors out of a national market is called:

A. noncompetitive pricing
B. forward pricing
C. pillaging pricing
D. predatory pricing

Answer: B
Medium
Page: 549

54. __________ pricing refers to the fact that a firm's pricing strategy in one market may have an impact of its rivals' pricing strategy in another market.

A. Dual-action
B. Multi-point
C. Parallel
D. Cross

Answer: B
Easy
Page: 550

55. Selling a product for a price that is less than the cost of producing it is called:

A. reverse pricing
B. dumping
C. outsourcing
D. price reengineering

Answer: C
Medium
Page: 550

56. If a South Korean steel manufacturer sold steel in the U.S. for a price that was less than the cost of producing the steel, that would be an example of:

A. reverse pricing
B. price reengineering
C. dumping
D. outsourcing

NEW PRODUCT DEVELOPMENT

Answer: B
Medium
Page: 553

57. Which of the following is not a characteristic of countries where new-product development is strong?

A. more money is spent on basic and applied research
B. competition is modest
C. underlying demand is strong
D. consumers are affluent

Answer: A
Hard
Page: 554

58. One study of product development in 16 companies in the chemical, drug, petroleum, and electronics industries suggested that only about __________ of R&D projects result in commercially successful products or processes.

A. 20 percent
B. 40 percent
C. 60 percent
D. 80 percent

Answer: C
Medium
Page: 555

59. Close integration by R&D and __________ is required to ensure that product development projects are driven by the needs of customers.

A. materials management
B. production
C. marketing
D. human resources management

Answer: B
Easy
Page: 556

60. Basic research centers have all of the following characteristics except:

A. fundamental research is conducted
B. are typically located in remote locations apart from conventional research talent
C. are the innovative engines of the firm
D. attempt to develop the basic technologies that become new products

TRUE-FALSE QUESTIONS

INTRODUCTION

Answer: T
Easy
Page: 532

61. A global marketing strategy that views the world's consumers as similar in their tastes and preferences is consistent with the mass production of a standardized output.

Answer: F
Easy
Page: 533

62. The four elements that constitute a firm's marketing mix are product attributes, distribution strategy, communications strategy, and promotions strategy.

THE GLOBALIZATION OF MARKETS

Answer: F
Medium
Page: 533

63. The current consensus among academics, in regard to Theodore Levitt's arguments on the globalization of markets, is that Levitt is right on target.

MARKET SEGMENTATION

Answer: T
Easy
Page: 535

64. Market segmentation refers to identifying distinct groups of consumers whose purchasing behavior differs from others in important ways.

Answer: T
Medium
Page: 536

65. The goal of market segmentation is to optimize the fit between the purchasing behavior of consumers in a given segment and the marketing mix, thereby maximizing sales to that segment.

Answer: F
Hard
Page: 536

66. When managers of in international business consider market segmentation in foreign countries, they need to be cognizant of two main issues - the differences between countries in the structure of market segments and geographic location.

Answer: F
Hard
Page: 537

67. The most important aspect of cultural differences is probably the impact of governmental structure.

Answer: T
Medium
Page: 538

68. Contrary to Levitt's suggestions, consumers in the most developed countries are often not willing to sacrifice their preferred attributes for lower prices.

DISTRUBUTION STRATEGY

Answer: F
Medium
Page: 539

69. The main differences among countries' distribution systems are retail concentration, channel breadth, and channel depth.

Answer: T
Medium
Page: 539

70. A fragmented retail system is one in which there are many retailers, no one of which has a major share of the market.

Answer: F
Medium
Page: 539

71. Developed countries typically have a low level of retail concentration.

Answer: T
Easy
Page: 539

72. Channel length refers to the number of intermediaries between the producer (or manufacturer) and the consumer.

Answer: F
Easy
Page: 540

73. An exclusive distribution channel is one that is difficult for outsiders to access.

Answer: T
Medium
Page: 540

74. One of the reasons that the Japanese marketplace is so difficult for foreign companies to penetrate is channel exclusivity.

Answer: F
Medium
Page: 541

75. The longer the channel, the lower is the aggregate markup, and the lower the price that consumers are charged for the final product.

COMMUNICATION STRATEGY

Answer: T
Easy
Page: 541

76. International communication occurs when a firm uses a marketing message to sell its products in another country.

Answer: T
Medium
Page: 542

77. The best way for a firm to overcome cultural barriers is to develop cross-cultural literacy.

Answer: F
Medium
Page: 542

78. Cultural effects occur when the receiver of the message (the potential consumer in this case) evaluates the messaged based on the status or image of the sender.

Answer: F
Medium
Page: 542

79. In highly developed countries such as the United States, noise levels are extremely low.

Answer: T
Medium
Page: 542

80. A push strategy emphasizes personal selling rather than mass media advertising in the promotional mix.

Answer: F
Hard
Page: 543

81. A push strategy is generally favored by firms in consumer goods industries that are trying to sell to a large segment of the market.

Answer: T
Hard
Page: 543

82. A pull strategy relies on access to advertising media.

PRICING STRATEGY

Answer: T
Easy
Page: 546

83. Price discrimination exists whenever consumers in different countries are charged different prices for the same product.

Answer: F
Hard
Page: 547

84. The price elasticity of demand is a measure of the responsiveness of demand for a product to changes in product attributes.

Answer: T
Medium
Page: 549

85. Predatory pricing is the use of price as a competitive weapon to drive weaker competitors out of a national market.

Answer: T
Medium
Page: 549

86. Multipoint pricing refers to the fact that a firm's pricing strategy in one market may have an impact of its rivals' pricing strategy in another market.

Answer: F
Medium
Page: 550

87. Dumping occurs whenever a firm sells a product for a price that is more than double the cost of producing it.

NEW PRODUCT DEVELOPMENT

Answer: T
Medium
Page: 554

88. Other things being equal the rate of new product development seems to be greater in countries where competition is intense.

Answer: T
Hard
Page: 554

89. One study of product development in 16 countries in the chemical, drug, petroleum, and electronics industries suggested that only about 20 percent of R&D projects result in commercially successful products or processes.

Answer: F
Medium
Page: 555

90. Close integration between R&D and marketing is required to ensure that product development projects are driven by the firm's production department.

ESSAY QUESTIONS

Easy
Page: 533

91. Describe what is meant by the term "marketing mix." What factors cause a firm to vary its marketing mix across markets?

Answer: Marketing mix is a term that describes the set of choices that a firm offers to its customers. The four elements that constitute a firm's marketing mix are product attributes, distribution strategy, communication strategy, and pricing strategy. Many international businesses vary their marketing mix from country to country to take into account local differences. The potential differences between countries cover a wide range of factors, including culture, economic conditions, competitive conditions, product and technical standards, distribution systems, government regulations, and the like. According to the author of the textbook, as a result of the cumulative effects of these differences, it is rare to find a firm operating in an industry where it can adopt the same marketing mix worldwide.

Hard
Page: 536

92. What are the factors that influence a firm's ability to sell the same product worldwide? Ideally, is it better for a firm to sell the same product worldwide or would a firm rather customize its products for each individual market?

Answer: The three main factors that limit the ability of a firm to sell the same product to all of overseas markets are cultural differences across markets, economic differences across markets, and product and technical standards that differ from country to country.

Cultural Differences Across Markets: In regard to cultural differences across markets, countries vary along a wide range of dimensions. These dimensions include social structure, language, religion, tradition, education, physical stature, and forms of recreation. As a result, consumers in different countries have different tastes and preferences. For example, Japanese people tend to be smaller in stature than Americans. Consequently, American apparel manufacturers must be sensitivity to that when exporting clothing products to Japan. On the other hand, there is some evidence that tastes are converging worldwide, on a number of levels. For instance, Coca-Cola is a near global product, and its taste varies little worldwide. McDonalds Hamburgers are very similar worldwide, as are Levi Jeans and other apparel products. These examples, however, are the exception rather than the rule. In general, cultural differences across markets make it difficult to sell the same product worldwide.

Economic Differences Across Markets: Just as important as differences in culture are differences in the level of economic development across markets. Firms based in highly developed countries such as the U.S. tend to build a lot of extra performance attributes into their products because their customers want them. Conversely, consumers in developing countries (who have much less buying power) are typically content with much plainer products. This factor makes it difficult to sell the same product worldwide.

Product and Technical Standards Differences Across Markets: Differing product standards mandated by governments can rule out mass production and marketing of a standardized product in many settings. For instance, many appliance that are made for North American consumers cannot be plugged into the wall and run in Europe because of differing voltage requirements. Hundreds of these types of examples exist, which require exporters to customize their products to be suitable for individual foreign markets.

Whether firms prefer product standardization or customization is a difficult question. It is easy to quickly jump to the conclusion that a standardized product would be preferable, because it lends itself to economies of scale across the marketing mix. However, products that must be customized for individual markets have the benefit of representing a "best fit" between the consumer and the product. This may enable a firm to charge a higher price, and recapture some of the economies of scale advantages of a standardized product.

Medium
Page: 537

93. How do economic differences between countries affect the important of different product attributes?

Answer: As a general rule, consumer behavior is influenced by the level of economic development of a country. Firms based in highly developed countries tend to build a lot of extra performance attributes into their products. Consumers in less developed nations do not usually demand these extra attributes, where the preference is for more stripped down products. In fact, consumers in the most advanced counties often do not want globally standardized products that have been developed with the lowest common denominator in mind. Consumers in these countries are prepared to pay more for products that have added features and whose attributes are customized to their own tastes and preferences.

Hard
Page: 538

94. Explain what is meant by distribution strategy. What are the main differences among countries' distribution systems? Ultimately, how does a firm determine its distribution strategy in individual foreign markets?

Answer: A firm's distribution strategy is the way that it gets it product in the hands of consumers. Wholesale, retail, and direct sales are examples of distribution strategies. An international firm's distribution strategy is limited by the nature of the distribution systems that are available in its host countries. The main differences among countries' distribution systems are threefold: retail concentration, channel length, and channel exclusivity. Retail concentration refers to the number of retailers that supply a particular market. In some countries the retail system is very concentrated, and in other countries it is very fragmented. In a concentrated system, a few retailers supply most of the market. In a fragmented system, no one retailer has a major market share. In Germany, for example, four retail chains control 65 percent of the market for food products. This is an example of a very concentrated system. Channel length refers to the number of intermediaries between the producer and the consumer. If the producer sells directly to the consumer, the channel is very short. If the producer sells through several agents and wholesalers, the channel is very long. The most important determinant of channel length is the degree to which the retail system is fragmented. Fragmented retail systems tend to promote the growth of wholesales to serve retailers, which lengthens channels. Finally, channel exclusivity refers to how difficult the channel is to penetrate. For example, it is often difficult for a new firm to get access to shelf space in U.S. grocery stores because retailers tend to prefer to carry the products of long-established manufacturers like Procter & Gamble and General Mills. Channel exclusivity is very high in Japan, which makes the Japanese market so difficult to penetrate effectively. In Japan, relationships between manufacturers, wholesalers, and retailers often go back decades. Many of these relationships are based on the understanding that distributors will not carry the products of competing firms.

Ultimately, a firm's choice of distribution strategy in its international markets is influenced by which channels are available (i.e. channel exclusivity may eliminate some choices) and by the relative costs and benefits of each remaining alternative. The relative costs of each remaining alternative are affected by the three factors discussed above. For instance, if a food products company entered a foreign market that has very long, exclusive channels (which is often the case when the market if fragmented), selling to wholesalers might make the most economic sense. It would be difficult (if not impossible) for the importer to obtain shelf space in local supermarkets without the help of local wholesalers. Conversely, if the channels were short (which is often the case in highly concentrated markets), the importer may be able to sell directly to the retailer.

Medium
Page: 539

95. Describe the concept of channel length? How does a firm determine its channel length?

Answer: Channel length refers to the number of intermediaries between the producer (or manufacturer) and the consumer. If the producer sells directly to the consumer, the channel is very short. If the producer sells through an import agent, a wholesaler, and a retailer, the channel is long. The choice of a short or long channel is primarily a strategic decision for the producing firm. However, some countries have longer distribution channels than others. The most important determinant of channel length is the degree to which the retail system is fragmented. Fragmented retail systems tend to promote the growth of wholesalers to serve retailers, which lengthens channels.

Easy
Page: 542

96. In the context of international communication, describe the concept of "noise." Is the noise level higher in developed or developing countries? Why?

Answer: Noise tends to reduce the probability of effective communication. Noise refers to the amount of other messages competing for a potential consumer's attention, and this too varies across countries. In highly developed countries such as the U.S., noise is extremely high. Fewer firms vie for the attention of prospective customers in developing countries, and the noise level is lower.

Medium
Page: 542

97. In regard to communication strategy, what is the difference between a push versus a pull strategy? Provide an example of an appropriate application of a push strategy and an example of an appropriate application of a pull strategy.

Answer: The main decision with regard to communications strategy is the choice between a push and a pull strategy. A push strategy emphasizes personal selling rather than mass media advertising in the promotional mix. A pull strategy depends more on mass media advertising to communicate the marketing message to potential customers.

A push strategy is favored by firms that sell industrial products or other complex products. One of the strengths of direct selling is that it allows the firm to educate potential customers about the features of the product. Push strategies also tend to be emphasized (somewhat by default) when distribution channels are short and when few print or electronic media are available. An example of when a push strategy would be appropriate is a machine tool company that is selling a new manufacturing robotics product. The direct selling nature of the push strategy would provide the firm a forum to educate their potential customers relative to the merits of the new product.

A pull strategy is generally favored by firms in consumer goods industries that are trying to sell to a large segment of the market. For such firms, mass communication has cost advantages, and direct selling is rarely used. Pull strategies are also used when distribution channels are long. In most cases, using direct selling to push a product through many layers of a distribution channel would be impractical. As a result, a pull strategy, which makes use of print or electronic media to get its message across, is much more practical. An example of when a pull strategy would be appropriate is a soft drink company marketing its product in a new country that has fairly long distribution channels but sufficient media available.

Medium
Page: 544

98. Describe the advantages of using a standardized world wide advertising campaign.

Answer: The advantages of a standardized worldwide advertising campaign are threefold. First, there are significant economic advantages in pursuing such a strategy. A standardized campaign helps lower the costs of ad creation by spreading the fixed development costs over a larger number of outlets. Second, creative talent can be more readily and efficiently tapped. Third, a standardized campaign can help develop a global brand image.

Hard
Page: 546

99. For a firm to practice price discrimination, what conditions must hold?

Answer: For price discrimination to work the firm must be able to keep national markets separate and different price elasticities of demand must exist in different countries.

Medium
Page: 549

100. Discuss the concept of predatory pricing. Is predatory pricing ethical? What, if anything, should governments do to limit the influence predatory pricing by importers on domestic industries? Explain your answer.

Answer: This question is designed to stimulate classroom discussion and/or encourage students to "think" about the ethics of predatory pricing. Predatory pricing is the use of price as a competitive weapon to drive weaker competitors out of a national market. Once the competitors have left the market, the firm can raise prices and enjoy high profits. For such a pricing strategy to work, the firm must normally have a profitable position in another national market, which it can use to subsidize aggressive pricing in the market it is trying to monopolize. Many Japanese firms have been accused of pursuing this strategy, along with firms from other countries.

CHAPTER 18

GLOBAL HUMAN RESOURCES MANAGEMENT

MULTIPLE-CHOICE QUESTIONS

INTRODUCTION

Answer: C
Easy
Page: 564

1. Human resource management refers to the activities an organization carries out to utilize its __________ effectively.

   A. customers
   B. external stakeholders
   C. human resources
   D. suppliers

Answer: A
Easy
Page: 564

2. Determining a firm's human resource strategy, staffing, performance evaluation, management development, compensation, and labor relations are all:

   A. human resource management practices
   B. internal-external management practices
   C. value-chain management practices
   D. stakeholders management practices

Answer: B
Easy
Page: 564

3. The activities that an organization carries out to utilize its human resources effectively are referred to as:

   A. positive-sum management
   B. human resource management
   C. stakeholder management
   D. personnel psychology management

Answer: D
Easy
Page: 564

4. A(n) __________ manager is a citizen of one country who is working abroad in one of his or her firm's subsidiaries.

   A. ethnocentric
   B. cross-divisional
   C. cross-cultural
   D. expatriate

Answer: A
Medium
Page: 564

5. Jennifer Smith works for Intel (a U.S. based firm) but is assigned to Intel's sales office in Japan. Under these circumstances, Jennifer would be called a __________ manager.

A. expatriate
B. cross-divisional
C. ethnocentric
D. cross-cultural

THE STRATEGIC ROLE OF INTERNATIONAL HRM

Answer: D
Hard
Page: 564

6. Which of the following does not correctly match an international business strategy with its methodology?

A. multidomestic, try to create value by emphasizing local responsiveness
B. international, try to create value by transferring core competencies overseas
C. global, try to create value by realizing experience curve and location economies
D. transnational, try to create value by operating in as many foreign countries as possible

STAFFING POLICY

Answer: B
Easy
Page: 565

7. __________ is concerned with the selection of employees for particular jobs.

A. Compensation policy
B. Staffing policy
C. Performance appraisal
D. Training policy

Answer: A
Easy
Page: 565

8. The policy concerned with the selection of employees for particular jobs is referred to as:

A. staffing policy
B. organization policy
C. internal stakeholder policy
D. compensation policy

Answer: D
Medium
Page: 565

9. The term corporate culture refers to an organization's:

A. policies, rules, and regulations
B. standing among its peer firms
C. compensation system
D. norms and value systems

Answer: A
Hard
Page: 565

10. According to our textbook, in firms pursuing __________ strategies, we might expect the HRM function to pay significant attention to selecting individuals who not only have the skills required to perform particular jobs but who also "fit" the prevailing culture of the firm.

A. transnational and global
B. multidomestic and transnational
C. international and global
D. multidomestic and international

Answer: D
Medium
Page: 565

11. The international strategy that requires the lowest need for cultural controls is:

A. global
B. transnational
C. international
D. multidomestic

Answer: B
Medium
Page: 566

12. Which of the following is not one of the three types of staffing policies in international businesses?

A. polycentric
B. multicentric
C. ethnocentric
D. geocentric

Answer: A
Medium
Page: 566

13. The three types of staffing policies in international businesses are:

A. ethnocentric, polycentric, and geocentric
B. multicentric, betacentric, and polycentric
C. ethnocentric, intercentric, and multicentric
D. extracentric, geocentric, and betacentric

Answer: A
Medium
Page: 566

14. The three types of staffing policies in international business are the ethnocentric approach, the polycentric approach, and the:

A. geocentric approach
B. networkcentric approach
C. multicentric approach
D. unocentric approach

Answer: B
Medium
Page: 566

15. A __________ staffing policy is one in which all key management positions are filled by parent-company nationals.

A. unocentric
B. ethnocentric
C. intracentric
D. globalcentric

Answer: C
Medium
Page: 566

16. An ethnocentric staffing policy is one in which all key management positions are filled by:

A. host company nationals
B. the best people available, regardless of whether they are parent company nationals or host company nationals
C. parent company nationals
D. contract employees typically obtained from a consulting firm

Answer: D
Medium
Page: 566

17. In many Japanese and South Korean firms, such as Toyota, Matsushita, and Samsung, the majority of key positions in international operations are held by home-country nationals. This is a description of a __________ approach to international staffing.

A. geocentric
B. polycentric
C. multicentric
D. ethnocentric

Answer: C
Hard
Page: 566

18. Which of the following is not a reason that firms pursue an ethnocentric staffing policy?

A. the firm may believe there is a lack of qualified individuals in the host country to fill senior management positions
B. the firm may see an ethnocentric staffing policy as the best way to maintain a unified corporate culture
C. the firm may believe there is a lack of qualified individuals in its own parent company to fill senior management positions
D. if a firm is trying to create value by transferring core competencies to a foreign operation, it may believe that the best way to do this is to transfer parent country nationals who have knowledge of that competency to the foreign operation

Answer: A
Hard
Page: 567

19. There are two reasons that the ethnocentric staffing policy is on the wane in most international businesses. These are:

A. an ethnocentric staffing policy limits advancement opportunities for host country nationals and an ethnocentric policy can lead to "cultural myopia"
B. an ethnocentric staffing policy is the most expensive of the alternatives and an ethnocentric policy limits advancement opportunities for parent country personnel
C. an ethnocentric staffing policy limits the cultural awareness of parent country personnel and an ethnocentric policy can lead to "cultural myopic"
D. an ethnocentric staffing policy is the most expensive of the alternatives and an ethnocentric policy limits the cultural awareness of parent company personnel

Answer: D
Medium
Page: 567

20. A __________ staffing policy requires host-country nationals to be recruited to manage subsidiaries, while parent-country nationals occupy key positions at corporate headquarters.

A. intercentric
B. geocentric
C. ethnocentric
D. polycentric

Answer: A
Hard
Page: 567

21. A polycentric staffing policy requires __________ to be recruited to manage subsidiaries, while __________ occupy key positions at corporate headquarters.

A. host-country nationals, parent-country nationals
B. parent-country nationals, contract employees from an international employment firm
C. parent-country nationals, host-country nationals
D. contract employees from an international employment firm, host country nationals

Answer: B
Medium
Page: 567

22. According to our textbook, the major drawback with a polycentric approach, is:

A. the firm is more likely to suffer from cultural myopia than under an ethnocentric approach
B. the gap that can form between host-country managers and parent-country managers
C. that it is the most expensive approach to implement
D. statistics show that it is the least effective of the alternative approaches

Answer: C
Medium
Page: 568

23. A __________ staffing policy seeks the best people for key jobs throughout the organization, regardless of nationality.

A. intercentric
B. polycentric
C. geocentric
D. ethnocentric

Answer: D
Hard
Page: 568

24. Which of the following is not an advantage of the geocentric approach to staffing?

A. it enables the firm to make the best use of its human resources
B. it enables the firm to build a cadre of international executives who feel at home working in a number of cultures
C. the multinational composition of the management team that results from geographic staffing tends to reduce cultural myopia
D. a geocentric approach may require a compensation structure with a standardized international base pay level higher than national levels in many countries

Answer: B
Medium
Page: 568

25. According to our textbook, other things being equal, a __________ staffing policy seems to be the most attractive.

A. polycentric
B. geocentric
C. multicentric
D. ethnocentric

Answer: D
Medium
Page: 568

26. Which of the following international strategies is most compatible with an ethnocentric staffing policy?

A. transnational
B. global
C. multidomestic
D. international

Answer: A
Medium
Page: 568

27. Which of the following international strategies is most compatible with an polycentric staffing policy?

A. multidomestic
B. transnational
C. international
D. global

Answer: B
Medium
Page: 568

28. Which of the following international strategies is most compatible with an geocentric staffing policy?

A. international and global
B. global and transnational
C. multidomestic and transnational
D. transnational and international

Answer: B
Medium
Page: 569

29. Which of the international staffing policies has the potential to produce resentment in the host country?

A. multicentric
B. ethnocentric
C. polycentric
D. geocentric

Answer: A
Hard
Page: 569

30. Two of the three staffing policies rely on extensive use of expatriate managers. These are:

A. ethnocentric, geocentric
B. polycentric, intercentric
C. ethnocentric, intracentric
D. polycentric, geocentric

Answer: B
Easy
Page: 569

31. The premature return of an expatriate manager to his or her home country is referred to as:

A. expatriate relief
B. expatriate failure
C. expatriate rotation
D. expatriate timing

Answer: D
Easy
Page: 569

32. __________ is the premature return of an expatriate manager to his or her home country.

A. Expatriate timing
B. Expatriate rotation
C. Expatriate timing
D. Expatriate failure

Answer: B
Hard
Page: 569

33. One estimate of the costs of expatriate failure is that the average cost per failure to the parent company can be as high as __________ times the expatriate's annual domestic salary plus the cost of relocation.

A. 1.5
B. 3.0
C. 5.0
D. 6.5

Answer: D
Hard
Page: 570

34. According to a study conducted by R.L. Tung, __________ of U.S. multinationals experience expatriate failure rates of 10 percent or more.

A. 17 %
B. 33 %
C. 58 %
D. 76 %

Answer: C
Medium
Page: 570

35. Which of the following was not identified by R.L. Tung as a reason for expatriate failure among U.S. expatriate managers?

A. inability of spouse to adjust
B. difficulties with new environment
C. poor pay
D. personal or emotional problems

Answer: B
Medium
Page: 570

36. Which of the following was identified by R.L. Tung as the number one reason for expatriate failure among U.S. expatriate managers?

A. inability to cope with larger overseas responsibilities
B. inability of spouse to adjust
C. manager's inability to adjust
D. other family problems

Answer: D
Hard
Page: 570

37. The results of a study by R.L. Tung indicated that the most consistent reason for expatriate failure for Japanese expatriate managers was:

A. inability of spouse to adjust
B. personal or emotional problems
C. lack of technical competence
D. inability to cope with larger overseas responsibilities

Answer: B
Hard
Page: 570

38. A recent study by International Orientation Resources, a HRM consulting firms, found that 60 percent of expatriate failures occur because of three reasons. These are:

A. the inability to cope with larger overseas responsibilities, the lack of technical competence, and poor pay
B. the inability of a spouse to adjust, the inability of the manager to adjust, and other family problems
C. poor pay, the inability of a spouse to adjust, and the lack of managerial competence
D. the inability to cope with larger overseas responsibilities, other family problems, and the inability to cope with living overseas

Answer: A
Medium
Page: 571

39. Mendenhall and Oddou identified four dimensions that seem to predict success in expatriate selection. These are:

A. self-orientation, others-orientation, perceptual ability, and cultural toughness
B. cognitive ability, subjective ability, positive affect, and cultural awareness
C. self-orientation, cognitive ability, subjective ability, and cultural toughness
D. subjective ability, others-orientation, perceptual ability, and cultural awareness

Answer: D
Medium
Page: 571

40. Mendenhall and Oddou identified four dimensions that seem to predict success in expatriate selection: self-orientation, others-orientation, perceptual ability, and:

A. cognitive ability
B. global-orientation
C. foreign language ability
D. cultural toughness

Answer: C
Medium
Page: 571

41. Mendenhall and Oddou identified four dimensions that seem to predict success in expatriate selection: self-orientation, others-orientation, cultural toughness, and:

A. global-orientation
B. cognitive ability
C. perceptual ability
D. foreign language skills

Answer: A
Medium
Page: 571

42. According to Mendenhall and Oddou, __________ strengthens an expatriate's self-esteem, self-confidence, and mental well-being.

A. self-orientation
B. others-orientation
C. perceptual ability
D. cultural toughness

Answer: C
Medium
Page: 571

43. According to Mendenhall and Oddou, __________enhances an expatriate's ability to interact effectively with host-country nationals.

A. cultural toughness
B. perceptual ability
C. others-orientation
D. self-orientation

Answer: B
Hard
Page: 571

44. Which of Mendenhall and Oddou's predictors of expatriate success seems critical for managing host-country nationals?

A. cultural toughness
B. perceptual ability
C. self-orientation
D. others-orientation

Answer: A
Hard
Page: 573

45. Only __________ of the firms in the study conducted by R.L. Tung use formal procedures and psychological tests to assess the personality traits and relational abilities of potential expatriates.

A. 5 %
B. 15 %
C. 25 %
D. 35 %

TRAINING AND MANAGEMENT DEVELOPMENT

Answer: A
Medium
Page: 574

46. Historically, most international businesses have been more concerned with __________ than __________.

A. training, management development
B. technical development, training
C. management development, training
D. personnel development, training

Answer: C
Easy
Page: 574

47. The type of training that seeks to foster an appreciation for the host country's culture is refereed to as:

A. practical training
B. language training
C. cultural training
D. technical training

Answer: A
Easy
Page: 574

48. __________ is aimed at helping the expatriate manager and family ease themselves into day-to-day life in the host country.

A. Practical training
B. Cultural training
C. Technical training
D. Managerial training

Answer: D
Hard
Page: 575

49. According to one study of repatriated employees, __________ didn't know what their position would be when they returned home.

A. 10-20 %
B. 25-35 %
C. 45-55 %
D. 60-70 %

Answer: B
Medium
Page: 575

50. __________ programs are designed to increase the overall skill levels of managers through a mix of ongoing management education and rotations of managers through a number of jobs within the firm to give them varied experiences.

A. Organizational development
B. Management development
C. Personnel development
D. Technical development

PERFORMANCE APPRAISAL

Answer: B
Medium
Page: 577

51. __________ makes it difficult to evaluate the performance of expatriate managers objectively.

A. Unmindful bias
B. Unintentional bias
C. Inadvertent bias
D. Unconscious bias

Answer: C
Medium
Page: 577

52. In most cases, two groups evaluate the performance of expatriate managers. These are:

A. international HRM consultants and host-national managers
B. a committee of peer expatriate managers and home-office managers
C. host-national managers and home-office managers
D. host-national managers and a committee of peer expatriate managers

COMPENSATION

Answer: A
Medium
Page: 578

53. The most common approach to expatriate pay is the:

A. balance sheet approach
B. standard of living approach
C. merit approach
D. correspondence approach

Answer: C
Medium
Page: 578

54. In regard to expatriate pay, the __________ equalizes purchasing power across countries so employees can enjoy the same living standard in their foreign posting that they enjoyed at home.

A. correspondence approach
B. merit approach
C. balance sheet approach
D. standard of living approach

Answer: B
Medium
Page: 579

55. A __________ is extra pay the expatriate receives for working outside his or her country of origin.

A. parity adjustment
B. foreign service premium
C. allowance
D. expatriate special exemption

Answer: A
Medium
Page: 579

56. The form of compensation that compensates an expatriate for having to live abroad, in many cases isolated from friends and family, is referred to as a:

A. foreign service premium
B. expatriate special exemption
C. allowance
D. parity adjustment

Answer: B
Hard
Page: 580

57. Four types of allowances are often included in an expatriate's compensation package. These are:

A. travel allowances, emergency allowances, training allowances, and relocation allowances
B. hardship allowances, housing allowances, cost-of-living allowances, and education allowances
C. emergency allowances, leave allowances, training allowances, and cost-of-living allowances
D. housing allowances, leave allowances, cost-of-living allowances, and relocation allowances

Answer: A
Medium
Page: 580

58. A __________ allowance is paid when an expatriate is being sent to a difficult location.

A. hardship
B. affliction
C. affirmative duty
D. relocation

Answer: D
Medium
Page: 581

59. In regard to the types of allowances often included in an expatriate compensation package, a __________ allowance is often paid to ensure that the expatriate will enjoy the same standard of living the foreign posting as at home.

A. housing
B. hardship
C. education
D. cost-of-living

INTERNATIONAL LABOR RELATIONS

Answer: A
Easy
Page: 581

60. The __________ function of an international business is typically responsible for international labor relations.

A. HRM
B. public relations
C. marketing
D. legal

TRUE-FALSE QUESTIONS

INTRODUCTION

Answer: T
Easy
Page: 564

61. Human resource management refers to the activities an organization carries out to use its human resources effectively.

STAFFING POLICY

Answer: T
Easy
Page: 565

62. Staffing policy is concerned with the selection of employees for particular jobs.

Answer: F
Hard
Page: 565

63. Firms pursuing a multidomestic strategy have a high need for a strong unifying culture, and the need is somewhat lower for firms pursuing a global strategy and is lowest of all for firms pursuing international and transnational strategies.

Answer: F
Medium
Page: 566

64. A polycentric staffing policy is one in which all key management positions are filled by parent-country nationals.

Answer: F
Medium
Page: 567

65. An ethnocentric staffing policy requires host-country nations to be recruited to manage subsidiaries, while parent-country nationals occupy key positions at corporate headquarters.

Answer: T
Medium
Page: 567

66. One advantage of adopting a polycentric staffing policy is that the firm is less likely to suffer cultural myopia than under a ethnocentric approach.

Answer: T
Medium
Page: 568

67. A geocentric staffing policy seeks the best people for key jobs through the organization, regardless of nationality.

Answer: F
Hard
Page: 568

68. According to our textbook, all other things being equal, an ethnocentric staffing policy seems to be the most attractive.

Answer: F
Hard
Page: 568

69. An ethnocentric staffing policy is compatible with a multidomestic strategy.

Answer: T
Hard
Page: 568

70. A geocentric staffing policy is compatible with both global and transnational strategies.

Answer: F
Hard
Page: 569

71. Ethnocentric and polycentric staffing policies rely extensively on the use of expatriate managers.

Answer: T
Easy
Page: 569

72. The premature return of an expatriate manager to his or her home country is referred to as expatriate failure.

Answer: F
Medium
Page: 569

73. Although the frequency of expatriate failure is high, the cost is relatively low for the multinational firms involved.

Answer: T
Medium
Page: 570

74. According to a study by R.L. Tung, the number one reason for expatriate failure among U.S. multinationals is the inability of the expatriate manager's spouse to adjust.

Answer: T
Medium
Page: 570

75. Mendenhall and Oddou identified four dimensions that seem to predict success in a foreign posting: self-orientation, others-orientation, perceptual ability, and cultural toughness.

Answer: T
Medium
Page: 571

76. Perceptual ability is the ability to understand why people of other countries behave the way they do.

Answer: F
Medium
Page: 573

77. Cultural toughness refers to the fact that how well an expatriate adjusts to a particular posting tends to be related to the number of previous international assignments the expatriate has successfully completed.

TRAINING AND MANAGEMENT DEVELOPMENT

Answer: F
Medium
Page: 573

78. Training is a much broader concept than management development.

Answer: T
Medium
Page: 574

79. Historically, most international businesses have been more concerned with training than with management development.

Answer: T
Easy
Page: 574

80. Cultural training seeks to foster an appreciation for the host country's culture.

Answer: F
Medium
Page: 574

81. French is the language of world business.

Answer: T
Medium
Page: 574

82. Practical training is aimed at helping the expatriate manager and family ease themselves into day-to-day life in the host country.

Answer: F
Hard
Page: 575

83. According to one study of repatriated employees, over 90 percent knew what their position would be when they returned home.

Answer: T
Medium
Page: 575

84. Management development programs are designed to increase the overall skill levels of managers through a mix of ongoing management education and rotations of managers through a number of jobs within the firm to give them varied experiences.

PERFORMANCE APPRAISAL

Answer: T
Medium
Page: 577

85. Unintentional bias makes it difficult to evaluate the performance of expatriate managers objectively.

COMPENSATION

Answer: T
Medium
Page: 578

86. The most common approach to expatriate pay is the balance sheet approach.

Answer: F
Medium
Page: 579

87. An expatriate's base salary is normally double the base salary for a similar position in his or her home country.

Answer: T
Medium
Page: 579

88. A foreign service premium is extra pay an expatriate receives for working outside his or her country of origin.

Answer: F
Medium
Page: 580

89. A hardship allowance is paid when an expatriate takes a foreign assignment and is not accompanied by his family

Answer: T
Medium
Page: 580

90. A housing allowance is normally given to expatriates to ensure that they can afford the same quality of housing in the foreign country as at home.

ESSAY QUESTIONS

Medium
Page: 564

91. Describe the concept of human resources management. What extra challenges confront an international business in this area?

Answer: Human resource management (HRM) refers to the activities an organization carries out to utilize its human resources effectively. These activities include staffing, training and management development, performance appraisal, compensation, labor relations, and determining the firm's human resources strategy. To maximize human resources effectiveness, all of these activities should be performed with the firm's overall strategy, goals, and objectives in mind.

International businesses are faced with a number of extra challenges in this area. These extra challenge result primarily from the fact that countries differ in terms of their cultures, customs, philosophies of management, compensation systems, etc. As a result, a firm must adjust its HRM program (to varying degrees) to be compatible with each country that it does business in. In addition, selecting expatriate managers it is a challenge. An expatriate manager must have the technical skills necessary to do the job, along with a personal disposition and a family situation that is conductive to living in a foreign country for an extended period of time. The relatively high expatriate failure rate experience by U.S. multinationals attests to the difficulty of this challenge. Finally, international businesses must decided how to structure their overseas operations, which involves determining the appropriate roles of parent country and host country management personnel.

Hard
Page: 566

92. Discuss the differences between an ethnocentric approach, a polycentric approach, and a geocentric approach to staffing for international businesses. What is the rationale behind each of these approaches? How does a firm's staffing policy relate to the strategy that it is pursuing in a foreign country?

Answer: *Ethnocentric Approach*: An ethnocentric staffing policy is one in which all-key management positions are filled by parent country nationals. Firms pursue an ethnocentric staffing policy for three reasons. First, the firm may believe there is a lack of qualified individuals in the host country to fill senior management positions. Second, the firm may see an ethnocentric staffing policy as the best way to maintain a unified corporate culture. For instance, many Japanese firms prefer that Japanese managers head up their foreign operations, because these managers will be intimately familiar with the firm's culture and values. Third, if the firm is trying to create value by transferring core competencies to a foreign operation, it may feel that the best way to do this is to transfer parent country nationals who have knowledge of that competency to the foreign operation.

Polycentric Approach: A polycentric staffing policy requires host country nationals to be recruited to manage foreign operations, while parent country nationals occupy key positions at corporate headquarters. The principle advantage of adopting a polycentric approach is that the firm is less likely to suffer from cultural myopic. Host country managers are unlikely to make the mistakes arising from cultural misunderstandings that expatriate managers are subject to. Another advantage of the polycentric approach is that it is less expensive than other approaches to implement. By hiring host country personnel to fill management positions, the firm will not incur a significant amount of expatriate expense.

Geocentric Approach: A geocentric staffing policy tries to identify the best people available for management jobs, regardless of nationality. There are several advantages to this approach. First, it enables the firm to make the best personnel selections possible, without regard to nationality. In other words, a firm is not handcuffed in regard to whom it can hire because of a candidate's nationality. Second, a geocentric policy enables the firm to build a cadre of international executives who feel at home working in a number of different cultures. This is a critical consideration if the firm has future international business expansion in mind. The multicultural composition of the management team that results from geocentric staffing tends to reduce cultural myopic and enhances local responsiveness.

A firm's staffing policy does related to the overall global strategy it is trying to pursue. Overall, an ethnocentric approach is compatible with an international strategy, a polycentric approach is compatible with a multidomestic strategy, and a geocentric approach is compatible with both global and transnational strategies. Large international businesses may pursue a combination of these strategies to achieve the optimal staffing policy/international strategy mix.

Medium
Page: 567

93. How does staffing work in a polycentric organization? What are the advantages of this approach to staffing? With what type of strategy does it fit best?

Answer: A polycentric staffing policy is one in which host country nationals are recruited to manage subsidiaries in their own country, while parent country nationals occupy the key positions at corporate headquarters. While this approach may minimize the dangers of cultural myopia, it may also help create a gap between home and host country nationals. The policy is best suited for firms pursuing a multidomestic strategy.

Medium
Page: 569

94. What is an expatriate manager? What are some of the steps that an international business can take to enhance the success of their expatriate manager program?

Answer: An expatriate manager is a citizen of one country who is working abroad in one of his or her firm's subsidiaries. For example, if a manager for Disney (an American company) was moved from Orlando, Florida to Paris, France to work at Euro Disney, he or she would be an expatriate manager.

Selecting expatriate managers is a challenge because an individual who takes an assignment in a foreign country must have both the technical skills necessary to do the job and the personality disposition and family situation conductive to living and working overseas. The success of an expatriate program begins with the proper "selection" of expatriate personnel. Mehdenhall and Oddou have identified four dimensions that seem to predict success in foreign postings: self-orientation, others-orientation, perceptual ability, and cultural toughness. These factors should be considered in expatriate selection. Expatriate selection should be followed by expatriate training and management development. The training should include cultural training, language training, and practical training focused on living in a foreign country. Expatriates should also be prepared for repatriation. Upon returning home, a former expatriate manager can find himself or herself without a clear job or career path if repatriation is not an ongoing consideration during the expatriate period.

Other HRM issues should be carefully designed to accommodate the complex issues involved in employing expatriate managers. These issues include performance appraisal and compensation. Firms should work hard to reduce bias in performance appraisals, by both parent company and host country supervisors. Compensation programs should be thoughtfully prepared to adequately compensate expatriate managers for overseas assignments.

Difficult
Page: 569

95. What are the major reasons why U.S. managers fail in expatriate assignments? What are the major reasons why Japanese managers fail in expatriate assignments? What conclusions can you draw from the similarities or differences?

Answer: For U.S. multinationals, the reasons for expatriate failure are: (1) inability of the spouse to adjust, (2) employee's inability to adjust, (3) other family problems, (4) the employee's personal or emotional maturity, and (5) inability to cope with the larger overseas responsibility. For the Japanese firms the reasons for expatriate failure are: (1) inability to cope with the larger overseas responsibilities, (2) difficulties in the new environment, (3) personal or emotional problems, (4) lack of technical competence, and (5) inability of the spouse to adjust. Perhaps the most striking difference between these two lists is that the importance of the spouse was most important for U.S. expatriate managers but ranked only fifth for Japanese. This differences reflects the traditional separation of work from home life in Japanese culture.

Medium
Page: 574

96. What is the purpose of cultural training for an expatriate? How can "culture shock" be avoided?

Cultural training seeks to foster an appreciation for the host country's culture. The belief is that understanding a host country's culture will help the manager empathize with the culture, which will enhance his or her effectiveness in dealing with host-country nationals. It has been suggested that expatriates should receive training in the host country's culture, history, politics, economy, and so on. If possible, it is also advisable to arrange for a familiarization trip to the host country before the formal transfer, as this seems to ease culture shock. Given the problems related to spouse adaptation, it is important that the spouse, and perhaps the whole family, be included in cultural training programs.

Medium
Page: 574

97. Critically evaluate the following statement: "English is the language of international business. As a result, there is little need for an expatriate who knows English well to learn the local language."

Answer: For fairly short term assignments, this statement isn't too far off the mark - in many multinational firms business is typically conducted in English. Yet not speaking the local language will limit an expatriate's ability to be accepted by co-workers, and gather subtle information that can be lost when translated into English. Knowing the local language can also help expatriates and their families adjust to their surroundings.

Medium
Page: 575

98. What are management development programs? How can international businesses use management development programs as a strategic tool?

Answer: Management development programs are designed to increase the overall potential of employees by providing them training and a variety of experiences. For instance, a management development program might involve regularly scheduled educational programs, training, workshops covering a wide range of issues, and a program of rotating employees through foreign assignments to provide them international experience.

As a strategic tool, management development programs can play an important role in international businesses. These program can help a firm build a corporate culture that is sensitive to international business issues. In addition, in house company training programs, workshops, and off-site training can foster a sense of unity among the employees as well as the development of technical skills. In addition, the introduction of company songs, uniforms, T-shirts, and other firm specific initiatives can help build a manager's identification with the company and company spirit.

All of these initiatives can help build unity among the employees and the units of a firm, which may be particularly important for international businesses that have a number of disperse locations.

Management development programs are designed to increase the overall skill levels of managers through a mix of ongoing management education and rotations of managers through a number of jobs within the firm to give them varied experiences.

Medium
Page: 578

99. Discuss the issue of expatriate compensation. Suppose you worked for a firm that transferred you from the United States to a developing country in Asia or South America. How do you think you should be compensated relative to your peers in similar jobs at home?

Answer: This question is designed to encourage classroom discussion and/or to encourage students to "think" about how expatriate managers should be compensated. The issue of expatriate compensation is a difficult one. Substantial differences exist in the compensation of executives at the same level in various countries. These differences raise the question: should a firm pay its expatriate managers the prevailing wage rate in the country that they are working in, or should a firm pay all of its expatriate managers at the same level of responsibility a similar amount of pay? There is no standard answer to this question. The most common approach to expatriate pay is the balance sheet approach. This approach equalizes purchasing power across countries so employees can enjoy the same standard of living in their foreign postings that they enjoyed at home. In addition, this approach provides financial incentives to offset qualitative differences between assignment locations.

Consistent with this approach, the components of the typical expatriate compensation package are a base salary, a foreign service premium, allowances of various types, tax differentials, and benefits. In some cases, expatriates receive extra "hardship" allowances for living is a particularly difficult location. All together, an expatriate's compensation package may amount to three times what he or she would receive at home. Bear in mind, however, that the expatriate may be living and working in a difficult overseas assignment.

Ask your students to comment on this issue. It provides an interesting forum for classroom discussion.

Medium
Page: 581

100. What is the principle role of labor unions? What concerns does organized labor have about multinational firms?

Answer: The principle role of labor unions is to try to get better pay, greater job security, and better working conditions for the members through collective bargaining with management. Unions' bargaining power is derived largely from their ability to threaten to disrupt production, either by strike or some other form of work protest. This threat is credible, however, only insofar as management has no alternative but to employ union labor.

With this in mind, a principle concern of domestic unions about multinational firms is that a company can counter their bargaining power with the power to move production to another country. Another concern is that international businesses will keep highly skilled tasks in its home country and farm out only low skilled tasks to foreign plants. A final concern arises when international businesses attempt to import employment practices and contractual agreements from its home country. When these practices are alien to the host country, organized labor fears the change will reduce its influence and power.

CHAPTER 19

ACCOUNTING IN THE INTERNATIONAL BUSINESS

MULTIPLE-CHOICE QUESTIONS

INTRODUCTION

Answer: C
Easy
Page: 590

1. _________ has often been referred to as "the language of business."

A. Marketing
B. Finance
C. Accounting
D. Management

Answer: D
Easy
Page: 590

2. _________ information is the means by which firms communicate their financial position to the providers of capital, investors, creditors, and government.

A. Marketing
B. Demographic
C. Clerical
D. Accounting

Answer: B
Easy
Page: 590

3. _________ information is the means by which firms report their income to the government, so the government can assess how much tax the firm owes.

A. Clerical
B. Accounting
C. Demographic
D. Marketing

COUNTRY DIFFERENCES IN ACCOUNTING STANDARDS

Answer: A
Medium
Page: 591

4. Which of the following statement accurately describes the accounting systems that exist in various countries?

A. in each country, the accounting system has evolved in response to the demands for accounting information
B. accounting standards are not malleable, and once set do not change over time
C. accounting systems influence the local business environment, but are not themselves influenced by the local environment
D. accounting systems are not shaped by the environments in which they operate

Answer: D
Medium
Page: 591

5. Which of the following is not one of the five main variables that can influence the development of a country's accounting system?

A. the relationship between business and the providers of capital
B. political and economic ties with other countries
C. the level of inflation
D. membership in a trade region

Answer: A
Medium
Page: 591

6. The three main external sources of capital for business enterprises are:

A. individual investors, banks, and government
B. insurance companies, pension funds, and banks
C. banks, mutual funds, and pension funds
D. government, bonds, and banks

Answer: B
Medium
Page: 591

7. The three main external sources of capital for business enterprises are individual investors, banks, and:

A. pension funds
B. government
C. insurance companies
D. mutual funds

Answer: D
Medium
Page: 592

8. In the United States, the major source of capital for business enterprises is:

A. banks
B. government
C. pension funds
D. individual investors

Answer: C
Medium
Page: 592

9. In the U.S. and Great Britain, the financial accounting system is oriented towards:

A. providing individual investors with the information they need to make decisions about purchasing or selling corporate bonds, but not stocks
B. providing individual investors with the information they need to make decisions about purchasing or selling corporate stocks, but not bonds
C. providing individual investors with the information they need to make decisions about purchasing or selling corporate stocks and bonds
D. denying individual investors with the information they need to make decisions about purchasing or selling corporate stocks and bonds

Answer: B
Medium
Page: 592

10. In countries such as Switzerland, Germany, and Japan, the capital needs of business enterprises are provided primarily by:

A. individual investors
B. banks
C. government
D. pension funds

Answer: A
Hard
Page: 593

11. Since the passage of NAFTA, the accounting systems in the United States, Canada, and Mexico have:

A. seemed set to converge on a common set of norms
B. drifted further apart than before the trade agreement was consummated
C. remained as far apart as before the trade union
D. experienced no change

Answer: C
Medium
Page: 593

12. In many countries, including Germany, Japan, and the United States, accounting is based on the historic:

A. gold standard
B. par value
C. cost principle
D. value standard

Answer: B
Medium
Page: 593

13. The __________ assumes the currency unit used to report financial results is not losing its value due to inflation.

A. established value standard
B. historic cost principle
C. secure value principle
D. historic value standard

Answer: A
Hard
Page: 593

14. The historic cost principle affects accounting most significantly in the area of:

A. asset valuation
B. depreciation expense
C. financial ratio analysis
D. the valuation of intangibles

Answer: C
Medium
Page: 593

15. __________ adjusts all the items in a financial statement, including assets, liabilities, costs, and revenues, to factor out the effects of inflation.

A. Historic accrual accounting
B. Permanent ratio analysis
C. Current cost accounting
D. Contemporary asset accounting

Answer: C
Medium
Page: 593

16. Which of the following is not true regarding accounting systems in developed nations?

A. tend to have large, complex organizations whose accounting problems are far more difficult than those of small organizations
B. tend to have sophisticated capital markets in which business organizations raise funds from investors and banks
C. the providers of capital do not require that the organization they invest in and lend to provide comprehensive reports of their financial activities
D. the work forces tend to be highly educated and skilled and can perform complex accounting functions

Answer: C
Medium
Page: 593

17. Researchers have found that the extent to which a culture is characterized by __________ seems to have an impact on accounting systems.

A. a masculine orientation
B. an individualistic orientation
C. uncertainty avoidance
D. high power distance

Answer: A
Hard
Page: 594

18. Research suggest that countries with __________ cultures tend to have strong independent auditing professions that audit a firm's accounts to make sure they comply with generally accepted accounting procedures.

A. low uncertainty avoidance
B. high power distance
C. individualistic
D. masculine

Answer: D
Easy
Page: 594

19. __________ countries have identical accounting systems.

A. Many
B. A good number of
C. No
D. Few

Answer: D
Medium
Page: 594

20. Which of the following groups of countries was not signaled out in our textbook as having similar accounting systems?

A. British-American-Dutch group
B. South American group
C. Europe-Japan group
D. Asia-Africa group

NATIONAL AND INTERNATIONAL STANDARDS

Answer: B
Easy
Page: 594

21. __________ are rules for preparing financial statements; they define what is useful accounting information.

A. Auditing gestalts
B. Accounting standards
C. Accounting heuristics
D. Auditing mores

Answer: D
Easy
Page: 594

22. __________ specify the rules for performing an audit, which is the technical process by which an independent person gathers evidence for determining if financial accounts conform to required accounting standards and if they are also reliable.

A. Accounting standards
B. Auditing gestalts
C. Accounting principles
D. Auditing standards

Answer: C
Medium
Page: 594

23. An unfortunate result of national differences in accounting and auditing standards is:

A. some countries have more sophisticated standards than others
B. differences in accounting standards prevent some countries from conducting trade with one another
C. the general lack of comparability of financial reports from one country to another
D. the adverse impact that the differences in accounting standards has on currency fluctuations

Answer: A
Hard
Page: 594

24. __________ accounting standards favor the use of current value for replacement assets, while __________ law generally prohibits revaluation and prescribes historic cost.

A. Dutch, Japanese
B. German, British
C. American, French
D. South Korean, Spanish

Answer: B
Hard
Page: 594

25. Research and development costs must be written off in the year they are incurred in __________, but in Spain they may be deferred as an asset and need not be amortized as long as benefits that will cover them are expected to arise in the future.

A. Germany
B. the United States
C. the United Kingdom
D. Japan

Answer: A
Medium
Page: 596

26. __________ occurs when a firm based in one country enters another country's capital market to raise capital from the sale of stocks or bonds.

A. Transnational financing
B. Cross-boarder acquisition
C. Global capital accumulation
D. Multinational funding

Answer: C
Medium
Page: 596

27. Transnational financing occurs when a firm based in one country enters another country's capital markets to raise capital from:

A. commercial banks
B. pension funds
C. the sale of stocks and bonds
D. private individuals

Answer: C
Medium
Page: 596

28. A German firm raising capital by selling stock through the London Stock Exchange is an example of:

A. multinational funding
B. cross-boarder acquisition
C. transnational financing
D. global capital accumulation

Answer: C
Medium
Page: 596

29. __________ occurs when an investor based in one country enters the capital market of another nation to invest in the stocks or bonds of a firm based in that country.

A. Global venturing
B. Cross-boarder capital accumulation
C. Transnational investment
D. Multinational leveraging

Answer: A
Medium
Page: 596

30. Transnational investment occurs when an investor based in one country enters the capital market of another nation to:

A. invest in the stocks and bombs of a firm based in that country
B. loan money to a firm based in that country
C. purchase a company based in that country
D. form a joint venture with a firm based in that country

Answer: A
Easy
Page: 596

31. __________ has been made in recent years to harmonize accounting standards across countries.

A. A substantial effort
B. Some effort
C. Very little effort
D. No effort

Answer: A
Medium
Page: 596

32. The International Accounting Standards Committee is a __________ of the standardization of accounting standards across countries.

A. major proponent
B. critic
C. reluctant proponent
D. major force against

Answer: C
Hard
Page: 596

33. The IASC is governed by a __________ member board of representatives.

A. 5
B. 11
C. 14
D. 21

Answer: D
Hard
Page: 596

34. The __________ is responsible for formulating international accounting standards.

A. International Federation of Accountants
B. International Monetary Fund
C. World Bank
D. International Accounting Standards Committee

Answer: C
Hard
Page: 596

35. The __________ handles ethical issues pertaining to international accounting.

A. International Accounting Standards Committee
B. International Accounting Rules Committee
C. International Federation of Accountants
D. International Commission on Accounting Rules and Standards

Answer: A
Medium
Page: 596

36. The IASC was born in 1973 as an outgrowth of an effort by Canada, the United States, and Great Britain to develop:

A. international accounting standards
B. international auditing standards
C. an international accounting code of ethics
D. an international norm for reporting depreciation expenses

Answer: C
Hard
Page: 596

37. By the end of the mid-1990s, the IASC had issued over __________ international accounting standards.

A. 12
B. 22
C. 30
D. 55

Answer: A
Medium
Page: 597

38. The impact of the IASC standards has probably been least noticeable in __________ because most of the standards issues by the IASC have been consistent with opinions already articulated by a major accounting standards board in that country.

A. United States
B. Japan
C. Great Britain
D. Germany

Answer: C
Hard
Page: 598

39. In 1994, the SEC for the first time accepted three international account standards on cash flow data, the effects of hyperinflation, and:

A. depreciation expense
B. valuing intellectual property
C. business combinations for cross-border filings
D. the effects of currency rate fluctuations

MULTINATIONAL CONSOLIDATION AND CURRENCY TRANSLATION

Answer: C
Easy
Page: 598

40. A __________ financial statement combines the separate financial statements of two or more companies to yield a single set of financial statements as if the individual companies were really one.

A. collated
B. fragmented
C. consolidated
D. statutory

Answer: D
Easy
Page: 598

41. Multinational firms that are composed of a parent company and a number of subsidiaries located in various other countries typically issues a __________ financial statement.

A. statutory
B. fragmented
C. collated
D. consolidated

Answer: B
Medium
Page: 599

42. The purpose of consolidated financial statements is to provide accounting information about a group of companies that recognize their:

A. economic sovereignty
B. economic interdependence
C. economic independence
D. economic autonomy

Answer: B
Medium
Page: 600

43. Preparing consolidated financial statements is becoming __________ for multinational firms.

A. an impossibility
B. the norm
C. the exception
D. an impracticality

Answer: B
Hard
Page: 600

44. Foreign subsidiaries of multinational firms normally keep their accounting records and prepare their financial statements in:

A. the currency of the country in which they are headquartered
B. the currency of the country is which they are located
C. the currency of a neutral third country
D. a generic currency established by the IMF

Answer: D
Medium
Page: 601

45. Companies can use two main methods to determine what exchange rate should be used when translating financial statement currencies. These are:

A. the accrual method and the transitory method
B. the cash method and the accrual method
C. the temporal method and the transitory method
D. the current rate method and the temporal method

Answer: B
Medium
Page: 601

46. Companies can use two main methods to determine what exchange rate should be used when translating financial statement currencies. These are the current rate method and the:

A. transitory method
B. temporal method
C. cash method
D. accrual method

Answer: A
Medium
Page: 601

47. Companies can use two main methods to determine what exchange rate should be used when translating financial statement currencies. These are the temporal method and the:

A. current rate method
B. cash method
C. temporal method
D. transitory method

Answer: B
Medium
Page: 601

48. Under the __________ method, the exchange rate at the balance sheet date is used to translate the financial statements of a foreign subsidiary into the home currency of the multinational firm.

A. temporal
B. current rate
C. cash rate
D. transitory

Answer: C
Medium
Page: 601

49. The __________ method translates assets valued in a foreign currency into the home-country currency using the exchange rate that exists when the assets are purchased.

A. transitory
B. cash rate
C. temporal
D. current rate

Answer: B
Medium
Page: 602

50. US-based multinational firms must follow the requirements of Statement 52, "Foreign Currency Translation," issued by the __________ in 1981.

A. International Accounting Standards Committee
B. Financial Accounting Standards Board
C. U.S. Federal of Accountants
D. U.S. Commission on Accounting Rules and Standards

ACCOUNTING ASPECTS OF CONTROL SYSTEMS

Answer: B
Easy
Page: 602

51. For most firms, the __________ is the main instrument of financial control.

A. financial statement
B. budget
C. profit and loss statement
D. cash flow

Answer: A
Medium
Page: 602

52. According to one survey of control practices within multinational enterprises, the most important criterion for evaluating the performance of a foreign subsidiary is the subsidiary's:

A. actual profits compared to budgeted profits
B. actual revenues compared to projected revenues
C. actual expenses compared to projected expenses
D. return on investment compared to projected return on investment

Answer: D
Medium
Page: 603

53. Most international businesses require all budgets and performance data within the firm to be expresses in the _________, which is normally the home currency.

A. "indigenous currency"
B. "original currency"
C. "domestic currency"
D. "corporate currency"

Answer: C
Medium
Page: 603

54. Lessard and Lorange point out three exchange rates that can be used to translate foreign currencies into the corporate currency in setting budgets and in the subsequent tracking of performance. These exchange rates are:

A. the arrears rate, the temporal rate, and the ending rate
B. the initial rate, the spot rate, and the future rate
C. the initial rate, the projected rate, and the ending rate
D. the arrears rate, the current rate, and the future rate

Answer: A
Medium
Page: 603

55. Lessard and Lorange point out three exchange rates that can be used to translate foreign currencies into the corporate currency in setting budgets and in the subsequent tracking of performance. These are the initial rate, the projected rate, and the:

A. ending rate
B. arrears rate
C. temporal rate
D. spot rate

Answer: C
Medium
Page: 603

56. In the context of the Lessard-Lorange Model, the __________ is the spot exchange rate when the budget is adopted.

A. arrears rate
B. projected rate
C. initial rate
D. precipitating rate

Answer: A
Medium
Page: 603

57. In the context of the Lessard-Lorange Model, the __________ is the spot exchange rate forecast for the end of the budget period.

A. projected rate
B. anticipated rate
C. initial rate
D. ending rate

Answer: B
Medium
Page: 605

58. The price at which goods and services are transferred between the subsidiaries of a multinational firm is referred to as the:

A. action price
B. transfer price
C. shift price
D. movement price

Answer: C
Medium
Page: 605

59. International business often manipulate _________ to minimize their worldwide tax liability, minimize import duties, and avoid government restrictions on capital flow.

A. movement price
B. shift price
C. transfer price
D. action price

Answer: D
Hard
Page: 605

60. International businesses often manipulate their transfer prices for all of the following reasons except:

A. the minimize their worldwide tax liability
B. to avoid government restrictions on capital flow
C. to smooth out the exchange rates between countries
D. to minimize import duties

TRUE-FALSE QUESTIONS

COUNTRY DIFFERENCES IN ACCOUNTING STANDARDS

Answer: T
Easy
Page: 590

61. Accounting has often been referred to as "the language of business."

Answer: F
Easy
Page: 590

62. As a result of attempts to harmonize standards by developing internationally acceptable accounting conventions, very few differences between national accounting systems still remain.

Answer: F
Medium
Page: 591

63. The three main external sources of capital for business enterprises are individual investors, banks, and pension funds.

Answer: T
Medium
Page: 592

64. In the United States, individual investors are the major source of capital for business organizations.

Answer: T
Hard
Page: 592

65. In countries such as Switzerland, Germany, and Japan, a few large banks satisfy most of the capital needs of business enterprises.

Answer: F
Medium
Page: 593

66. In many countries, including Germany, Japan, and the United States, accounting is based on the contemporary cost principle.

Answer: T
Hard
Page: 593

67. The historic cost principle affects accounting most significantly in the area of asset valuation.

Answer: F
Hard
Page: 593

68. Current cost accounting adjusts all items in a financial statement to reflect currency exchange rates.

Answer: T
Medium
Page: 593

69. Uncertainty avoidance refers to the extent to which cultures socialize their members to accept ambiguous situations and tolerate uncertainty.

Answer: F
Medium
Page: 593

70. Using the cultural typologies developed by Hofstede, researchers have found that the extent to which a culture is characterized by a high power distance seems to have an impact on accounting systems.

NATIONAL AND INTERNATIONAL STANDARDS

Answer: T
Easy
Page: 594

71. Accounting standards are rules for preparing financial statements; they define what is useful accounting information.

Answer: T
Medium
Page: 596

72. Transnational financing occurs when a firm based in one country enters another country's capital markets to raise capital from the sale of stocks or bonds.

Answer: F
Medium
Page: 596

73. A Danish firm raising capital by borrowing money from a London banker is an example of transnational financing.

Answer: T
Medium
Page: 596

74. Transnational investment occurs when an investor based in one country enters the capital market of another nation to invest in the stocks or bonds of a firm based in that country.

Answer: F
Medium
Page: 596

75. An investor based in Australia buying rare coins from a dealer in Canada would be an example of transnational investment.

Answer: F
Easy
Page: 596

76. Very few efforts have been made in recent years to harmonize accounting standards across countries.

Answer: T
Medium
Page: 596

77. The International Accounting Standards Committee is a major proponent of standardizing accounting practices across countries.

Answer: T
Medium
Page: 596

78. The International Federation of Accountants handles ethical issues pertaining to international accounting practices.

Answer: F
Medium
Page: 596

79. A key characteristic of the International Accounting Standards Committee is that it has substantial power to enforce its standards

MULTINATIONAL CONSOLIDATION AND CURRENCY TRANSLATION

Answer: T
Easy
Page: 598

80. A consolidated financial statement combines the separate financial statements of two or more companies to yield a single set of financial statements as if the individual companies were really one.

Answer: F
Medium
Page: 600

81. Preparing consolidated financial statements is becoming the exception rather than the norm for multinational firms.

Answer: F
Medium
Page: 600

82. Foreign subsidiaries of multinational firms normally keep their accounting records and prepare their financial statements in the currency of the country in which they are headquartered.

Answer: T
Medium
Page: 601

83. Under the current rate method, the exchange rate at the balance sheet date is used to translate the financial statements of a foreign subsidiary into the home currency of the multinational firm.

Answer: F
Hard
Page: 601

84. The temporal method translates assets valued in a foreign currency into the home-country currency using the exchange rate that exists when the assets are sold.

ACCOUNTING ASPECTS OF CONTROL SYSTEMS

Answer: T
Easy
Page: 602

85. The budget is the main instrument of financial control.

Answer: T
Medium
Page: 603

86. Most international businesses require all budgets and performance data within the firm to be expressed in the "corporate currency," which is normally the home currency.

Answer: T
Medium
Page:603

87. The projected rate is the spot exchange rate when the budget and performance are being compared.

Answer: F
Medium
Page: 603

88. The ending rate is the spot rate forecast for the end of the budget period.

Answer: T
Medium
Page: 603

89. The initial rate is the spot exchange rate when the budget is adopted.

Answer: T
Easy
Page: 605

90. The price at which goods and services are transferred between subsidiary companies in a multinational firms is referred to as the transfer rate.

ESSAY QUESTIONS

Easy
Page: 590

91. What if the purpose of accounting information? Is a good accounting system critical to the smooth running of a firm?

Answer: Accounting information is the means by which firms communicate their financial position to the providers of capital, which include investors, creditors, and government. It enables the providers of capital to assess the value of their investments or the security of their loans and to make decisions about future resource allocations. Accounting information is also the means by which firms report their income to the government, so the government can assess how much tax the firm owes. It is also the means by which the firm can evaluate its performance, control its internal expenditures, and plan for future expenditures and income. Thus, a good accounting function is critical to the smooth running of a firm.

Medium
Page: 591

92. What are the five main factors that influence the development of a country's accounting system?

Answer: The five main factors that influence the development of a country's accounting system are as follows:

- The relationship between business and the providers of capital.
- Political and economic ties with other countries.
- The level of inflation.
- The level of a country's economic development.
- The prevailing culture in a country.

Medium
Page: 593

93. What is the historic cost principle? When is the application of the historic cost principle appropriate?

Answer: The historic cost principle assumes the currency unit used to report financial results in not losing value due to inflation. Firms record sales, purchases, and the like at the original transaction price and make no adjustment in the amounts later. The historic cost principle affects accounting most significantly in the area of asset valuation. If inflation is high, it underestimates a firm's assets, so the depreciation charges based on these underestimates can be inadequate for replacing assets when they wear out of become obsolete. The appropriateness of the historic cost principle varies inversely with the level of inflation in a country. In countries where inflation is low, the historic cost principle makes sense. In countries suffering from high inflation, however, historic prices may not at all reflect current reality.

Medium
Page: 593

94. What is the distinctive attribute of "current cost accounting?"

Answer: Current cost accounting adjusts all items in a financial statement - assets, liabilities, costs, and revenues - to factor out the effects of inflation.

Easy
Page: 596

95. When does transnational financing occur? Provide an example of transnational financing.

Answer: Transnational financing occurs when a firm based in one country enters another country's capital market to raise capital from the sale of stock. A Danish firm raising capital by sell stock through the London Stock Exchange is an example of transnational financing.

Easy
Page: 598

96. What is a consolidated financial statement? Do multinational firms typically issue consolidated financial statements? If so, why?

Answer: A consolidated financial statement combines the separate financial statements of two or more companies to yield a single set of financial statements as if the individual companies were really one. Most multinational firms are composed of a parent company and a number of subsidiary companies located in various other countries. Such firms typically issue consolidated financial statements, which merge the accounts of all the companies, rather than issuing individual financial statements for the parent company and each subsidiary.

Medium
Page: 60`

97. Regarding currency transactions, what is the difference between the current rate method and the temporal rate method?

Answer: While the current rate method uses the exchange rate at the date the financial statement is issued (i.e. the fiscal year end), the temporal rate method uses the exchange rate at the time the transaction originally took place.

Easy
Page: 603

98. What does the term "corporate currency" refer to?

Answer: Most international businesses require all budgets and performance data within the firm to be expressed in the "corporate currency," which is normally the home currency of the company.

Hard
Page: 603

99. What are the three exchange rates that can be used to translate foreign currency into the corporate currency in setting budgets and in the subsequent tracking of firm performance?

Answer: The three exchange rates are as follows:

- The initial rate, the spot exchange rate when the budget is adopted.
- The projected rate, the spot exchange rate forecast for the end of the budget period (i.e., the forward rate)
- The ending rate, the spot exchange rate when the budget and performance are being compared.

Medium
Page: 604

100. Describe the concept of transfer pricing.

Answer: The price at which goods and services are transferred between the various subsidiaries of a firm is referred to as transfer pricing.

CHAPTER 20

FINANCIAL MANAGEMENT IN THE INTERNATIONAL BUSINESS

MULTIPLE-CHOICE QUESTIONS

INVESTMENT DECISIONS

Answer: A
Easy
Page: 613

1. __________ budgeting quantifies the benefits, costs, and risks of an investment.

A. Capital
B. Economic
C. Functional
D. Tactical

Answer: C
Easy
Page: 613

2. __________ budgeting enables top managers to compare, in a reasonably objective fashion, different investment alternatives within and across countries to they can make informed choices about where the firm should invest its scarce financial resources.

A. Global
B. Tactical
C. Capital
D. Temporal

Answer: D
Hard
Page: 614

3. According to our textbook, which of the following is not one of the three factors that complicate the capital budgeting process.

A. the connection between cash flows to the parent and the source of financing must be recognized
B. political and economic risks, including foreign exchange risk, can significantly change the value of a foreign investment
C. a distinction must be made between cash flows to the project and cash flows to the parent company.
D. the majority of international firms used cash based accounting

Answer: A
Medium
Page: 514

4. Political risk tends to be greater when the following two conditions prevail.

A. social unrest or disorder are taking place and the underlying nature of the society makes the likelihood of social unrest high
B. a weak judiciary exists and inflation is high
C. the underlying nature of the society makes the likelihood of social unrest high and unemployment is high
D. the country has a history of political unrest and inflation is high

Answer: C
Easy
Page: 614

5. When political risk is high, there is a __________ probability that a change will occur in the country's political environment that will endanger foreign firms there.

A. low
B. moderate
C. high
D. near zero

Answer: B
Hard
Page: 615

6. __________ magazine publishes an annual "country risk rating," which incorporates assessments of political and other risk.

A. *Globalization*
B. *Euromoney*
C. *World Trade*
D. *International Finance*

Answer: A
Medium
Page: 615

7. The likelihood that economic mismanagement will cause drastic changes in a country's business environment that hurts the profits and other goals of a business enterprise is referred to as:

A. economic risk
B. political risk
C. capital risk
D. fiduciary risk

Answer: B
Medium
Page: 618

8. Adjusting discount rates to reflect a location's riskiness:

A. is not permitted
B. is widely practiced
C. is permitted, but is seldom practiced
D. is not technically possible

FINANCING DECISIONS

Answer: C
Medium
Page: 619

9. When considering its options for financing a foreign investment, an international business must consider two primary factors. These are:

A. if IMF guaranteed financing is available and interest rates in the foreign country
B. if World Bank financing is available and the inflation rate in the foreign country
C. how the foreign investment will be financed and how the financial structure of the foreign affiliate should be configured
D. if loan subsidies are available and wage rates in the foreign country

Answer: A
Medium
Page: 619

10. When considering its options for financing a foreign investment, an international business must consider two primary factors. These are how the foreign investment will be financed and:

A. how the financial structure of the foreign affiliate should be configured
B. if loan subsidies are available
C. the inflation rate in the foreign country
D. the unemployment rate in the foreign country

Answer: D
Medium
Page: 619

11. There is a __________ difference in the financial structures of firms based in different countries.

A. barely noticeable
B. moderate
C. subtle
D. quite striking

Answer: A
Medium
Page: 620

12. According to recent empirical research, country differences in financial structure __________ to country differences in tax structure.

A. do not seem related in any systematic way
B. are highly related in a systematic way
C. are related, but not in a systematic way
D. are moderately related in a systematic way

GLOBAL MONEY MANAGEMENT: THE EFFICIENCY OBJECTIVE

Answer: B
Easy
Page: 621

13. __________ management decisions attempt to manage the firm's global cash resources - its working capital - most efficiently.

A. Capital
B. Money
C. Fiduciary
D. Tactical

Answer: B
Easy
Page: 621

14. __________ costs are the cost of exchange.

A. Debit
B. Transaction
C. Fiduciary
D. Action

Answer: D
Medium
Page: 621

15. Which of the following is an example of a transaction cost?

A. interest rate expense
B. plant and equipment
C. employee wages
D. a transfer fee for moving cash from one location to another

Answer: C
Hard
Page: 621

16. According to the United Nations, __________ of international trade involves transactions between the different national subsidiaries of transnational corporations.

A. 15 percent
B. 30 percent
C. 40 percent
D. 55 percent

GLOBAL MONEY MANAGEMENT: THE TAX OBJECTIVE

Answer: A
Hard
Page: 621

17. The OECD country with the highest corporate income tax rate is:

A. Germany
B. Italy
C. Japan
D. U.S.

Answer: C
Hard
Page: 622

18. The OECD country with the lowest corporate income tax rate is:

A. Japan
B. U.S.
C. Finland
D. Mexico

Answer: C
Medium
Page: 622

19. In the context of global firms, double taxation occurs when:

A. a firm is taxed in a foreign country at twice its domestic tax rate
B. a firm does business in a country that collects income tax twice a year
C. the income of a foreign subsidiary is taxed both by the host-country government and by the parent company's home government
D. a firm is taxed on both its gross sales and its net income

Answer: A
Medium
Page: 622

20. A __________ allows an entity to reduce the taxes paid to the home government by the amount of taxes paid to the foreign government.

A. tax credit
B. tax exemption
C. tax abatement
D. tax debit

Answer: C
Medium
Page: 622

21. A tax __________ between two countries is an agreement specifying what items of income will be taxed by the authorities of the country where the income is earned.

A. alliance
B. convention
C. treaty
D. pact

Answer: D
Medium
Page: 622

22. An agreement between the U.S. and Germany that specifies that a U.S. firm need not pay tax in Germany on any earning from its German subsidiary that are remitted to the U.S. in the form of dividends is an example of a tax:

A. heuristic
B. alliance
C. convention
D. treaty

Answer: B
Medium
Page: 622

23. A __________ specifies that parent companies are not taxed on foreign source income until they actually receive a dividend.

A. special abatement
B. deferral principle
C. special exception
D. ad hoc provision

Answer: C
Easy
Page: 623

24. A __________ is a country with an exceptionally low or even no, income tax.

A. tax sanctuary
B. tax refuge
C. tax haven
D. tax shelter

Answer: B
Medium
Page: 623

25. A tax haven is a country with:

A. an extremely high tax rate
B. an exceptionally low to zero tax rate
C. a moderate tax rate
D. no tax laws

MOVING MONEY ACROSS BORDERS: ATTAINING EFFICIENCIES AND REDUCING TAXES

Answer: B
Medium
Page: 623

26. All of the following are examples of techniques used by international firms to transfer liquid funds across boarders except:

A. dividend remittances
B. countertrade
C. fronting loans
D. royalty payments

Answer: B
Medium
Page: 623

27. Which of the following is an example of a technique used by international firms to transfer liquid funds across boarders?

A. countertrade
B. dividend remittances
C. letters of credit
D. special debits

Answer: D
Medium
Page: 623

28. __________ is the use of more than one technique to transfer liquid funds across international boarders.

A. Double sourcing
B. Bundling
C. Concurrent sourcing
D. Unbundling

Answer: A
Medium
Page: 623

29. By using a mix of techniques to transfer liquid funds from a foreign subsidiary to the parent country, __________ allows an international business to recover funds from its foreign subsidiaries without piquing host-country subsidiaries with large "dividend drains."

A. unbundling
B. bundling
C. concurrent sourcing
D. double sourcing

Answer: D
Medium
Page: 623

30. __________ is probably the most common method by which firms transfer funds from foreign subsidiaries to the parent country.

A. The use of countertrade
B. Transfer pricing
C. The payment of consulting fees
D. The payment of dividends

Answer: C
Medium
Page: 624

31. __________ represent the remuneration paid to the owners of technology, patents, or trade names for the use of that technology or the right to manufacturer and/or sell products under those patents or trade names.

A. Dividents
B. Subsidies
C. Royalties
D. Special levies

Answer: A
Medium
Page: 624

32. Royalties may be levied in one of two ways: as a fixed monetary amount per unit of the product the subsidiary sells or as:

A. a percentage of a subsidiary's gross revenues
B. a percentage of a subsidiary's net revenues
C. a percentage of a subsidiary's return on assets
D. a percentage of a subsidiary's return on sales

Answer: B
Medium
Page: 624

33. A __________ is compensation for professional services or expertise supplied to a foreign subsidiary by the parent company or another subsidiary.

A. royalty
B. fee
C. dividend
D. retainer

Answer: A
Hard
Page: 624

34. Royalties and fees have certain tax advantages over dividends, particularly when:

A. the corporate tax rate is higher in the host country than in the parent's home country
B. the corporate tax rate in the host country and the parent's home country are equal
C. the corporate tax rate is higher in the parent's home country than in the host country
D. no income is earned

Answer: C
Easy
Page: 624

35. The price at which goods and services are transferred between entities with a firm is referred to as the:

A. conveyance price
B. switching price
C. transfer price
D. transaction cost

Answer: A
Medium
Page: 625

36. Which of the following statements is false regarding transfer pricing?

A. most governments like it
B. transfer pricing can help a firm reduce its tax liability
C. transfer pricing can help a firm reduce its exposure to risk
D. firms can use transfer pricing to circumvent taxes

Answer: B
Medium
Page: 626

37. A __________ is a loan between a parent and its subsidiary channeled through a financial intermediary, usually a large international bank.

A. transfer loan
B. fronting loan
C. dividend loan
D. transaction loan

Answer: D
Medium
Page: 626

38. In a __________ loan, the parent company deposits funds in an international bank, and the bank then lends the same amount to the foreign subsidiary.

A. transaction
B. transfer
C. debit
D. fronting

TECHNIQUES FOR GLOBAL MONEY MANAGEMENT

Answer: D
Hard
Page: 627

39. Rather than having each foreign subsidiary hold its own cash balances, firms prefer to hold cash balances at a centralized depository for three main reasons. These are:

A. by pooling cash reserves centrally, the firm can deposit larger amounts, pooling cash reserves reduces overall international political risk; and by pooling its cash reserves, the firm can reduce foreign exchange risk
B. by centralizing its cash reserves, the firm can reduce foreign exchange risk; pooling cash reserves reduces overall international economic risk; and if the centralized depository is located in a major financial center, it should have access to information about good short-term investment opportunities that the typical subsidiary would lack
C. by pooling cash reserves centrally, the firm can command higher interest rates; by centralizing its cash reserves, the firm can reduce foreign exchange risk; and by pooling its cash reserves, the firm can reduce the total size of the cash pool it must hold in highly liquid assets
D. by pooling cash reserves centrally, the firm can deposit larger amounts; if the centralized depository is located in a major financial center, it should have access to information about good short-term investment opportunities that the typical subsidiary would lack; and by pooling its cash reserves, the firm can reduce the total size of the cash pool it must hold in highly liquid accounts

Answer: B
Easy
Page: 629

40. Multilateral __________ allows a multinational firm to reduce the transaction costs that arise when many transactions occur between its subsidiaries.

A. spooning
B. netting
C. sparing
D. concealment

Answer: A
Easy
Page: 629

41. The technique that allows a multinational firm to reduce the transaction costs that arise when many transactions occur between its subsidiaries is referred to as multilateral:

A. netting
B. simulation
C. gathering
D. concealment

Answer: C
Medium
Page: 629

42. Netting reduces transaction costs by:

A. lower service fees
B. introducing efficiencies
C. reducing the number of transactions
D. increasing the quality of transactions

Answer: D
Hard
Page: 629

43. Under __________ netting, if a French subsidiary owes a Mexican subsidiary $6 million and the Mexican subsidiary simultaneously owes the French subsidiary $4 million, a bilateral settlement will be made with a single payment of $2 million from the French subsidiary to the Mexican subsidiary, the remaining debt being canceled.

A. parallel
B. double entry
C. simultaneous
D. bilateral

MANAGING FOREIGN EXCHANGE RISK

Answer: C
Easy
Page: 631

44. When we speak of __________, we are referring to the risk that future changes in a country's exchange rate will hurt the firm.

A. currency risk
B. economic risk
C. foreign exchange risk
D. political risk

Answer: A
Medium
Page: 631

45. When we speak of foreign exchange risk, we are referring to the risk that:

A. future changes in a country's exchange rate will hurt the firm
B. changes in a country's exchange rate will increase interest rates
C. changes in a country's exchange rate will increase tariffs
D. a firm will devalue its currency

Answer: C
Medium
Page: 631

46. Foreign exchange exposure is normally broken into three categories. These are:

A. political exposure, translation exposure, and demographic exposure
B. economic exposure, political exposure, an market exposure
C. transaction exposure, translation exposure, and economic exposure
D. transfer exposure, political exposure, and strategic exposure

Answer: A
Medium
Page: 631

47. Foreign exchange exposure is normally broken into three categories. These are transaction exposure, translation exposure, and:

A. economic exposure
B. demographic exposure
C. market exposure
D. political exposure

Answer: D
Medium
Page: 631

48. Foreign exchange exposure is normally broken into three categories. These are transaction exposure, economic exposure, and:

A. strategic exposure
B. fiduciary exposure
C. political exposure
D. translation exposure

Answer: B
Medium
Page: 631

49. __________ exposure is typically defined as the extent to which the income from individual transactions is affected by fluctuations in foreign exchange values.

A. Fiduciary
B. Transaction
C. Economic
D. Translation

Answer: D
Medium
Page: 631

50. The extent to which the income from individual transactions is affected by fluctuations in foreign exchange values is referred to as:

A. translation exposure
B. market exposure
C. technical exposure
D. transaction exposure

Answer: A
Medium
Page: 631

51. __________ exposure is the impact of currency exchange rate changes on the reported consolidated results and balance sheet of a company.

A. Translation
B. Transfer
C. Transaction
D. Market

Answer: D
Medium
Page: 631

52. The impact of currency exchange rate changes on the reported consolidated results and balance sheet of a company is referred to as:

A. market exposure
B. transaction exposure
C. fiduciary exposure
D. translation exposure

Answer: D
Medium
Page: 631

53. __________ is the extent to which a firm's future international earning power is affected by changes in exchange rates.

A. Political exposure
B. Market exposure
C. Tactical exposure
D. Economic exposure

Answer: C
Medium
Page: 631

54. __________ exposure is concerned with the long-run effect of changes in exchange rates on future prices, sales, and costs.

A. Market
B. Technical
C. Economic
D. Political

Answer: B
Medium
Page: 632

55. In addition to buying forward and using swaps, firms can minimize their foreign exchange exposure through __________ payables and receivables.

A. fronting and backing
B. leading and lagging
C. opening and closing
D. increasing and decreasing

Answer: C
Medium
Page: 632

56. A __________ strategy involves attempting to collect foreign currency receivables early when a foreign currency is expected to depreciate and paying foreign currency payables before they are due when a currency is expected to appreciate.

A. lagging
B. fronting
C. leading
D. backing

Answer: B
Medium
Page: 632

57. A __________ strategy involves delaying collection of foreign currency receivables if that currency is expected to appreciate and delaying payables if the currency is expected to depreciate.

A. backing
B. lagging
C. leading
D. fronting

Answer: B
Medium
Page: 632

58. __________ and __________ involves accelerating payments from weak-currency to strong-currency countries and delaying inflows from strong-currency to weak-currency countries.

A. Fronting, backing
B. Leading, lagging
C. Backing, fronting
D. Lagging, leading

Answer: B
Hard
Page: 632

59. Because lead and lag strategies can put pressure on a weak currency, many governments:

A. strongly encourage leads and lags
B. limit leads and lags
C. prohibit leads and lags
D. require leads and lags

Answer: A
Medium
Page: 632

60. Local debt financing can provide a hedge against:

A. foreign exchange risk
B. political risk
C. consumer risk
D. economic risk

TRUE-FALSE QUESTIONS

INVESTMENT DECISIONS

Answer: T
Easy
Page: 613

61. Capital budgeting quantifies the benefits, costs, and risks of an investment.

Answer: F
Easy
Page: 613

62. Tactical budgeting enables top managers to compare, in a reasonably objective fashion, different investment alternatives within and across countries so they can make informed choices about where the firm should invest its scarce financial resources.

Answer: T
Easy
Page: 614

63. When analyzing a foreign investment opportunity, the company must consider the political and economic risks that stem from the foreign location.

Answer: F
Medium
Page: 614

64. When political risk is high, there is a fairly low probability that a change will occur in a country's political environment that will endanger foreign firms there.

Answer: F
Hard
Page: 615

65. *Asia Money* magazine publishes an annual "country risk rating," which incorporates assessments of political and other risks.

Answer: F
Medium
Page: 615

66. Market risk is defined as the likelihood that economic mismanagement will cause drastic changes in a country's business environment that hurt the profit and other goals of a business enterprise.

Answer: T
Medium
Page: 618

67. Adjusting discount rates to reflect a location's riskiness seems to be a fairly widely practiced.

FINANCING DECISIONS

Answer: F
Easy
Page: 619

68. The cost of capital is typically higher in the global capital market than a firm's domestic market.

Answer: T
Easy
Page: 619

69. There is a quite striking difference in the financial structures of firms based in different countries.

Answer: F
Medium
Page: 620

70. Country differences in financial structure relate in a systematic way to country differences in tax structure.

GLOBAL MONEY MANAGEMENT: THE EFFICIENCY OBJECTIVE

Answer: T
Easy
Page: 621

71. Money management decisions attempt to manage the firm's global cash resources.

Answer: T
Medium
Page: 621

72. For any given period, a firm must hold certain cash balances.

Answer: F
Easy
Page: 621

73. Transfer costs are the cost of exchange.

Answer: T
Medium
Page: 621

74. Multilateral netting can reduce transaction costs.

GLOBAL MONEY MANAGEMENT: THE TAX OBJECTIVE

Answer: F
Hard
Page: 622

75. The OECD country with the highest corporate tax rate is Sweden.

Answer: T
Medium
Page: 622

76. Double taxation occurs when the income of a foreign subsidiary is taxed both by the host-country government and by the parent company's home government.

Answer: F
Medium
Page: 622

77. A tax abatement allows an entity to reduce the taxes paid to the home government by the amount of taxes paid to the foreign government.

Answer: T
Medium
Page: 622

78. A tax treaty between two countries is an agreement specifying what items of income will be taxed by the authorities of the country where the income is earned.

Answer: T
Medium
Page: 622

79. A deferral principle specifies that parent companies are not taxed on foreign source income until they actually receive a dividend.

MOVING MONEY ACROSS BORDERS: ATTAINING EFFICIENCIES AND REDUCING TAXES

Answer: F
Medium
Page: 623

80. Fronting loans is probably the most common method by which firms transfer funds from foreign subsidiaries to the parent company.

Answer: F
Medium
Page: 624

81. Royalties are typically levied as a percentage of net income.

Answer: F
Easy
Page: 624

82. The price at which goods and services are transferred between entities within the firm is referred to as the conveyance price.

Answer: T
Medium
Page: 624

83. Transfer prices can be used to position funds within an international business.

Answer: F
Hard
Page: 625

84. Most governments like and encourage transfer pricing.

Answer: T
Medium
Page: 626

85. A fronting loan is a loan between a parent and its subsidiary channeled through a financial intermediary, usually a large international bank.

TECHNIQUES FOR GLOBAL MONEY MANAGEMENT

Answer: T
Medium
Page: 629

86. Netting reduces transaction costs by reducing the number of transactions.

Answer: T
Medium
Page: 629

87. Multilateral netting is an extension of bilateral netting.

MANAGING FOREIGN EXCHANGE RISK

Answer: F
Medium
Page: 631

88. Translation exposure is typically defined as the extent to which the income from individual transactions is affected by fluctuations in foreign exchange values.

Answer: T
Medium
Page: 631

89. Economic exposure is the extent to which a firm's future international earning power is affected by changes in exchange rates.

Answer: T
Medium
Page: 632

90. Leading and lagging involves accelerating payments from weak-currency to strong-currency countries and delaying inflows from strong-currency to weak-currency countries.

ESSAY QUESTIONS

Medium
Page: 613

91. What is the purpose of capital budgeting? How is the process more complicated for international businesses?

Answer: The purpose of capital budgeting is to try to quantify the benefits, costs, and risks of an investment. Among factors complicating the process for an international business are:

- A distinction must be made between cash flows to the project and cash flows to the parent company.
- Political and economic risks, including foreign exchange risk, can significantly change the value of a foreign investment.
- The connection between cash flows to the parent and the source of financing must be recognized.

Hard
Page: 614

92. Critically evaluate the following statement: "When evaluating a foreign investment opportunity, the parent should be interested in the cash flows that it will receive rather than the cash flows the project generates."

Answer: The statement is basically correct. When evaluating a foreign investment opportunity, the parent should be interested in the cash flows that it will receive - as opposed to the cash flows the project generates - because the cash flows it receives are ultimately the basis of returns to shareholders. Shareholders will not perceive blocked earnings as contributing to the value of the firm, and creditors will not count on them when calculating a firm's ability to service its debt.

Medium
Page: 619

93. What are the two main factors that an international business must consider when evaluating its options for financing a foreign business?

Answer: When considering its options for financing a foreign investment, an international business must consider two factors. The first is how the foreign investment will be financed. If external financing is required, the firm must decide whether to borrow from sources in the host country or elsewhere. The second factor is how the financial structure of the foreign affiliate should be configured.

Easy
Page: 621

94. What is the relationship between transaction costs and transfer fees? Are transaction costs and transfer fees significant, or just a minor charge for doing business?

Answer: Transaction costs are the cost of exchange. Every time a firm changes cash from one currency into another currency it must bear a transaction cost - the commission fee it pays to foreign exchange dealers for performing the transaction. Most banks also charge a transfer fee for moving cash from one location to another; this is another transaction cost. The commission and transfer fees arising from intrafirm transactions can be substantial; according to the United Nations, 40 percent of international trade involves transactions between the different national subsidiaries of transnational corporations.

Easy
Page: 622

95. What is a tax credit?

Answer: A tax credit allows an entity to reduce the taxes its pays to the home government by the amount of taxes paid to the foreign government.

Medium
Page: 622

96. What is a tax treaty between two countries? Provide an example of a tax treaty?

Answer: A tax treaty between two countries is an agreement specifying what items of income will be taxed by the authorities of the country where the income is earned. For example, a tax treaty between the United States and Germany may specify that a U.S. firm need not pay tax in Germany on any earnings from its German subsidiary that are remitted to the United States in the form of dividends.

Hard
Page: 624

97. What are the four main advantages of manipulating transfer prices?

Answer: The four main gains that can be derived by manipulating transfer prices are as follows:

- The firm can reduce its tax liabilities by using transfer prices to shift earnings from a high-tax country to a low-tax one.
- The firm can use transfer prices to move funds out of a country where a significant currency devaluation is expected, there by reducing its exposure to foreign exchange risk.
- The firm can use transfer prices to move funds from a subsidiary to the parent company (or a tax haven) when financial transfers in the form of dividends are restricted or blocked by host-country governmental policies.

Medium
Page: 626

98. Describe the advantages of fronting loans.

Answer: There are two reasons why firms use fronting loans. First, fronting loans are a way of circumventing host government restrictions on the remittance of funds from a foreign subsidiary to the parent company; countries are unlikely to stop the repayment of loans as this can stifle future investments. The second reason for using fronting loans it that there may be tax advantages.

Medium
Page: 631

99. What is the difference between transaction exposure and translation exposure?

Answer: Transaction exposure is typically defined as the extent to which the income from individual transactions is affected by fluctuations in foreign exchange values. In contrast, translation exposure is the impact of currency exchange rate changes on the reported consolidated results and balance sheet of a company.

Medium
Page: 632

100. What is the difference between a lead strategy and a lag strategy?

Answer: A lead strategy involves attempting to collect foreign currency receivables early when a foreign currency is expected to depreciate and paying foreign exchange currency payables before they are due when a currency is expected to appreciate. A lag strategy involves delaying collection of foreign currency receivables if that currency is expected to appreciate and delaying payables if the currency is expected to depreciate.